Book One
Washington State Labor and Industries and the Attorneys behind it Revised
"How to Fight and Win"

Book Two
Labor & Industries Secret City Files

Written by _____ Kal Keller

Cal's Realm of Nightmares
Art & Photos by Kal Keller

ISBN-13: 978-0-6152-0551-9

Standard Copyrights License
2008

All Illustrations Kal Keller

Table of Contents
Non Fiction Book One of five
Introduction 5

Chapter 1 Injured on the Job — 9
Chapter 2 Out of Work — 19
Chapter 3 Part Time Work — 33
Chapter 4 Attorney Ethics — 37
Chapter 5 The Wringer — 44
Chapter 6 Surgery — 63
Chapter 7 L&I Physicians — 82
Chapter 8 Referrals — 98
Chapter 9 Secret Files — 109
Chapter 10 How Long is the Wait — 112
Author Commentary — 134

Book 2

If there are obstacles, the shortest line between two points may be the crooked one.

Chapter 11. Doctors of osteopathic medicine — 138
Chapter 12. Physical Therapy — 142
Chapter 13. Privileged Client Information — 146
Chapter 14. Your Medicine — 154
Chapter 15. Focus your time objectively — 164
Chapter 16. Threats and warnings — 173
Chapter 17. Employers and their Rights — 179
Chapter 18. Objective Medical Evidence — 192
Chapter 19. Presenting Objective Evidence — 204
Chapter 20. Child Labor — 214
Chapter 21. Breaking your will to Fight — 225
Conclusions — 239
    Addendum — 250
    This book is non-fiction
Bonus Book City Laws ignore Federal Regulations — 251-304
Summation-Telling names — 305-324
Zero Tolerance Policy on Government corruption — 324-336

4
Notes

Cal's Realm of Nightmares

Introduction

You must learn and understand the system. We will explain step by step what you will experience after a work related injury. I trusted in the system once in my life, I believe in the American way of life. We will expose Washington State Labor & Industries for what they truly represent and then we will dissect Monterey County, California and teach you city and county law and Federal Regulations that you can use to combat the odds against you.

This text book will allow you to know what they know and then some. It breaks down every law that affects you so that you can understand your choices better. These books will give you volumes of knowledge bringing you into the loop. Raw truth, we have not held back unless it proved to injure innocent persons. We are kicking ass and telling names, there is no room for corruption in Government in our American way of life.

Bee Roses Entertainment have interviewed over two-hundred injured workers collecting L&I monies along with more than 50 L&I employees.

While I was conducting some of these interviews I was threatened and intimidated by my attorneys not to write this book. Not everybody is meek or stupid, some people feel outraged and cheated, dubbed to be closed out. This book will give solutions and answers to the most frequently asked questions about filing a claim with an inside look at the Department.

Within Washington State, it is against the law to sue the State Government for stupidity, laziness, incompetence or lying. The law also requires that you need a Certified State Attorney Licensed by them to represent your case. From the beginning, the cards are stacked against you.

You will learn the best ways to combat the odds; most importantly you will know when your Attorney is lying to you. Believe me that Attorneys first do not believe you and listen to your Employer, working with them to faze you out. In this book, you will learn what to expect and what how to prepare, along with what is coming around every corner.

First, you lose your ambition, then you are late for the mortgage, insurance is hard to keep going and it has been ten years. You are about ready to lose your house, you have children then it gets tough. Indeed, think about it. Most persons live payday to payday, imagine if for three months you received no pay at all from your employer, and too injured to go back to work. You can always call an L&I Agent/Attorney and schedule a Hearing, yea, good luck.

Certainly, they know who signs their paychecks. Do you know that every part and parts of your body is in a Government book with a price tag attached to it? You can suffer all the pain and suffering throughout this fiasco unfortunately there is no compensation for pain and suffering. *They can pain and suffer the bees-wax out of you.* Underpaid employees and others that work for L&I detest what they see happening around them. Desk Clerks, Secretaries, and L & I will tell you that they can barely wait to read this book. I have been researching this book and writing down my findings for seven years. I dedicate this book to the unfortunate employees who hate their jobs but stay at it trying to help you find vanishing files or Records. Everything was going fine until I mentioned to my lawyer that I belonged to a certain club. Soon after that, attitudes changed and a racist remark flew at me. This private meeting closed with uneasy feelings and I felt hate directed at me.

"City laws allow you to sue for pain and suffering."

I learned that there were some things, which you must keep to yourself in this home of the free. Americans become victims of a suspicious nature before the persons in power become suspect. We vote and over-ruled by the legislature, they control Washington State Labor and Industries. The buck falls there. Think about it, so many Attorneys have your privileged information and I am writing this book. It must be "mighty" tempting not to use them to defend their pasts. Of course, Attorneys that have my personal information that has it to use or not to use against me. They keep it as an insurance policy. People heal as they get older, all people, some for the better, and others for the worse.

I have studied the way our personal and secret records are manipulated, surely used against us to discredit us. Private meetings between private powerful persons decide your fate. Certainly, Attorneys will have their own information about you to share and compare notes.

Deciding what is best for their private Firms and negotiates an estimated value for the exchange, and then decides what is best for their client. Some of your files are shredded, vanish or over-looked before your case is decided.

"Attorney's interests come first."

Equality is not an issue here because L&I and your employer have the advantage of the laws and money to try to make you disappear. It can get intense with L & I placing heavy burdens on you and your attorney threatening to quit if you do not do exactly what he says.

We will go into depth with companies such as Temp Services and Contractors. A good example is Lab Construction LLC, I am sad to report to you that they constructed a high-rise condominium, shopping mall resort at a cost of over a hundred million dollars. These are Canadian Contractors licensed in the USA to work. The photographs that I had taken featured in this book including critical mistakes in designs with the structure. These photographs will show girders and concrete beams positioned and poured incorrectly along with predictions of a future disaster relating to this building. You can find this building at 50 Elliot St. in Seattle, Washington. All Bee Roses Feathers Entertainment Books include illustrations, pictures or photographs.

Do you know how many persons are collecting and applying for compensation for a job injury today? You will when you read this book and it will make you think twice about what the system is operating now. The Numbers are staggering; 'I will say that much now.'

This story is a true story based on eyewitness accounts and legal documents. **"Names were altered to protect the innocent."** I love our country and the people living in it, therefore I cannot judge those I love, I will allow you to be the Judges.

Salinas California in Monterey County and the Monterey system of Government will alert you to the possible threat of terrorists targeting Monterey County; more measures need to be taken to protect Monterey.

We need drastic changes in our policies toward Americans and we the people demand these changes now. We are the fabric of this great nation, not the privileged few or the powerful but we, and only we can correct the problems created by government departments causing disorder.

8
This is your page.

_____

Chapter 1

"Injured on the Job"

Christmas Eve 1999, a day that I will never forget... These are some of the tasks and thoughts during the events at the time of my injury and three more days that I labored after the injury on the jobsite before given authorization to see their doctor. By that time, two tendons had snapped in my right arm and there were more then several fractures in my right thumb.

Yes, they did hire a professional, I am a commercial and Residential Journeyman Carpenter but not even an expert can do the job of three to six men. In addition to reading the blueprints and getting the regulations right, along with the building of the main foundation of a giant structure; it was more then one professional that you needed on the jobsite but three, one for making sure the specs were correct, one for keeping the work area clean and the excavation required. This involves assuring that the correct steel is used and the right tension applied on the wire tension cables reaching into the sky secured onto the next deck pillar of this vast complex.

It also means providing laborers to clean work areas hard to reach and to pump the water out of the holes. The Union jobs across the street had all their people and were well-organized teams worked like clockwork. They had to follow Federal Guidelines; only state guidelines set for independent contractors. They became entrepreneurs for money, bosses in America a step above the law protected by Labor and Industries and special interest groups. As Americans should we allow this job-grabbing lawlessness to continue?

December 22, 1999

Today, I got some help. A man showed up for work. It did not take long to know that he was good at what he did. There was one problem; he was still intoxicated from the night before. It was obvious that Dick was a good person and had a rough life. It takes a hard man to become a Form Carpenter. Especially if you have to carry 4x5 and 5x8, concrete panels that stuck concrete had dried onto by the crew that used them before Lab Construction LLC rented them.

I believe that it was one of the boss's crews. There were three owners at the time of this construction and some heavy contacts. Jerry was reckless and in pain. It was muddy and the holes filled with water. I will not give the dept and the square of the girders, beams, or footings, walls, any information, in the technical designs of the Complex will not, be exposed. However, we will show faults in construction using photographs as it rose into the giant it is now, if the job wasn't scrapped.

We worked the day out the two of us being a great team but that was not enough; we needed supplies, the correct tools and more manpower, day labor employment agencies. Two Lead men cannot do the work of a whole crew. We worked in the rain and toughed it out.

It was mid-afternoon when my hand became a victim, smashed by a 'hand mall with a 16-ounce hammer handle' swung by Jerry. He hit the head in an angle and at the same time, we struck a steel girder buried deep in the stone. The impact sent a tuning fork effect up my arm and through my body.

I complained about my arm to the supervisor, after some encouragement, he laughed it off. He claimed that I was not injured enough to see a physician and to continue working on the construction of this complex on 50 Elliot St.

With the rising tide gauged by the almanac, this structure made to withstand time for a hundred years or more will tumble in twenty-years if the structure is not redesigned and corrected, backed in the areas of poor construction and moved back at least fifty yards.

Unfortunately, Global warming did not read the Almanac and waters are rising over twice the rate of our history. 50 Elliot St is a sitting time bomb ready to slide into the ocean with one bad storm, an Earthquake, perhaps a terrorist attack; it is a disaster waiting to happen.

This disaster will maim and kill approximately two thousand people, more if it occurs in the middle of summer.

December 23, 1999

Inspectors could have shut down the job as bad as the specs were and the moving of stakes if it gets constructed?

Provide a workplace free from recognized hazards.
Provide and use means to make your workplace safe.
Prohibit employees from entering, or being in, any place of work that is not safe. Construct your Workplace so it is safe.
Prohibit alcohol and narcotics from your workplace.
Take responsibility for the safe condition of tools and equipment used by employees. Establish, supervise, and enforce rules that lead to a safe and healthy work environment that are effective in practice
Control chemical agents.

These are laws that your employer must follow

Provide a workplace free from recognized hazards. **WAC 296-800-11005**

Provide and use means to make your workplace safe. **WAC 296-800-11010**

Prohibit employees from entering, or being in, any workplace that is not safe.
WAC 296-800-11015

Construct your workplace so it is safe.   **WAC 296-800-11020**

Prohibit alcohol and narcotics from your workplace.   **WAC 296-800-11025**

Prohibit employees from using tools and equipment that are not safe   **WAC 296-800-11030**

Establish, supervise, and enforce rules that lead to a safe and healthy work environment that are effective in practice. **WAC 296-800-11035**

Control chemical agents.   **WAC 296-800-11040**

Protect employees from biological agents. **WAC 296-800-11045**

Washington State Contractors must follow these laws; in a future chapter, we will discuss Jobsite inspectors. *"Are these laws followed?"*

Working one year for a bad contractor can equal five or more years of your life from toxic materials and mishaps. These laws and others easily found on the internet yet how many of us take them seriously. We know that it is best not to complain if you want to stay employed. I know for a fact that all that truly matters is getting the job done at the least possible cost to the contractor.

Today Jerry and I were moving forms and then assembling them. We had to clean and plane the ground, and the steel sloppily poured so there were thousands of burs, had to be muscled or hammer out whatever way worked best. I hired on as a journeyman carpenter and was disappointed that there were no labors on the job and it was off the prints, several inches off. In fact, because of the lack of workers and the neglect by the owner to stay on top of this job, the final dimensions have vanished. It was a piece together job with the Foreman and Supervisor asking me to interpret the blue prints and design the seats for the tension cables reaching far into the sky, I helped bout all final dimensions were set by one of the owners..

Boomer promised me a crew and laborers to be waiting for me on this job, now I was the only lab construction LLC carpenter on the site. I installed the forms with Jerry showing up when he could and knew that the width and height were correct. I am sure that on the next stage of the project the men had to improvise to make the design fit. We worked as a team and together we climbed a mountain. Hung-over or not Jerry kicked butt to help me finish before the trucks arrived. I was glad that another Contractor loaned me one of his men to try to finish this phase of the project. I learned that Boomer was ill prepared and undermanned for the Projects he had acquired. Whenever Boomer saw me, he tried to make my life difficult. Gave me jobs that I had to use my right hand working on hardware and brackets knowing that my hand and arm were injured. Boomer knows that I saved the job and then tries to dishonor our country by not paying the disability for the injured hand and allowing alcohol and drug use among his crews. Boomer and many of his people are from Canada working as General Contractors in Washington, why should they care?

The day ended at 6:30PM and began at 6:30AM, my hand was

puffed and swelled, I asked Boomer if I could see a physician and he told me no, it is just sprang a wrist. It was not bad enough to see a Doctor and I returned home across the Puget Sound and wrapped my hand. In the morning when I awakened, my hand was red blue and twice the size. I knew that I had to go to work so I worked that day.

Christmas Eve Day 1999

Employee's Responsibility: To play an active role in creating a safe and healthy place of work and comply with all applicable safety and health rules.

I only worked until 1PM because finally one of the owners allowed me to see a physician for my job injury.

First Aid was a bad word working for Boomer. All the carpenters that I observed had broken up or mangled hands but they were healed and working. When a young man one is immortal but as the years go by your hand or knee or hip, whatnot? Will began growing lump or bones forming bone spurs. Anyway at 50 Elliot Street we had none of the below items.

Make sure that first-aid trained personnel are available to provide quick and effective first aid.

Make sure appropriate first-aid supplies are readily available.

Make sure first-aid trained personnel are available to provide quick and effective first aid. If you have the right friends then you can get away with murder in this realm of nightmares. Later chapters of this book will discuss these friends.

All morning we installed backing to hold the weight of the pouring concrete and using a defective hand mall to hammer down 4-inch steal pins. On a job this size hundreds of these pins are used. I was at their mercy and obligated to finish the site ready for the coming pour.

While the amount of fatal work injuries in private construction continued to be the most of any industry sector, the number of fatalities was 4 percent lower in 2004 and 2005. I wonder what it was like in 2000.

Overexertion was the number one job injury in Washington State; this number comes under skilled labor construction, or concrete related Private Contractors employees suffer these injuries the most because of the bosses neglecting to hire enough of a work force safely do the job to save money. That means that the men working are always moving about the jobsite under and around heavy equipment and steel hazards without the proper safety precautions taken to do the job right. The bosses push you and tell you that if want to earn the big money you have to be willing to also make sacrifices. I say hire the persons needed to do the job safely and correctly, but that is only my opinion. Overexertion has one of the lowest benefits and the least guilt put on the employer, go figure.

I visited the doctor office and filled out a job injury form, stating how the accident occurred and when, now it officially filed, L&I supposedly officially cover your bills.

Once forced and I returned to work, the physician had missed the snapping tendons and they swelled my hand more. My boss gave me a simple task to do repetitiously that was not to exceed 5lbs per lift. Of course, I had to lift more then ten pounds and given tough labor work to do while my hand was in a huge brace. Treated badly and regarded as if I was stupid. I kept taking photographs. It was obvious to any naked eye that my fingers were turning red except for persons working for L&I, my Attorney had important agendas, more clients then the firm could handle competently we all suffered.

I was speaking with the chamber of commerce in Seattle today and learned that the city is bustling with construction; I have spent three days searching for this jobsite on Elliot Ave and on the internet. It seems to have vanished after millions of dollars invested in building construction. I will be investigating this fact as I wonder where most of the money dolled out and how Canada's laws played into this scheme. This book will give explicit interviews given by some of the persons behind this job and the type of persons that they were. Business is the mainstream of American life but we can do without the pirates. Was the mock building of this project, intended as a way to cheat the taxpayers of Washington State? Makes you wonder about the possibilities?

The *Family and Medical Leave Act of 1993* (FMLA), (29 U.S.C. 2601 et seq.) requires employers to provide employees up to 12 weeks of unpaid leave each year to care for a newborn, adopted, or foster child. Leave also "must be granted" for care of a seriously ill child, parent, or spouses. In addition, employees may use unpaid family and medical leave for personal illnesses. Medical insurance benefits "must be continued" during the leave and employees *"must be reinstated"* into the same or an equivalent position after leave.

The law forced state and local governments to revise long-standing personnel policies and created unfunded costs related to extending medical insurance coverage to employees on family and medical leave, to temporary hiring of replacement workers, and to additional training and personnel counseling activities. The law contains special provisions for federal government employees, state and local governments are treated the same as private entities.

Leave policies of state or local governments determined solely by the employment policies of those governments. The public accountability of elected official sand the collective bargaining powers of employee unions will provide adequate protection for workers. Federal Laws protect us:

The Occupational Safety and Health Act of 1970 (OSHA). (29 U.S.C. 651-678) establishes standards for safe, healthy, and productive work environments. **State governments and their political subdivisions as well as the United States government, "are specifically excluded."** from the definition of an "employer" under the act.

In the case of state governments and their political subdivisions, OSHA has no requirements unless a state volunteers to participate in the federal program. States that volunteer to administer the federal OSHA program within their jurisdiction are required to extend federal requirements to all public employees in the state. *"You can wager that the contractors in Washington State know that most OSHA laws do not apply within Washington State."*

Twenty-three states have assumed responsibility for operating the federal OSHA program. Two additional states have federally approved OSHA plans only for state and local government employees. Even in the remaining states, however, there may be an impact, or a perception of an impact, because some OSHA requirements simulated in state laws or perceived as mandatory even though they aren't. ***"Are they telling us that OHSA is a big bluff, possibly compared to placebos for a basis of laws?"***

Numerous complaints expressed about OSHA policies in both participating and non-participating states attest to the widespread misunderstanding about the law's coverage and the substantial compliance costs. Making all states exempt from OSHA, would allow all states to set their own health and safety standards, taking into consideration their priorities and budgetary constraints. Such a policy would give states flexibility similar to that given federal agencies. ***Flexibility, I can think of better words to use to describe this supposed state of mandates.***

The Boren Amendment requires states to establish reimbursement rates to pay hospitals, nursing facilities and intermediate care facilities for services provided to persons eligible for assistance through the Medicaid program. The mandated federal criteria provide that the reimbursement rates must be "reasonable and adequate to meet the costs which must be incurred by efficiently and economically operated facilities in order to provide care and services inconformity with applicable State and Federal laws, regulations, and quality and safety standards . . . ."

The intent of the Boren Amendment was to give states a means of controlling costs related to reimbursement claims from providers of Medicaid services. Rather than basing reimbursements on a cost-related payment requirement for hospitals and nursing home services, the amendment allows states to pay for services based on a predetermined reimbursement rate, giving states a basis for denying reimbursement for costs determined to be in excess of that necessary to provide "efficiently and economically" delivered services. ***"In this manner, if the physicians do not send the paperwork that L&I wants to receive along with the one-sided evaluations, physicians get receive payment for services rendered next year or not at all."***

Although flexibility was intended the use of vague and undefined terms in the amendment created problems that were compounded by the federal government's decision not to issue regulations defining the vague terms. To add further confusion, the law, while requiring reimbursement rates to be "determined in accordance with methods and standards developed by the State," also requires the federal government to be satisfied with the state-determined rates. To implement this requirement the Federal Government requires state processes for determining rates and the rates themselves to be a part of Medicaid State Plans, subject to approval by the Secretary of Health and Human Services. *"Is this anything like passing the buck?"*

The vagueness of the legislative language combined with the lack of regulatory definitions has resulted in substantial litigation, with some courts viewing the Boren Amendment as a cost based payment standard in which all cost incurred by the providers must be reimbursed. In these instances, states may be liable for significant sums to cover the retroactive rate increases ordered by the court for the group of providers involved in the suit even if the federal government approved their rate schedule. In some cases, the additional payments made because of a court-ordered retroactive rate increase are not eligible for cost sharing from the federal government.

Because Medicaid is a state administered program and states are responsible for the quality and safety of medical services, states "should be allowed" to conduct reimbursement rate negotiations with Medicaid service providers without preconditions set by federal law. Litigation against states by medical service providers should be limited to matters related solely to the state's own laws and policies. *"This rule leaves the imagination open; Attorneys can invent their own laws."*

The *Americans with Disabilities Act of 1990* **(ADA) (P.L. 101-336)** prohibits discrimination against individuals with disabilities in employment, public services, and public accommodations. Any state or local Government policies found to be inconsistent with ADA provisions corrected as soon as feasible.

ADA provides important and necessary social benefits, but it is creating problems for state and local governments because of expensive retrofitting and service delivery requirements, confusing and ambiguous statutory language, and insufficient technical assistance provided by the federal government. Further, virtually no federal funding appropriated to cover most state and local compliance costs. With tight budgets and limited time to correct structural obstacles to improve public accommodation it has been difficult for many governments to implement the extensive changes required. Structural changes to existing buildings to meet "program accessibility" requirements were to be made by January 26, 1995, a deadline not met by many state and local governments.

In addition the use of the terms, "reasonable accommodation," Undue hardship, "readily achievable," Countless other broad expressions in the law have subjected state and local governments to numerous lawsuits over legal interpretations of ADA. The penalties for noncompliance are severe, and legal costs can be substantial. *"I tried to stay in compliance but once they began over prescribing me I stopped treatment."*

Federal enforcement of ADA is uncoordinated with eight federal departments having some enforcement power. The prime responsibility for processing complaints under ADA is the Justice Department and the Equal Employment Opportunity Commission. The Federal Communications Commission manages telecommunications issues. The National Council on Disability is an independent federal agency that identifies emerging issues and recommends disability policy to the President and Congress. The Architectural and Transportation Barriers Compliance Board provide some educational and technical assistance regarding accessibility.

"We have given you many words that are supposed to mean something, now allow me to explain. These laws have meaning only as we the people demand it. Reforms are needed and corrupt lawyers and politicians should go to jail because it is the American way. These words do not mean anything if your family is hungry and you need a job. As we said in the beginning, the deck is stacked against the injured from the start."

The End of Chapter one

Chapter 2
"Out of Work"

Your first compensation check gets to you in three or four months if all went well. Then you receive three quarters or so of your pay, remember that you have been borrowing money for months and your local business owners and friends do expect you to pay them back the money you borrowed. Possibly behind on the rent by now and you and your spouse are fighting more then not. The check came after the collection agencies called and the first eviction notice had arrived on your door. Do not panic, all this has a remedy be it a temporary solution.

With children your checks from L&I amount to more but not enough to make the difference you wished for. If you are about to retire before you are injured then expect a fight that could drive you into your grave. I have interviewed married couples collecting for two decades and with my own eyes saw the shape her husband was in, he was suffering and unable to work. Without warning, his checks had stopped and the Judge ruled against him making this poor family lose the only income they had to support themselves.

"Are you living paycheck to paycheck, and if you get injured on the job will the bank give you a break, will the gas and electric companies say, pay us when you can,
I doubt it."

There is no settlement for pain and suffering, no compensation at all, nothing, nada, zilch, zero. In many cases, waiting for their turn to come I witnessed normal persons become desolate or go mad. If you are an ethical person then you have a big problem. Expected to agree with your law firm on all things yet, they tell you their reasoning for neither it nor the purpose behind the cause. You get evaluated more if you are telling the truth by tour medical personal then they are of isolating the injury so expect a long wait. While you are waiting for this, so process to transpire surgery "is scheduled." Then you are suspect again. You get an ulcer from the stress and ruled not job related, you have doctors and therapists to see whose offices are an hour apart. Strenuous evaluations and stress therapy, physical therapy, perhaps a physiatrist?

"However, it is not their fault that your life is going all to hell, yeah sure."

Not much I can do about finding a solution for jumping through hoops, you must learn to jump high when they say jump. An injured worker will find it difficult to find sympathy even from family members or spouses. If you want understanding then you might wait forever.

Now you have a number that begins with a capital letter. Your attorney will tell you to wait until he calls you; while you wait the other side is moving fast against you as your own attorney tries to catch up on case files of others waiting like you are. Once you are, at this point all control over your life is in the hands of Attorneys.

A judge upheld the Washington State's workplace ergonomics rules July 12. The ruling rejected a business coalition's challenge to the plan for reducing musculoskeletal disorders (MSDs).

"We are pleased with the judge's decision," said Department of Labor and Industries Director Gary Moore. *"This is good news for the workers of the state of Washington who suffers more than 50,000 ergonomic related injuries every year. These are costly injuries and this ruling will save employers money on the bottom-line. This decision takes us a step closer to preventing these painful, debilitating injuries."*

Seems to me that they look good, taking our rights away from us. There are going to be two classes in America, the employers and the employees as long as these lobbyists keep convincing our elected Officials to vote against the workers of Washington.

What can we do about this syndicate type government; I do not have a clue because they seem to be anchored deep in influence and drunken driving, hit and run, cases sentenced with a slap on the wrist. How many Officials have aliens working bare minimum wage or less legal or illegal deciding your compensation? Scary, is it not.

The ruling rejected a business coalition's contention that the department exceeded its authority under state law, acted arbitrarily and capriciously, and did not properly follow rule-making requirements.

All kinds of places help, but what do you give in return? I am sure that what dignity you have remaining will search some more and find Catholic Charities. Salvation Army, Community Action ... medical bills arising from an on-the-job injury and for payment of lost wages delayed because of a court order imposed by the court.

Workers with job injuries may apply for SDI when workers' compensation payments ... Free "Guide to Church Insurance and Risk Management" resource.

The Occupational Safety and Health Administration announced the draft of a national ergonomics standard Friday that could require businesses to redesign their work places.

OSHA's six-part proposal could require businesses to redesign their workplaces in order to avoid repetitive motion injuries. It would affect workers susceptible to injuries as varied as carpal tunnel syndrome from working at a keyboard, muscular injuries from lifting patients in a nursing home, and repetitive motion hazards from scanning groceries at a supermarket. *"I guess we just missed out, what about our injuries and futures? I do not know how you feel but I feel that as an individual I must be expendable."* Who would have thought that I would become a Publisher, and now a Media Corporation?

As a Journalist, I am free to say my opinion and state my views without revealing my sources, which makes our country great. You can vent your opinion at **keller2529@hotmail.com** and we will publish it for you.

I believe that our President has done an outstanding job and believe that it is Congress, which let President Bush down. During wartime we need to stand together not stand apart. If there is not an overwhelming majority then our great president is correct in focusing on the war against terrorism allowing our Representatives to free-lace state law making. There are 110,000 unintentional deaths a year. In one way or another, they are job-related to one party or the other. Perhaps a job done poorly could qualify for this role. It is up to our; lawmakers to protect us from greedy entrepreneurs and the President keep our borders safe from our enemies. It is time that they started doing there jobs by agreeing for the same objective, victory at home and abroad. Out of work with nothing to do but be depressed. I would not advise it, I would advise you to have your therapy and physician records copied on a monthly basis as you go to the evaluations and physician appointments. Do not let your attorney know and do not give the law firm your records. Turn them over during discovery because their records came after the facts. They are always a step ahead of you, this will give you a better chance to receive exactly what you deserve, compensation for your injuries not mandated but considered as an individual.

  The following is good advice and I would memorize them if I were you. There is not a conspiracy against you, money is against you, I would not call protocol and   Proper Operating Procedure as a conspiracy would you? Well, I suppose it depends on the rules and there are so many of them along with tricks and cameras. 1. You are never out of work because you have to work hard following the rules just complying because if you are non-compliant then you lose your benefits. They try to give you more then you can do so you are always on edge.

  2. This is a great time to keep a log and organize your records.

  3. Never, miss an appointment and always be there on time.

  4. Remember these two rules A. When you raise your voice, you are ranting and raving or delusional.

    B. If an Agent or attorney working for L&I yells at you or your own attorney yells at you they are being sensible, and yes, possibly held against you.

  5. Always be respectful everyplace they send you so go with the program. First, be sure that is what you want.

  6. Learn to recognize tricks and watch for cameras, the most innocent move can condemn your case.

  7. Nurse your injury.

  8. What they say and then do can change without your knowledge.

  9. If you can, always bring a witness to an evaluation or doctor appointments.

  10. Try your best to find the time for your family while juggling a heavy caseload. Follow these ten rules while collecting compensation and

things will go much smoothly for all of you in dire straights.

Home when not on the road the only one that truly appreciates you is your dog because he or she goes along with you. A loyal pet is the best therapy for any injury or Illness, ask a Wise person if you want a second opinion.

Understanding is what an injured person craves for, and blame seems to haunt their every step. The wringer is state sponsored victimization project.

I suppose that you cannot judge somebody that you love, unless it is money, that you love and greed runs your life. I have investigated their homes and the great comfort Attorneys enjoy and amazed at their god-like demeanors served by the hired aliens; I wonder how they could afford it? I suppose there are good investments in the area and a smart person can get ahead in life quickly knowing the right people. Certainly, there are ways a shrewd attorney can find the end of a rainbow, and means to an end. I love Attorneys, they own us so why not love them but I can bitch if I want to. Following are some laws and guidelines that you need to know so you can be ware of what is happening around you, watching the actions carefully as they enter your case file.

BACKGROUND

Unfortunately, in many cases, injured workers suffer an injury or illness that makes it impossible to return to their job of injury. L&I or the self insured employers then begin a process that, in many cases, leads to an "employability" or "able to work" assessment. **(This happened to me and then I returned to work, only divided from the crews and the butt of rude jokes. My assignments were tedious and difficult creating more stress in the fractures of my thumb. This included working heights and climbing ladders with a broken arm and drugged on pain-killers and valium, with snapping tendons.)**

The problem is this: L&I adopted a standard in 1985 that defined "employability" or "able to work" as the ability to work at a job, that pays at least the federal minimum wage. Since 1985, about 75,000 workers injured so severely that they could not return to their job of injury found "employable." Their benefits have been terminated and they have been left in many cases, unemployed or working at jobs with substantially less income than their wage at the time, they were injured. They have received no vocational training, as they are ineligible once they "are found employable" at federal minimum wage. Workers who have spent years developing their skills deemed they can be employed at a minimum wage job, regardless of what they were earning at the time they were injured.

The problem is this: L&I adopted a standard in 1985 that defined "employability" or "able to work" as the ability to work at a job, that pays at least the federal minimum wage. Since 1985, about 75,000 workers injured so severely that they could not return to their job of injury deemed "employable." Their benefits terminated and left in many cases, unemployed or working at jobs with substantially less income than their wage at the time, they were injured. They have received no vocational training, as they are ineligible once they "are found employable" at federal minimum wage. Workers who have spent years developing their skills told that they can be employed at a minimum wage job, regardless of what they were earning at the time they were injured.

LABOR'S POSITION -- The resolution proposed in the 1998 Performance Audit. To quote, "The standard for employability as it relates to vocational rehabilitation benefits **should be some portion of wages at the time of injury rather than the federal minimum wage**." Labor is proposing a standard of 80% of wage of injury. A worker unable to return to their job of injury would be eligible for vocational retraining unless they were, in a vocational assessment, **determined to be able to work at a job that paid 80% or better of their wage of injury.**

"I will advise you that it is a roll of the dice and that few injured workers benefit from any of this. I can write another book named Labor and Industries Variables."

Benefit Levels

BACKGROUND -- Washington is a relatively low-cost, relatively high-benefit state. Because workers make a significant contribution to workers' compensation premium, they have enjoyed benefits, acknowledged to be among the top 25% in the country. *"I cannot believe that Washington residents enjoy so much unless it is a selected few of* *the majority that collect these monies."*

Calculated time-loss benefits are based on a worker's earnings at the time of injury using a formula that also takes into account family size. In addition, the formula provides for cases where an employer pays for some level of support for health care coverage prior to injury and ceases health care payment after a work-related injury or disease. In those cases, the employer contribution to the health care premium "is considered" in calculating time loss benefits so injured workers have additional resources to address health care needs unrelated to the injury or work-related disease. (This is the *Cockle* decision.)

Any injured worker can receive a maximum benefit regardless of the formula factors. Under no circumstances can an injured worker receive more than 120% of the state average wage, (approximately $40,000), regardless of how much they were earning at the time of injury. Most injured workers receive substantially less than the maximum.

Finally, time-loss benefits are set on the worker's earnings at the time of injury. *"This I learned can be ignored or fabricated or not considered"* By now you can see that so many persons and agencies have influence and power that policies are designed by those who are most influenced by Private contributors and private interest groups. While you are injured and disabled, you can learn about laws designed to make it difficult for an average person.

Appeals & Protests

BACKGROUND -- When an injured worker files a workers' compensation claim, the Department of Labor and Industries then decides if the claim is compensable and what benefits, if any, are due to the worker. By statute, an employer or injured worker has 60 days to protest an L&I decision. (The main reason an employer would protest is that claims may affect its "experience rating," which may result in a higher premium.) *"Workers are expendable."*

If an employer or worker is dissatisfied with L&I's decision on the protest, they may then appeal to the Board of Industrial Insurance Appeals. *"See what I mean, make time work for you and be sure that you have the correct physicians treating your injury."*

The problem is this: when an employer protests an L&I decision finding an injured worker's claim compensable, the claim is put in abeyance and usually Time-loss benefits cease. Because the protest resolution can take *months*, this creates an undue financial hardship for the injured worker and his or her family. Similarly, appeals to the Board of Industrial Insurance Appeals suspend the worker's time-loss and medical benefits pending, this decision. Most of the time, a board decision takes 18 months.

LABOR'S POSITION -- The solution seems simple. Whatever L&I's initial decision is, it ought to stand pending the next decision, whether it is a protest to L&I or an appeal to the Board. Organized labor supports this common sense approach. **(By the way, more than 70% of the Board's final decisions uphold L&I's initial decision that a worker's claim is compensable.)**

"Now you know that you have to learn where you stand when you are out of work. There is no such thing as boring, I thus far gave you more then enough to keep you busy while you are out of work, and your spouse can be a great assistance if you have one. The worst thing that can happen is L&I learning that you have no family base, then they think nobody cares what happens to you anyways so you become meat for the beast, a casualty of political warfare with the flying buck never running out of fuel."

With very few exceptions, workers' compensation insurance is a mandatory purchase for every business in the state. While a few large, cash-rich companies may qualify for self-insurance, all others must purchase insurance from an external source. Moreover, since Washington is one of only five states that forbids private insurers from Underwriting policies, most employers are forced to purchase insurance from the sole provider the Department of Labor and Industries. The Department is therefore in both the government regulatory business (it oversees the safety of workplaces, among other things) and the insurance business.

The Department of Labor and Industries is the third largest agency in state government, with more than 2,600 full-time staff and an annual budget of almost half a billion dollars. Since the Department is the sole insurer for all businesses, the insurance program it administers is also extremely large: the program provides insurance to over 160,000 employers, covers roughly 1.9 million workers, and collected about $1.2 billion in premiums in 2003. *"Seems to me that with that much money going around and so many injured workers running through the wringer for lack of funds, the bucks stop here and there and find homes in the pockets of who knows who? There is no way to know."*

The cost of purchasing the mandatory compensation insurance is a serious concern for many businesses. A recent survey by the Washington chapter of the National Federation of Independent Business (conducted before the 2004 rate increase was announced), found that worker's compensation costs were one of the top three "most serious problems" for small business owners, trailing only the cost and availability of liability and health insurance.

"These business owners as being significantly more problematic than Business and Occupation taxes, environmental regulations, unemployment insurance taxes, transportation for moving goods and services and hiring quality employees identified workers compensation insurance costs."

Industrial insurance laws through either the state fund or a self-insurance program cover almost all workers in Washington State, from clerical workers and bank executives to baristas and retail salespeople. Overall, it is estimated that a workers 'compensation program covers 90 to 97 percent of the American workforce.' In Washington and most other states, people who "employ" others temporarily for services such as house cleaning, garden work, appliance repair and newspaper delivery are not required to provide compensation insurance for the workers they hire. But almost every other type of worker who sustains an injury or occupational illness "in the course of employment" is covered and eligible to receive benefits. Moreover, the injury or illness need not be solely the result of work, since job-related aggravation of a pre-existing condition is compensable in Washington. *"Not if you ask your Attorney, he will differ with you. Protocols overshadow law, the Firm always comes first."*

"Pre-existing is a term used for applicants that do not qualify for compensation.

Perhaps on paper with words, it sounds peachy but in reality it is a sham."

In fact, Washington has more inclusive coverage laws than many other states, which often exempt key groups to help reduce business costs to employers. Fourteen states, for instance, exempt employers with fewer than 3 or 5 employees from purchasing insurance, and more than half have some special exemptions for agricultural workers. Washington does not have any numerical exemptions and the only agricultural exemption is for dependents under age 21 who live and work on a family farm.

3. Delays in injury reporting and claims initiation

The whole purpose of workers' compensation systems is to ensure prompt, reliable payment to injured workers - to provide "sure and certain relief" to workers and their families in the event of an injury. **Yet an astounding number of Washington workers do not receive benefits quickly because of the process followed by the Department.**

"It is like this: When the Government sets a mandate for a budget then it must be met. If the Budget is not met with compensation denials then the money comes from other places, Resources to help the injured and monies to pay medical bills and compensation. A balance is created using this system but thousands of innocent workers suffer because of mandated budgets L&I are held accountable to."

Many states have set and achieved goals to pay the vast majority of claims within 14 days of a worker submitting a claim. This is an important goal for the many families living paycheck to paycheck. Needless delays may make it impossible for a family to pay its monthly bills. In 1998, many states achieved this commonsense objective: 88% of injured workers in Oregon and 82% of injured workers in Wisconsin, for instance, received their first workers' compensation checks within two weeks of making a claim. In contrast, most injured workers in Washington must wait much longer to receive their first check. *"I will be more precise then they are. How does three to six months sound? They should say what it is, we are not children."*

This payment delay is largely the result of the Department upholding a "highly unusual if not unique" feature of the system. Workers in Washington report their injuries through their doctors instead of their employers, as is common in other states. Doctors can take days or weeks to complete and return the forms to the Department, but the Department does not begin the required 14-day countdown until the necessary paperwork is in hand. The audit team identified this characteristic as a "very serious weakness in the Washington system" and stated that no new legislation would be needed to change it, but the Department has not yet streamlined the process. Additionally, self-insured employers report the Department requires them to begin the 14-day countdown from the date of the injury, without applying this same standard to it. *"Special interest groups shine, red tape drowns out the victimized injured worker."*

The claims process does not improve much once the Department finally receives the paperwork from a doctor. The audit team found that the claims-initiation process requires claims to be passed through an unusually high number of departments and that it takes "more than six days to accomplish" what is just "90 minutes of actual work." *"They are not the people suffering, we is."*

Appeals process is lengthy and costly

6. The Washington workers' compensation system has many levels of dispute resolution that eat up time and resources. In most states, the appeals process is composed of just four steps, but in Washington, an appeal is subject to as many as **nine steps**. If the additional steps helped create improved outcomes they might be warranted, but the audit team found no evidence that this was the case. In fact, the team suggested that the large number of steps may cause claims managers to be less diligent in the initial review process since they feel they have a **"second chance to correct errors."**

"Perhaps our lawmakers should follow some well known laws that bring to mind how simple this picture is to visualize." There is no way to win, all the Attorneys belong to the same B.A.R Association and cover it each when it counts.

I. Every object in a state of uniform motion tends to remain in that state of motion unless an external force is applied to it.

II. The relationship between an object's mass *m*, its acceleration a, and the applied force *F* is $F = ma$ Acceleration and force are vectors (as indicated by their symbols being displayed in slant bold font); in this law the direction of the force vector is the same as the direction of the acceleration vector. Certainly perfect order operates systematically if it was observed by the public. I believe that there should be Public Representatives watching Labor and Industries and reporting there findings into the new directive that is most likely than not a pipe dream. If this did exist and the observers were picked from a lottery of the residents in the District that they lived, what would be the harm in applying such measures to governor our Governors.

III. For every action there is an equal and opposite reaction.

The second law states that the acceleration of a body is proportional to the force on it. This is consistent with our experience that the harder we push on a moveable body, the quicker its speed changes. The second law goes on to state that the constant of proportionality between the force and the acceleration is the "mass" of the body. In the form of an equation the second law reads **F**=m***a**, where **F** is the force vector, m is the scalar mass, and is the acceleration vector. The mass may be considered the property of a body that determines its resistance to changing its velocity.

Worker's Compensation provides compensation for employees who injured on the job. Compensation may include but not limited to weekly wages, medical expenses and pain and suffering, ***"pain and suffering is not compensated in Washington State."*** It can be a good idea to work with an attorney to ensure that you might, get compensation fairly for your losses. Often workers are injured on the job or on a construction site through no fault of their own.

Usually there may be many trades on a construction site. One trade or even the general contractor may accidentally cause another worker from a different trade to
be seriously injured.

In Washington, the general contractor of all work sites and/or an owner developer have a non-delegable duty to provide a reasonably safe work place and to enforce specific WISHA regulations. **(Washington Industrial Safety and Health Act)**

"Let us venture into these worlds of double-talk filled with shallow promises made into law."

WHISHA is Washington State's occupational safety and health program, designed to assure as far as reasonable possible, safe and healthful working conditions for all workers in out state. Established in 1973 when the Legislature passed the Washington Industrial Safety and Health Act, WISHA administered by the state's Department of Labor and Industries. Federal OSHA approves monitors and partially funds "state plan" programs. The OSH Act requires state plans to be at least as effective as OSHA.

WISHA prepares and adopts standards governing workplace safety and health conditions. The standards enforced by inspecting workplaces without advance notice, and by investigating employee complaints, accidents and fatalities. Compliance officers cite violations and may assess penalties. Employers and employees are notified of alleged violations, including proposed abatement requirements and an appeals process. *"I have known some of these inspectors and some of the staff go by the book but most are push-over's, cash, other bribes, new titles, there are many reasons to pass an inspection if a body thinks about it."* When WISHA receives reports of workplace hazards creating imminent danger of death or serious physical harm to employees, they are investigated promptly to ensure that the hazards are eliminated or restrained. WISHA notifies employees of their rights and obligations under the WISH Act, including protection against discharge or discrimination when employees exercise those rights. *"No way to enforce at secluded jobsites."*

WISHA encourages voluntary compliance by employers and employees in reducing safety and health hazards at their workplaces. Preventing workplace injuries and illnesses directly benefits employers by reducing workers' compensation claims and premium costs. A full range of consultation and outreach services are available. Consultants perform free workplace evaluations, providing employers with a written report of findings and recommendations about how to correct hazardous conditions.

No citations issued or penalties assessed. Consultants and compliance officer's verify the correction of any hazards or violations identified. *"In Washington the Employers come first, Seattle is a fast growing city and good contractors are hard to find for the surplus of jobs."*

Through training and outreach, WISHA provides information on how to prevent workplace hazards and accidents. Many workshops are offered on topics such as how to develop an effective workplace safety and health program, personal protective equipment, fall protection, ergonomics. And controlling claims costs. WISHA can also provide specialized training onsite at the workplace. Employers can borrow from a free video library'; with over 650 tapes covering topics such as back safety. Blood borne pathogens hazard communication, hearing conservation, preventing slips and falls and welding safety. The workshop and video catalogs are available on WISHA's web site. *"We here at brfe publishing LLC hope that we have given you some insight on what to expect and do if you get injured on the job."* Use your time out of work to get ahead in line for your industrial compensation claim.

The End Chapter 2

Chapter 3
"Part Time Work"

Here we are desperate and ready to find a job that you can do with your present injury. Every job application asks you if you ever collected worker's comp or had a job injury. *"You lost your job before you started it once you answer it correctly."* You can get an attorney that wills cover-up the work you make under the table and get comp and thousands contracting, working for attorney's hidden private properties or something else of the sort. Some extremely talented persons disabled, "on the job" that have exceptional abilities and talents. Attorneys can arrange the right physicians to get the painkillers needed by these talented injured workers to manipulate them into breaking the law. Since these attorneys make the laws, it just does not matter as long as you slide past their eyes, out of sight and out of mind; to be caught they have to single you out. There are ways around that too.

Injured workers have to share information about the events during their plight with a job injury and input the data into a computer. We can demand a change, who wants to work with or for a disgruntled Employer, and the sight of you irritates him? No American should experience the horrors of political corruption. Reading about it is one thing but when it affects your life, it is inside another ballpark.

If you are single then you bare this journey alone. If you have a spouse or a girlfriend or boyfriend then by now they are complaining. Pushing you to get a job, call
Relatives, steal, whatever the home situation might become is anybody's guess. You will find that a settlement is decades away, yet you need to survive and the compensation falls short of your normal needs.

The essentials of life are getting further from your reach and your attorney says do not worry, just wait this out. No matter what your home situation might be at this time one thing you can count on is desperation and disappointment towards Washington State Labor Industries, and the Attorneys behind it.

In recent years, the insurance industry's focus on cheaters and malingerers helped push through national workers' compensation reform, a profitable cost-cutting campaign supported by outrage over alleged abuse of the system. The problem, however, is that the fraud image is false for the vast majority of workers' compensation cases. Studies show that only 1 to 2 percent of workers' compensation claims are fraudulent. Certainly, the tens of thousands of workers killed every year were hardly aiming for a free ride on their employer's tab.

"It may be a false image but Labor and Industries takes this statistic to the outer limits of common sense."

There is no part time work, you are over-education for state sponsored vocational training, and you ask then what it is you should do? They ask you if you know how to use a broom or if you can deliver, pizza and you frown in despair. Did they forget that you are on medications and lost, that your next surgery is in two weeks? The Attorneys are calling your hearing short because they have to go and play golf; you are devastated as they laugh about it. You drive home passing help wanted signs on the roadsides, as your car is low on gasoline

Robert Stern of the Washington State Labor Council, AFL-CIO also sent a letter to Dateline reporter Tom Brokaw. He received no response. Dear Mr. Brokaw:

Approximately a week and a half ago, you broadcast a report on fraud by an injured worker in California. I frankly do not know whether this worker in fact committed fraud. I have no sympathy for workers who defraud the Industrial Insurance system. What is astonishing to me is that your report focused on what is accepted by the vast majority of academic experts to be, by far, the source of the lowest amount of fraud in the Industrial Insurance system. In every study done on fraud in Workers' Compensation, employer, insurer, and provider fraud were a dramatically greater problem than claimant fraud. At a time when injured workers throughout this nation are suffering enormously from "deform" of the system driven primarily by insurance providers, your report gave a seriously skewed presentation on the problems with the system.

"Robert Stern tried to help the people of America but his pleas were ignored."

I do not believe you have a serious interest in what is happening to injured workers, but if by chance, you do. I urge you to look at the recommendations that were made by the National Commission on Workers' Compensation during the Nixon administration. (An administration not particularly sympathetic to workers), then have your staff compare those recommendations to today's reality for injured workers. We should be ashamed of what we are doing to injured workers throughout this nation.

"My suggestion for some supplemental income is get a job on the internet. In this type of dire situation, you need a way out. Everybody can do only so much for you, and then you out-stay your welcome. Computers have the solutions to all your problems if you have the ability and time to search, unless your hands mangled or you are blind. Even then, voice-activated computers may help even those. If you ask for these items L&I must provide them if it will assist you in your job injury recovery."

I wish I did not feel cynical about sending you this e-mail. I am sorry that you have bitten the insurance industry bait, hook, line and sinker.

Robert Stern, Special Assistant to the President, Washington State Labor Council, AFL-CIO.

What is it going to take before we have to import labor because most American workers are injured during the job or because of the job? We as Americans are vulnerable to the alien workforce as they replace injured persons on the job. Is this what Americans want for their future? I doubt it; I think that Americans are feeling entrapped all the way around the spectrum of living in America, and helpless to change the flow for the better of the people, I believe that it is not too late; we have the time and before long realize that we are the power of America.

If you manage to find work then you are labeled and tagged for closing your case, I suggest that the work in this book is as much or more then a job. If you gotten a part time job you would miss appointments and stress your injury. L&I would suspect fraud and your injury would worsen.

Our investigations have uncovered a Mecca of names corrupted by greed and outside pressures, we will never publish these names but if we threatened in court then these names be posted on the web and in the New York Times the same day.

This chapter will be short like the days I spent searching for part-time work with my crushed hand. It is not worth the trouble but we will post organizations in Washington that do help families collecting workers compensation and truly care about your plight. I am revealing no secrets just common knowledge to the residents of Washington State.

The End of Chapter 3

Chapter 4
"Attorney Ethics"

This chapter will explain the lawful rules of attorney ethics and the perceptions created by it, along with ethics abused or ignored by many attorneys. Ethical values change from state to state and interpreted to suit the needs of the political agendas among the lawmakers community. Tailored to create revenue for attorneys and Judges Ethical laws are sketchy and create more work for attorneys. Words such as shall and may are words with double standards and interpreted by a Judge one way or the other, tailored to suit the needs of protecting attorneys and not their clients. This chapter will teach you how to use Attorneys Rules of Ethical Conduct to help you win your job injury compensation case.

Ethical Conduct Rules

The area of law dealing with ethics and professional responsibility extends to all industries with individuals serving in specialized capacities. For example, all U.S. physicians are required to follow the American Medical Association's Principles of Medical Ethics and the Radio-Television News Directors Association has a code of ethics their professional journalists must follow. Educators and community workers also have a code of professional practice and conduct. Some ethical conduct mandated by law for attorney's impact their client relationships. For example, an attorney has a duty to act with reasonable diligence and promptness in representing a client and must have the necessary legal knowledge and skills appropriate for representing the client. An attorney must also abide by a client's decisions concerning such issues, such as accepting a settlement offer, what plea to enter in a jury trial: and whether the defendant client will testify in court.

The law also governs how attorneys should behave with clients whose mental capabilities are impaired. A client's funds deposited for future costs must be maintained in a trust account. Additionally, attorneys cannot represent clients where there is a conflict of interest with current or former clients.

"How should Attorneys behave?"

Attorneys are forbidden from committing discriminatory acts, committing criminal acts (including assisting another person to commit a dishonest or fraudulent act) and from attempting to improperly influence a government or legal official. Falsifying evidence or witness testimony is another punishable action.

"I turned in objective medical evidence to my attorney and he refused to return them to me. They were Physical Therapy reports, medical reports, reports from specialized physicians and earned income." "These records were valuable for the treatment of my injury and litigation. Ethical responsibility of lawyers also extends to such issues as advertising and the manner in which they solicit clients, trial publicity, obligations to fulfill needs for pro bono services, and membership in legal services organizations, *"We have the right to know exactly where our attorneys go and who they deal with in handling your case."*

New laws or changes to existing laws can influence the area of ethics and professional responsibility law in other areas.

Sometime during your court proceedings, you will need an Arbitrator. The last thing that this person wants to do is get involved because usually it must be a Judge. This person is not supposed to know anything about you except the required paperwork filled out properly. They all tend to be indifferent to the client, not worth their time as far as they are concerned. This Hearing will decide the tide of the war between getting justice and compensation or ending like some, others have in the past.

From 1992 to 2001, a total of 2,170 workers died from suicides that occurred while the decedent was at work. These fatal self-inflicted injuries accounted for 3.5 Percent of the 61,824 overall workplace fatalities over the period.

This makes me wonder how many others intimidated by employers to reach limits that were unattainable thought about suicide. Labor and Industries could do much to prevent jobsite mass murders and suicides if they enforced the laws that they have in the books now. How will these persons be compensated and when? How many persons have lost their families and homes that are now living in the streets of cities all over America that have committed suicide? The questions will never end until all attorneys synchronize.

RPC RULE 1.12
FORMER JUDGE, ARBITRATOR, MEDIATOR OR OTHER THIRD PARTY NEUTRAL

The CFOI data also indicate that the risk of on the-job suicide was highest for men, older workers, the self-employed and agricultural workers. In addition, among the individual occupations, managers and administrators, not elsewhere classified, incurred the highest number of workplace suicides. However, police and detectives in public service faced the greatest "relative risk" of becoming a victim of workplace suicide.

The persons that we the people need the most are killing themselves over the stress of their jobs. What have Labor and Industry Officials done to help the persons that are making this country America? They use us as an expendable resource. A few sacrificed for the good of the whole until the few become the majority. You have to understand what it is you are up against and with all the red tape. It is not impossible if you do not stop trying and if you read all the books in this series. Books packed full of
information that you can use to stand your ground.

Twenty-nine thousand three-hundred and fifty Americans committed suicide in 2000, making it the 11thleading cause of death that year (homicide was 14th). Four times as many men committed suicide in 2000 than did women, and nearly 84 percent of all suicide victims were non-Hispanic whites. There were 3 times as many workplace homicides in 2000 than there were workplace suicides. Statistically, a man commits suicide in Ontario Canada every 10 hours, how many commit suicide can be compared and discredited but who will check on how many of these persons had previous job-related injuries? That will tell the story about the effectiveness of the procedures followed by Labor and Industries to ensure that the people get a fair deal.

"Compared to drinkers who did *not* report heavy drinking," said

Mark Veazie, assistant professor in the College of Public Health at the University of Arizona and lead author of the study, "those who reported heavy drinking were twice as likely to report injury in 1989 and 1990. However, most of this association appeared explained by the fact that heavy drinkers worked in occupations that are more dangerous and held jobs that required a high school education or less. This also appeared to be the case with drinkers who were classified as dependent on alcohol. Initially, they appeared to have a higher risk of injury at work."

Howland also noted several ways that heavy drinking could in fact be associated with workplace injury.

First," he said, "there is little doubt that acute exposure to alcohol, even in low doses, is a risk for injury, but it is also possible that heavy drinking has a residual impairing effect on next-day worker performance, even when blood alcohol is zero. This residual effect can occur even in the absence of hangover symptoms, such as headache, tremors, nausea, etc. The residual effects of heavy drinking have not received a lot of attention from alcohol researchers. There are, however, exceptions and some experimental studies have shown 'hangover effects' for injury. This paper adds to the small but important literature on residual effects of heavy drinking on worker performance and injury."

"All kinds of studies but no actions, all talk no results. I am the narrator of the facts; the man put through the wringer and escaped in one piece. There are anchor bolts, and other hardware in my wrist and hand holding the tendons together, constant surgeries for carpal tunnels. Constant pain along with the fact that I would be a hazard on any job that I worked has forced me into seclusion. All that I had to do was take anti-psychotic medicine and say I am mentally ill and stop writing and then I would be taken care of well. I am leaving out names as long as they leave me alone. My company was investigating them as they were investigating me. They underestimated me big time. In the coming chapters you will in detail the inside private offer that were made tome, without naming names but naming cities correctly. An offer; stop my writing and I would be set for life, but not in those words. Many persons believe that if you think you are right then you must be crazy."

Studies are great achievements but without counter measures to fix the system, the casualties from employment will collapse our great nation.

I am not pleased that authors compare alcoholism about your yearly wages or salary. Who are doing these studies and what are they drinking? I wonder. **"Selective statistical comparisons,"** I am not scared to tell you the truth no matter who hears it. Attorney ethics is control by those in seats and positions of power.

"Attorney ethics will make or break you. By law, they can quit your case at anytime they can quit for just about any reason. This happened to me while I was not present during trial, where is the ethics in that? They betrayed me as they have done countless others and the machine keeps rolling. Favors, if you have that then you are fortunate indeed. Rule of thumb, attorneys make ethics work for them and rule for them, if in their best interests the rulings suit their own needs the rulings will be in your favor."

Think good of others and they will become good. Seek the best in your colleagues and refrain from discussing them with others in the workplace.

Refrain form critique rather seek solutions. Don't misuse company equipment, stationary, and time.

Build a reputation of trustworthiness, integrity and being able to keep deadlines.

Do not make fun of your colleagues. Never swear, use foul language, or partake in profanity.

Do not yell or humiliate others. Keep your promises.

These are employee ethics that I believe are the most important to follow. I have a suggestion for another one: if you see an injury occur, you must report it to your supervisor.

Recent ethical, regulatory, and legal responses to enterprise wrongdoing is driving a sea change throughout organizations in the United States. There are many new regulatory guidelines in place, evidencing the urgent need to drive ethical behavior and establish integrity across both public and private organizations.

In the centuries before Christ, Wisdom appeared in two roles in Jewish scriptures. She was the creative, organizing; energizing, was the waste dispenser of ethical and practical advice. Little if anything is found in the *Gospel of Thomas* to support either function, even assuming that Thomas is here the dispenser of "wisdom". The Jewish Wisdom literature that has survived, while moving toward an affirmation of immortality, universalism, and a personal relationship of human with God, remained firmly based on the Law and Lord of Israel. In general, this body of writing combines advice about how to conduct oneself in the world, with promises of rewards for the righteous (who fear the Lord and obey his Law) and punishment for the wicked.

One can take solace in knowing that if you believe in god, then the persons responsible for your sufferings, severely punished in the next life. I believe that the Federal Government should take action on state insurance companies in operation with politicians.

Since the mid-seventies and increasingly since the beginning of the nineties, the ethical perspective has been moving more and more to the forefront of social thought. Every significant profession and every institution that thinks anything of itself has its "something ethics" to proclaim – environmental ethics, media ethics, research ethics, and even corporate ethics are the consequence. The latter has recently along with environmental ethics, gained most in significance. There are now a great number of national and international books, seminars, symposia, professorships, ethics networks, and journals exclusively devoted to business ethics. There can be no doubt that not only "ethics" is "in" business ethics is too.

"Lack of will power has caused more failure than lack of intelligence or ability."

It is not that our great country cannot find the answers; it is that they do not want to know them.

"I find that the harder I work the more luck I seem to have."

We know that attorneys regulate attorney ethical behavior so you do not have to be a brain surgeon to know that you are better off believing nothing until it is in your hands.

Some people, see things that are and ask, why? Some people dream of things that never were, and ask "Why not," some people have to go to work and do not have time for all that.

Thoughts are but dreams until their effects be tried.

Now is the time to realize that being injured on the job means going to hell if you live in Washington State? Where ethics are invented and it is never the bottom line but always the final word, who knows, your case could be decided over a game of golf between two opposing Attorneys, where is the ethical conduct in this situation?

The End of Chapter 4

Chapter 5
"The Wringer"

Times are okay, you have been collecting $2,500.00 monthly and you barely get by. Then the bomb hits when your boss decides to appeal your compensation to L&I and your checks stop for six months. You do not know what happened and you get an appointment to see your Primary care physician. After he refuses to see the obvious redness and swelling, ignores the high blood pressure your primary care doctor returns you back to work on limited duty. Now, welcome to the wringer.

"The above is only an example; you can put any amount in its place."

From this day on several doctors a hundred miles apart will evaluate you. You will not exit the wringer until your case is closed or you die.

During work hours, the others believe you are faking it and others show you their injuries and laugh at you. They work because if they complain then they lose their jobs. 'The Foremen's see that you're victimized and sympathize with you,' they refuse to help because they say that they do not count, it is impossible to go against the flow

Remember that when you go to your appointments always wash trim and clean your fingernails because many specialists judge you on this character. Some of the persons that judge you during evaluations suffer from a god-like complex. They feel aloof, a step above the average Joe or Jane. Many times you will be driving to your appointments after lunch from work; the cards are stacked against you.

Soon you feel like an exhibition or a lab rat as you try to make difficult appointments. Then when you arrive, you are scrutinized, asked stupid, repetitive questions, and then a book placed before you filled with photographs of persons. They mix them up and test your memory. During this time, video is on as you evaluated on your personal hygiene, then your posture, what you are wearing and finally your attitude and body signatures. I bet you did not know that your profile is data-processed into computers and data banks easily accessed by any decent hacker. Most days you will not get home until eight or nine at night. If you have an understanding wife that is assisting you then you are one of the fortunate ones. Otherwise, you feel like an expendable piece of furniture that has been around for to long.

    Paperwork piles and headaches are an everyday experience and fighting traffic is difficult taking medication. All ways in pain and painkillers stopped performing a year ago. Side effects from medications prevent you from getting a good night sleep and some nights sleep escapes you.

    Brent Ferry calls from Labor and Industries and he is your claims representative. You know that you are not supposed to speak with this agent, attorney, and profiler but you do anyways because you are desperate. Brent is typing every word you say but in his own opinionated manner. Brent tells you that your compensation was set to restart and that you should take $2000.00 settlement now while you can. By ethical law, Brent had broken the rules and had typed words you said in his own order. They are like weasels the night with the fox away. Brent was supposed to go through my Attorney and never to me. Know through experience that they can run you like a dog and ask you to resubmit the same forms repeatedly. They can claim that they were lost or never delivered, remember that it is not against the law for them to lie but if you're caught lying, then sentenced to prison. Double standards that you have to live with I cannot tolerate, nor will I. Never be late sending a document with a deadline attached to it. Missing a meeting is grounds to close your Compensation claim.

    The wringer keeps turning knocking you around passed one curve ball after another. That same night you go shopping and barely have enough monies to pay for the groceries, life can be ill fated if your life is in the hands of greedy attorneys saving for luxurious retirements.

    Deliberate misinformation documented in files, comments about your appearance, demeanor, attitude, if they like you then they give the evaluation that you need. For any reason, then it will be unfavorable to your case, perhaps if they do not like a certain look or a mannerism.

Color and ethnic background plays into decision-making by these independent evaluators. They say what they want, or say as directed to say by the persons that sign his or hers checks.

Blatant misinformation documented in files, comments about your appearance, demeanor, attitude, if they like you then they give the evaluation that you need.

For any reason, then it will be unfavorable to your case, perhaps if they do not like a certain look or a mannerism. Color and ethnic background plays into decision-making by these independent evaluators. They say what they want, or say as directed to say by the persons that sign his or hers checks. Many things affect your case such as the types of xrays requested and the lab work ordered. You will not find a grizzly bear in Florida. It depends what they search for on what they find wrong with you. That goes the same with cat scans and MRI's. Every so often, a specialist will glance at your injury and send a ten-page report citing that no remarkable evidence to report.

If you get anxiety attacks or angry then they say you had a preexisting problem and find a physician to elevate your mood prescribing drugs. Do not try and tell them at anytime that they were wrong because if you do not go to the doctor and take mind altering drugs you will be in noncompliance plus your attorney will quit.

Following are some photographs I had permission to take. You tell me how many safety violations you can find. Notice that I work as a one-man crew until the day of the pour.

Cal's Realm of Nightmares

A total mess when I arrived because of the lack of labors this is the job after I cleaned the jobsite. There was still plenty of water to pump and the rain was coming. I was promised a crew and labors at the jobsite. The owner and I discussed it at the Red Robin during the interview that I was hired. There was nobody there to help me and I started this job like any other job, cleaning the mess as I waited for the lumber to arrive. I was hired as a lead man building Concrete forms for the foundation of a huge shopping complex with condos.

I tried to find a reason why they were building this Project below sea-level and beneath a landslide? I found no logic in this venture except greed.

Cal's Realm of Nightmares

Cal's Realm of Nightmares

Iron-workers were days ahead, a week ahead of the Project while as one man I built the forms and installed them. It is easy to see the hazards on the jobsite and this was on a good day. Steel was dropped atop materials that were needed to continue working the job. I had pumped the water and was building forms. Sloppy concrete pours brought me down to my hands and knees using my straight claw hammer and a chisel and hammer to chip away the concrete from between the rebar before I could properly build and set my Simon forms.

Cal's Realm of Nightmares

    I received a man from another company and together we made more progress. We had to stack the plywood, move it to the proper location, and then we had to build the Simon forms customizing each form to fit the dimensions before us. You can see for yourselves the planks we needed to walk and move as we worked to get around the jobsite. Materials were simply dumped into the jobsite from the side of the road where we found our timber and hardware. Constantly raining and working soaked to the bone we continued to do our best to meet the deadline for the next pour.

Cal's Realm of Nightmares

My hand was crushed between a steel turnbuckle and an illegal sledgehammer provided by the owner of the job Contractor. This is where my hand swelled twice the size and I continued to work for three more days after reporting the injury and asking to see a physician, I was denied.

I was working alone again with the steel workers installing the backing. My helper called in sick. My hand was blue, purple and red with spasms and yet I was not allowed to seek medical treatment nor was any offered. It was difficult to move around the site because the steel and scattered left-over's.

Finally the crew showed up and I spent most of my time trying to get traffic control and briefing the Foreman on the job, basically how it was accomplished and who did it. First we added in the finishing touches to the job.

Copyrighted Material

56

Cal's Realm of Nightmares

I was never paid or thanked for seeing this job through to the end. Medical care was delayed and filled with surgeries, ongoing. I was given a 2% disability and barred from ever working again. I had been given permission by the owner of LAB Construction to photograph and document the building of this project that was more than a comedy, it was a farce.

End results, two surgeries and constant harassment from the Claims Manager. Where is you Attorney when you really need him. I will tell you where he is, playing golf with the enemy.

Cal's Realm of Nightmares

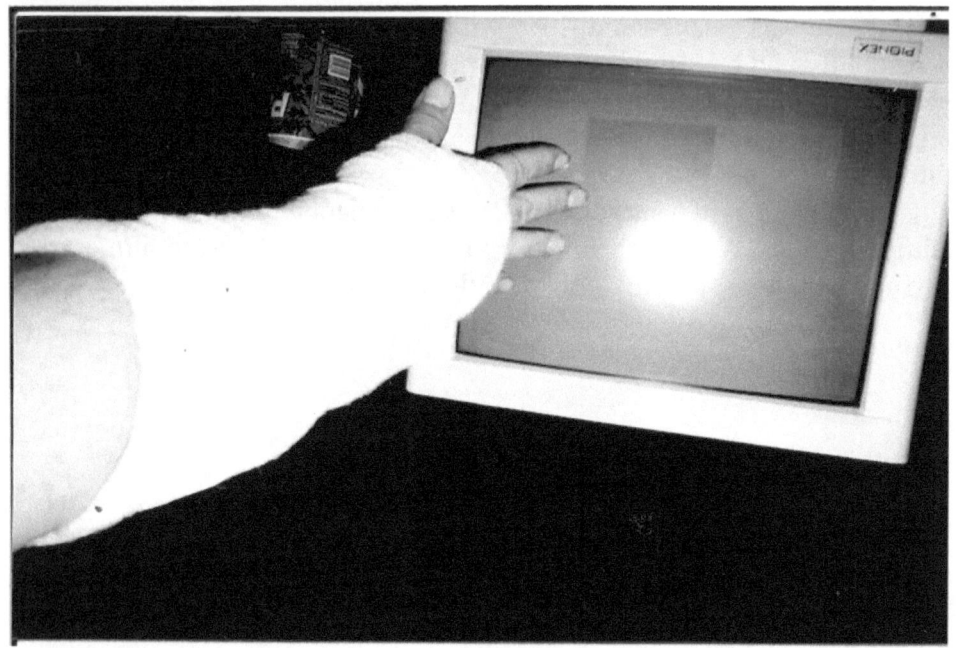

If you cannot depend on your Attorney to speak up for you, then it is always good to have a pet to tell your sad stories and cry with, as once more you are thrown into the wringer.

Cal's Realm of Nightmares

There was a labor but he worked for another contractor, I wanted to call him as a witness but my Attorney was against it. He worked for the Excavators and tried to help sometimes but it was rare that he did. I actually did the grading and hammered in the stakes for the pockets after pumping the water out, sawing plywood making panels, cleaning the sloppy pours beneath us covered with backfill, Jerry and I had to carry all the plywood and clean, pumping as we worked. Much of the time it was raining and cold but we kept working.

We set forms into place for 12 hours a day and Jerry was there more then he was not there so without his help, millions of dollars would have gone down the drain. We were never thanked for our great efforts that made it possible for the Pour to transpire.

My hand was aching and I asked to go to the doctor and denied my request. We had more work to do and all we needed was more supplies, but we could prepare what we did have at hand. By now, everybody agreed that my hand was seriously injured but I worked one more day. Boomer had to give the okay or I would get fired if I departed on my own to see a Doctor about my arm. These events continue to haunt me and I am sure that they will to the day I die, imagine feeling, perhaps knowing that you are expendable.

We hurried and worked the only way possible, which was recklessly and in a rush. Jerry scraped his leg and his knuckles were bleeding, gloves helped only so much with concrete. It was a lonely job with a supervisor stopping by to chat with us about everything and nothing, ignoring the fact that working was causing more swelling by the pounding of rock and steel. The foreman determined that it was a sprain. The next day we were almost ready but the pour came as we were adjusting the backing for the west panels.

Jerry and I finished the job when help arrived for the pour. You can see that not all the pours were prepared but the men that arrived soon reinforced the panels to get the job. I suggested to the Foreman of the pour to have this task done and after he ordered it so he thanked me. This foreman said that things were a mess and nobody had briefed him. I drove three hours to be there and brief the foreman and for my loyalty I was put into the Wringer. This was my last job. Notice that there is no traffic control and that the jobsite littered with hazards. Jerry is not a complainer and his hands appear as if a hand grenade exploded in them. He is in constant pain and will not dare to see a doctor.

It was in total throbbing agony, completely raising my blood pressure to a critical level. When it comes to staying out of it all, doctors' play by Labor and Industry rules, I photographed and told them I would publish my findings and they laughed at me at first. We will see if they think my suffering was funny now. Please do not talk golf with my attorney as you are deciding my case, your honor. It is a disgrace, I am extremely disappointed and know that this is going on now with another client in Washington State.

Isolated cases are now becoming average cases, part of the main caseloads. Physicians in special fields find work and so do foreign entrepreneurs. With millions of dollars stashed in several places without enough staff to manage it one can ponder the fact that monies vanish. Isolated cases like seeing a medical professional after you sustain a severe hand injury, or any other injury. Perhaps we the people been divided into individuals; I hope that this is not the case.

Labor and Industries deems writing as not a task classified as a job. The last thing they want is for you to become a writer and compose the horror you were pushed into onto pages in a book. Therefore no vocational training is offered in this field.

Some victims claim that after they went through the wringer they felt violated and did not want to speak about that particular subject. Is it no wonder that this corruption has gone on for so long. Churches, and before long your community, and then your friends begin acting as if you put yourself into the situation you are in so now bare it.

From the first time that I asked to see a physician and turned away, I was riding through the wringer. I hope that you remain safe on the job and if you are injured, then
get serious.

L&I Reps are nice, almost sweet and they sympathize with you but if it is not a simple case like a broken finger or carpal tunnel then you will enter the realm of the wringer. Everything becomes complicated and nothing is simple anymore. Your life and the lives around you possibly have changed forever.

A machine or device for pressing out liquid or moisture <a clothes *wringer*> b: something that causes pain, hardship, or exertion <his illness put them through the *wringer*>

Right out of the dictionary says it all. It is sort of like stage freight, once it happens to you, you feel all alone. Question this; as an American do you think that these practices are good for America?

The end of Chapter 5

Chapter 6
"Surgery"

    I doubt there are few people in the United States who have not heard of carpal tunnel syndrome. Most have a friend or family member who has had carpal tunnel syndrome and many have had a carpal tunnel release operation themselves. As with any common entity, there are all sorts of tales told about carpal tunnel syndrome, various ways to treat it, and even some real horror stories about bad outcomes. Carpal tunnel syndrome (CTS) has always been regarded in the medical community, as "simple problem" regrettably there has been very few comprehensive publications in either the medical or the lay literature to clear up some of the misinformation that surrounds carpal tunnel syndrome.

    Almost every wrist injury they dub carpal tunnel, this makes it easy for both your employer and Labor and Industry workers. Physicians can only search and identify what L&I allow to do so. L&I were on the telephone with my surgeon during my operations. If they did not approve it then it dismissed, in my eyes, this behavior is unethical. Do you have carpal tunnel, are you sure that is what is wrong with your hand, wrist and arm?

    This scenario works for foot problems that are syndromes and other injuries. They have it down to a science, like the casinos, L&I always win in the end.

    There are exceptions but theses exceptions kept secret. If you have something on them or they want something from you then you are one of the lucky ones. You can work and collect if you know the right people. The power that I witnessed daunts me and still haunts me; these people can zero in on anybody and make him or her history. Somebody had to tell it as it is so I am. Secrets are only secrets if you know that they will kill you if they find out you told the secret to another.

Here are some good tips about surgery for a job related injury.

1. be sure that surgery is a necessity.

2. Request a surgery sheet plan and have it copied. So you know what they are cutting into and the cost. How much money they are willing to pay for your operation.

3. Learn which procedures been turned down.

4. Research your surgeon's background.

5. Request copies of everything about the surgery.

6. Ask for a second opinion outside of your HMO.

A minor injury with a minimal amount of medical treatment and no lost time usually handled without a lawyer. Bumps, bruises, contusions, lacerations, or even a few stitches which are treated in the emergency room or with a few follow up visits to Doctor's Care will probably be processed routinely and not require you to get a lawyer.

On the other hand, if you have a severe injury you are more likely to benefit from the services of an attorney. A lawyer can help you get the proper medical care and compensation so you have the best outcome from your injury.

Sorry to say that you suffered a severe job injury, without an attorney, you most likely will get nothing. They have the market covered. If your employer seems to be angry with you for getting hurt or refuses to send you to a doctor, this may be a warning they do not plan to cooperate to get your benefits started. The employer is supposed to report the injury to their insurance company right away. The insurance company then "adjusts" the claim - investigates to determine if the injury is compensable and what benefits are owed. If the employer does not report the claim, the insurance company will not know about it and will not be processing the claim for benefits. This can cause all sorts of problems and delays. With a non-cooperative employer, it is probably a good idea for an injured worker to consult a lawyer. Previous studies had shown that patients who have surgery of the shoulder and spine due to an injury on the job tend to fare worse than other people having these surgeries. Attempting to shed light on whether this is also true for knee surgery, a new study suggests that patients who undergo reconstruction of their anterior cruciate ligament

(ACL) did just as well as patients undergoing the procedure for sports injuries.

Whenever there is an injury, inflammation ensues. Inflammation is a response of blood vessels and cells of the injured area that removes intrusive material so that healing
can begin. While inflammation has a purpose and a value, it must be kept in check for the healing process to go smoothly.

Back injuries represent the largest single contributor in injury cases and insurance claims in the manufacturing environment.

More than one out of five work-related injuries is a back injury.

Work injuries to the back occur nearly twice as often as any other injury.

Back injuries cause more than 100 million lost workdays annually.

Training and education employees on proper lifting techniques can prevent avoidable back injuries.

Personal risk factors such as age sex, strength and fitness influence workers potential for injury.

Several factors, including type of work, noise, temperature and design of the workspace can influence the safety of a workplace.

I had a back injury also that needed workers compensation and surgery. I want to thank California for fixing my back and giving me a decent award. Great therapy, honest physicians and an attorney who had my best interests in mind, as had the state of California. Washington State should pay California for lessons on operating L&I in their own state as California do. Most Attorneys in California refer to Washington State as enforcing draconian laws. Draconian may refer to: Laws created by Draco, an Athenian law scribe under which small offenses had heavy punishments; it goes the same with the entire Washington State law infrastructure.

Washing State should take a lesson from California Legislation and learn that good ethics save the state money.

What to do when an injury occurs on the job:
1. if it is a major injury, call 911 immediately and

render first aid.
   2. Get emergency medical aid; render assistance and first aid.
   3. Notify your supervisor > employer > medic.
   4. Fill out the Claim Form your employer must provide after learning about your injury or illness (This may be the State Form or the employer's form that contains all the data found on the state form)
   5. Get good medical care.
   I did not know these things because a book like this explaining the truth is not on the market until now.
   1. A claim must be filed for you to be eligible for benefits.
   2. Even an injury that does not require medical assistance should be reported. If you do not seek medical assistance, the claim will be filed as an incident. If you later need medical assistance, the incident will be changed to an injury and you will be eligible for benefits. (Examples; a cut that later becomes infected, a sprain that does not heal)

NOTE: If no claim was filed at the time of the incident / accident, you will not be eligible for benefits if you need medical assistance later.

   "Rules are rules and the outcome of any situation is how well these rules are followed."
   The number one cause of on-the-job injuries is physical overload. These injuries are cause by lifting (too heavy a load or lifting improperly), straining, overreaching, bending, and twisting. To protect your back against injury, learn and use proper lifting techniques, never bend or twist while lifting or carrying, and whenever possible, use a mechanical aid or get help with the load from another worker.
   "So many persons have back injuries because they are pushed and overwhelmed with more work then that person can do." Here are some tips . . .
   Non-traumatic Discectomy can provide an effective way to decompress and repair damaged discs without open surgery.
   Percutaneous Endoscopic Laser Discectomy is a technical surgery

under video-image through 1.7mm discoscope, following the making of just 0.6mm incision without general anesthesia.

The process is as followed.

The first step is identification of the Annulus fibrosus and confirmation of nerve root's absence through Endoscope. The second step is making an incision on fibrosus of disc avoiding the spinal nerve. Then mechanical removal procedure is followed with forceps on herniated disc.

This method is a new surgery therapy, in which any bones, any nerves and any muscles are not touched, with an inconvenience as degree as muscular injection.

The laser irradiation is so safe, because it is operated in watching through Endoscope and Monitor.

This is one of the desirable decompression methods to remove disc nucleus pulposus, and includes the merits of Endoscopic therapy and Laser therapy.

Microscopic Laser Discectomy

In this method, the minimal incision of skin may be possible without damage of surrounding structures, such as blood vessel, tissue, spinal cartilage, disc and muscles.

By using the automated nucleotome and recently developed microscopic laser it can be precisely irradiated to target, after incision of the skin with 1.5cm length and magnifying the target part with microscope, targeted tissue and scar are separated.

At there, damaged nucleus pulposus of disk is inhalated to decompress the inside of disc, and then laser diminishes the broken disc segments. Postoperative pain in this case is less than other conventional surgery and so the recover time is short. Hospital stays last more or less one day.

Most of all patients who have been treated in Wooridul hospital show the 95% successful surgery rate.

Percutaneous Cervical Disc Surgery

Conventional open surgery, in which the cervical spine is directly opened to remove herniated cervical disc. So it would be possible to bring about undesirable effects such as bleeding or neural injury.

This method developed from the combination of Percutaneous Manual Discectomy and Percutaneous Laser Disc Surgery, because pre-existing therapy could not remove herniated disc perfectly.

In this procedure, the patient has supine position with neck extension on the bed without general anesthesia.

After making 0.5cm sized incision on a wrinkle of the front neck, a fine needle put into inside of herniated cervical disc. Along with the needle, a 4mm slim tube inserted. Then, herniated cervical disc removed by using forceps.

At last, Holmium YAG Laser attached Endoscope is placed into the canule and then the herniated posterior disc is vaporized and diminished. There are several merits in this minimally invasive cervical disc surgery, compared to typical open surgery.

Arthroscopy is a minimally invasive surgery that allows for direct visualization of the exact site of the pathology via an endoscope. Unlike old-fashioned "open" back surgery, these advanced outpatient spine surgeries usually can avoid dissection of the muscle and removal of the bone. Because these surgeries are minimally invasive, patients with cervical, thoracic, or lumbar disc problems experience far less trauma.

Arthroscopic surgery patients can return to work and resume normal daily activities much sooner than patients who have had "open" back surgery.

"I am giving you a good look into the future if you suffered a back injury yesterday or last week at the jobsite, back injuries are always disbelieved until verified by a MRI."

Before surgery, your doctor will confirm that a herniated disc is causing your symptoms by using an imaging study, such as magnetic resonance imaging (MRI) or computed tomography (CT scan). Once confirmed, there are a variety of treatments that could first be explored when trying to treat herniated disc pain, the final of which is herniated disc surgery. Technology has recently made gains in minimal access spine procedures such as microscopic, endoscopic, or percutaneous discectomy. The difference between these techniques and open discectomy is the newly refined use of microscopes or endoscopes and small surgical instruments that necessitate only a much smaller incision. Smaller incisions result in less patient morbidity and quicker recovery from surgery.

Non-Surgical

Based on your doctors' recommendation, the first option will usually be a non-surgical action such as short periods of bed rest or medications that can reduce swelling and decrease pain. Physical therapy can also be an option to as well as customized exercises or epidural steroid injection therapy. Patients experiencing pain should meet with a doctor to discuss their symptoms in full detail, to pinpoint the cause, and then explore these non-surgical options.

Percutaneous Treatments

If these conservative treatments don't help, or if something less invasive than herniated disc surgery is desired, patients could turn to some new procedures that make use of small surgical instruments, which are inserted into the middle of the disc in order to destroy or remove the disc material. These instruments include suction devices, cutting tools, and laser. The goal of all of these methods is to remove or destroy the central disc (nucleus) in the hope that the disc material that pushed outward be drawn back into the disc. These procedures are not researched and are considered experimental.

Surgical: Percutaneous Discectomy

This is the least invasive of the surgical procedures surgery is considered if non-surgical treatment does not relieve symptoms. To relieve nerve pressure and leg pain, Percutaneous Lumbar Endoscopic Discectomy can be used and is different from standard lumbar disc surgery because there is no muscle dissection or bone removal. There is only one tiny incision to accommodate the micro instruments, inserted into the herniated disc. Most complications that occur with surgery are eliminated with percutaneous lumbar endoscopic discectomy. Generally, patients who do not obtain relief within three to six weeks may be considered for microsurgical disc removal, depending on the circumstances. The use of the percutaneous discectomy procedure usually does not limit or hinder the subsequent use of micro-surgical procedures to remove discs. You can expect to go home on the same day as a routine percutaneous discectomy.

Standard micro-surgical procedures or endoscopic surgery usually involves a partial disc removal or discectomy. In addition, the surgeon may need to access the herniated disc by removing a portion of the bone covering the nerve. Fortunately, these procedures can often be done utilizing minimally invasive techniques. Minimally invasive or endoscopic surgery does not require large incisions, but instead uses small cuts and tiny specialized instruments and devices such as a microscope and endoscope during the operation.

Thanks to a new, state-of-the-art procedure for total knee replacement developed by surgeons at the Detroit Medical Center's Sinai-Grace Hospital, the rehabilitation time for patients reduced from six months to six weeks.

If you have persistent pain, catching, or swelling in your knee, a procedure known as arthroscopy may help relieve these problems.

Arthroscopy allows an orthopedic surgeon to diagnose and treat knee disorders by providing a clear view of the inside of the knee with small incisions, utilizing a pencil-sized instrument called an arthroscope. The scope contains optic fibers that transmit an image of your knee through a small camera to a television monitor. The TV image allows the surgeon to thoroughly examine the interior of your knee and determine the source of your problem. During the procedure, the surgeon also can insert surgical instruments through other small incisions in your knee to remove or repair damaged tissues.

Knee surgery is in one respect like having kids both teach you that patience is a virtue.

Your neck is the vital passageway through which the spinal cord passes to connect the brain to the arms and legs and key bodily organs and tissues. The brain and spinal cord, with its important spinal and autonomic nerves, control and coordinate almost all body functions.

The seven cervical vertebrae (spinal bones) in the neck have highly mobile joints so that you can bend your head forward and backward, tilt it to either side and rotate the head an neck. Since the neck is exceptionally flexible, it lends itself easily to injury and pain.

Depending upon its severity, an insult to the head or neck may injure the supporting muscles, tendons and ligaments of the neck and perhaps interfere with essential circulation to the head and brain. A neck injury may even disrupt the functioning of the spinal cord and the autonomic nerves distributed by the cervical vertebrae. This can result in serious interference with the life-support communications network of the body.

"Bet you never thought about the neck pain you experience after work hours, have you?"

Some neck pain may be job related. Individuals who sit in the same position and face the same direction for long periods, such as secretaries and word processor operators, may experience neck stiffness and/or muscular spasms. Other jobs, such as those involving the repetitive motions which are common in industry, may also lead to neck pain. Workers who operate a drill press, power equipment or continuous assembly-line operations may feel fatigue and soreness in the supporting head-and-neck muscles. These and similar situations can bring on muscle tension and irritation of the nerves and blood vessels in the neck. Severe injuries happen in many ways and have long term effects.

"We have explored many common workers compensation injuries. There are injuries that are not in the books. Jobsite injuries can be quite gruesome and the compensation extremely low for the disability. Surgery is all bad, but necessary. We should be in control of the doctors that treat us and cut into us, not our employer. It should not be the state budget calling them as they see them."

It would be cheaper for employers if proper ethics were applied in Washington State, but surgeries are *costly, it is cheaper for them to burry you."* *For instance joking about my injury during a hearing conference call and having a conversation about golf was inappropriate at my final hearing as I was injured and fighting for a life. it made me give up all hope of continuing winning appeals once I knew absolutely that the cards were stacked against me.*

When your job requires you to stand on your feet for long periods, work in potentially hazardous areas or with potentially hazardous materials, you have some risk of foot injury. However, you can do a lot to prevent injuries by keeping your feet healthy and following safe work practices.

"In any given year, there are about 120,000 job related foot injuries, one-third of them toe injuries, according to the National Safety Council. You cannot take your feet for granted! In addition, your concern for them cannot be divided it should continue off the job, as well as at work."

Almost always surgery is the best way to repair a hip fracture. Doctors typically use nonsurgical alternatives, such as traction, only if you have a serious illness that makes surgery too risky. The type of surgery you have generally depends on the part of the hip that fractured the severity of the fracture and your age.

Construction workers are susceptible to every type of eye hazard known to the safety industry, and too many of them suffer eye injuries every day: Impact injuries from wood and paint chips, concrete pieces, and the like are common. Less common are injuries from ultraviolet (UV) radiation, liquid splashes and infrared radiation.

In a handbook titled *Personal Protective Equipment*, the Occupational Safety and Health Administration states that many eye injuries occur because employees wore either improper or ill-fitting eye protection–or none at all. In fact, a recent OSHA study estimated that only 34 percent of workers in building and construction wear nonprescription safety glasses; just 22 percent wear goggles. Workers who are injured because they did not wear eye protection usually say they thought it was not necessary.

"The U.S. Department of Labor estimates that 1,000 eye injuries occur every day in workplaces across America," says Dave. *"When you factor in medical expenses, lost time, and workers compensation costs from eye injuries, the total cost adds up to more than $300 million. And most of these injuries can be prevented with the use of proper eye protection."*

"Seattle is new and packed with fun. Construction is moving at a pace that cannot be filled with qualified contractors and subcontractors."

The 605 foot (184 meters) Space Needle designed by Edward E. Carlson for the 1962 World's Fair in Seattle. The futuristic structure, has become a symbol for the city
and is home to festive events such as the annual New Year's Eve fireworks display.

The structure has gone through many transformations. Early plans called for a tethered balloon. Carlson's plan called for a soaring needle topped by a disk reminiscent of a flying saucer. The structure required a 120-foot-square underground foundation. 467 cement trucks spent an entire day filling the hole. The completed foundation weighs as much as the Needle.

Massive steel beams form the slender legs and upper body. The structure designed to withstand a wind velocity of 200 miles per hour, but storms occasionally force the facility to close. Several earth tremors have caused the Needle to sway. However, the original designers doubled the 1962 building code requirements, enabling the Needle to withstand even greater jolts.

The Space Needle was completed in December 1961, and officially opened four months later on the first day of the World's Fair, April 21, 1962. The Space Needle is in the midst of a $20 million revitalization effort. Nearly every aspect of the 1962 World's Fair centerpiece has been or is being updated, including the entry level, restaurant, and Observation Deck, all the way down to the grounds surrounding the attraction. ***"This was by far the most dangerous project in Seattle and the jobsite injury occurrences were rare."***

"Seattle is a beautiful city that is growing at an astronomical rate. That is why we should be sure not to rush our building projects so that in case of an act of god
Seattle will remain standing."

The Seattle Art Museum features contemporary art, Northwest coast Native American art, Old Masters and African masks, along with rotating exhibits of works from their 21,000-object Seattle Art Museum collection and frequent traveling exhibitions.

The Emerald City is home to many award-winning museum exhibits including Native American, Seattle and Seattle Asian art; doll collections from Barbie to Madame Alexander; vintage airplanes; hands-on exhibits; Seattle and Washington history; snake identification resources, glass making and history and much more.

"Rain forest," The words conjure up images of exotic flowers, colorful birds, lush plant life, and high humidity. These ideas are true of the tropical rain forests of equatorial Central and South America. Few people, however, realize that a similar climate and circumstances exist in North America, which has produced an area known as the temperate rain forest. The images one has of the tropical rain forest are also true of the *old-growth forests* of the Pacific Northwest. The mild climate and location of the area have produced an ecosystem in which time passes very slowly. Trees in this forest grow to immense sizes and live incredibly long lives. The biomass of these forests, estimated to be between 500 and 2000 metric tons per hectare, exceeds that of the tropical rain forests. This factor also makes them valuable economically, and this has led to a reduction in their size.

"I have seen hundreds of illegal aliens working organized cutting down thousands of cedar trees. They are destroying the state of Washington and Labor and Industries do little to stop them. No permits, no licenses and a motor pool filled with trucks used to transport laborers and the bigger trucks they use to steal American wood. I was always well armed and brought a German Sheppard and a pit-bull along that tracked these millionaire poachers. How can we allow these criminals, nothing short of outlaws to steal our timber and haul them out of state, soon to be used in Japan bring up another issue? Why."

"No doubt, they have stolen tens of thousands of trees with immunity. Where are the Authorities? Everybody knows these acts of terrorism are being committed in Washington State yet nothing is done to quell this great danger to Washington State, and the stealing of our natural Resources"

"What is the big deal, it is our money in the first place. If injured

on the job, all Americans should have the right to receive the correct treatment with dignity and respect and then they be compensated. It should be an easy process, and it would take fewer attorneys if a better plan replaced the corrupted system that is in place now
and the code of ethics followed. Washington could prosper the heights never known to the state in its history."

Now let us learn about the great cedar trees: The Olympic temperate rainforest is a moist world of tall trees and dense shrubs in the understory.

Perhaps I am years away from seeing this happen, perhaps Washington will be ruled by the powerful and the rich and if that happens more then it is now, the residents of Washington will be at each other's throats trying to squeeze out a living from what is left-over.

There was a real good man who was always helping others. If they needed, he gave; when they wanted, he gave them food and clothing. When the Great Spirit saw this, he said, "That man has done his work; when he dies, where he is buried, a cedar tree will grow and be useful to the people: the roots for baskets, the bark for clothing, the wood for shelter."

Western Red Cedars were by far the most important trees in the forest for the Pacific Northwest coastal people. Their importance reflected in the custom of reciting a prayer to the spirit of the tree before it or some part of it is taken. This is part of the greater system, among most Native American peoples, of giving obeisance and respect to the natural resources that have sustained their lives for so long, to the Coastal people, the Red Cedar is the "tree of life."

Harvesting Red Cedars requires some ceremony, and includes appeasing the tree's spirits as well as those of the surrounding trees. This spirituality of the Red Cedar is part of an overall respect and reverence for nature. It is the basis for the deeply held philosophy that one does not take more than one needs, and one always makes sure that one puts something back in exchange for what was taken.

"What if an American family wanted to saw down a huge cedar tree and mill the wood to build a house he or she would go to jail. Yet, hundreds of alien contractors are blatantly stealing our cedar trees

without a DNR Agent anywhere, seems that the logging trucks were immune to inspection and I was fortunate to leave their domain on my own two feet."

I observed this activity for two years time and if anything, more aliens were standing alone to be picked up or in groups deep in the rainforests on nearly deserted Roads.

If you are injured on the job, L&I decide what treatments they will pay, I hope your workplace injury surgery is approved your if you have a surgery pending. *"This is good for them but for you your injury festers."*

Two related studies, using different methodologies, found that back surgery did produce slightly better outcomes than non-surgical treatment. Both studies are published in the Nov. 22/29 issue of the Journal of the American Medical Association.

"The bottom line is that surgery works," said Dr Todd Albert, co-author of one of the studies and vice chairman of the department of orthopedics and president of the Rothman Institute at Thomas Jefferson University in Philadelphia. *"Non-operative treatment can work, and people can do well with it, but surgery worked better."*

But surgery is definitely not for everyone, added another of the study's authors, Dr. Alan S. Hilibrand, associate professor of orthopedic surgery at Jefferson Medical College.

"The person who comes in with leg pain from a herniated disc has a good chance of getting better with no operative treatment and, unless they have certain unusual things going on, they should be treated non-operationally initially," he said. *If they're not getting better, they're likely to do well with surgery."*

In fact, in general, the procedure should be reserved for herniated discs causing leg pain (sciatica), not for back pain caused by degenerated discs, Hilibrand explained.

Misleading information or misinformation is a professional tool. *"The key words are shall, shall, may, and words such as these that are left to be interpreted by a Judge or Judges."* Herniated discs occur when the nucleus of a spinal disc -- the cushioned part of the spine -- pushes into the spinal canal due to a tear or rupture. Many people recover from herniated disc A League of Their Own, but others require operations.

As the study points out, there are high variations in rates of this operation in the United States and, generally, lower rates internationally. That raises the question of whether and when it is appropriate to perform the procedure.

For the first study, close to 500 patients with herniated disc and sciatica randomly assigned to undergo surgery or receive non-operative treatment, which included
physical therapy and counseling.

Those undergoing surgery had slightly better outcomes in the areas of pain and physical function as well as severity of sciatica, satisfaction with symptoms and Employment status.

One caveat: There was a high crossover, meaning many patients switched groups. This made direct comparisons more difficult, the authors said.

"I hope that this book is helping prepare for your compensation case or that you see L&I under a new light, if you are healthy and in the work force here in the
United States of America."

This is the end of chapter six and I am sure it has helped you understand the seriousness of this ongoing crisis in Washington State.

There are my opponents who claim I am making too much out of this but I must beg to differ with these persons. They are right when they say I am nobody and nobody will listen to me. Persons of great status and power in our Government do not get replies from Washington State. Letters are unanswered and Washington State politicians ignore pleas. Now is the time to make a difference and signal by voting for outrageous opponents. Who can say anyone can beat this conspiracy outside of a Federal Agency; and guidelines that Agents must follow prevent a job well done.

I noticed that the agents working as tellers and information topics among other persons of low or middle status has encouraged me to write this book. I have only just begun. People want to have justice but are afraid to ask for it because the persons doling out justice frighten them.

Keep in mind that from the beginning you are only a number and in the end that is all you will be to your Washington State

Government because all they see is the numbers and the State Budget liberally distributed among them. Saving money means more money in their pockets. This system was devised by Attorneys to work for their best interests. Never forget that once you are in their system that they own you.

What happens when you lose you arm that you depend on to earn a living taken out of your life and your boss is demanding that you return to work. .

Blood was unable to move, no circulation to speak of turned my hand bloody-red. I was shocked to hear that I was near non compliance in going back to work. *"What were they nuts, what other way is there to explain this? Indeed, there is another way."*

Police and detective work can be dangerous and stressful Competition should remain keen for higher paying jobs with State and Federal agencies and police departments in affluent areas; opportunities will be better in local and special police departments that offer relatively low salaries or in urban communities where the crime rate is relatively high.

Applicants with college training in police science or military police experience should have the best opportunities.

The state has ordered a 75-year-old Eastern Washington resident to pay back almost $59,000 in workers' compensation benefits that he collected illegally.

The Department of Labor and Industries ordered Alton Foster of Keller, Ferry County, to repay benefits he received from June 1996 to March 1999. Foster began receiving a pension in 1984 for a work-related injury that left him permanently disabled.

However, a department investigation showed Foster continued to collect benefits even though he returned to full-time employment in 1996.

He also filed annual statements during this time saying that his injury continued to prevent him from working.

During the time he collected the benefits illegally, Foster worked as a police officer with the Colville Confederated Tribes in Nespelem.

"They put us into this situation, trying to pay our bills anyway that we can knowing full well that we are risking our lives. Washington State puts you into this scenario and you were their fall guy, the patsy. Exactly like the thousands before your case you fall a victim to a combination of personal gain by agencies outside your knowledge and the budget of the State of Washington."

The repayment order includes the $39,000 Foster received in benefits plus a 50 percent penalty that state law allows in such fraud cases.

The department discovered the fraudulent payments by cross-matching its files with documents at the state Department of Employment Security. Records at Employment Security showed a work history for Foster, prompting the investigation. Labor and Industries manages the workers' compensation system in Washington. It provides coverage to about 163,000 employers and almost 1.4 million workers. *"This case was not fraud it was victimization of the Government by numbers."*

The Department of Labor and Industries' fraud program recovered more than $27 million in the first three months of this year, according to a report sent to the state Legislature and the Office of Financial Management. The money recovered represents delinquent workers' compensation premiums and improper payments to health-care providers and workers. *This means that people were targeted and baited.*

In 2004, the Legislature gave L&I additional money and legal authority to pursue fraud and abuse in the workers' compensation system. The Legislature also required L&I to file quarterly reports in fiscal year

2005, explaining how the agency was spending the money and how much money it recovered. The newest report, covering January, February and March of this year, highlights those efforts. Activities include:

Working with the Office of Inspector General, an L&I investigation led to a guilty plea and three years in federal prison for a man who created a company for the sole purpose of filing false claims for workers' compensation and employment security benefits. In addition to the prison sentence, the man has been ordered to repay L&I $127,444 in benefits, interest and penalties. *"This is one example for claims managers to use to persecute the innocent, how long had the Government allowed this to continue before making the arrest, and was there people on the inside? Makes a body wonder about this whole system, should not the Attorneys involved been heavily prosecuted? I would think so but there was no mention of it."* We are believed to be cheating the state until we prove that we are not. Is this any way to treat decent hard-working Americans? I think not.

In broad terms, **political corruption** is the misuse by government officials of their governmental powers for illegitimate private gain. Misuse of government power for other purposes, like repression of political opponents and general police brutality, is not considered political corruption. Illegal acts by private persons or corporations not directly involved with the government are not considered political corruption either

All forms of government are susceptible to political corruption. Forms of corruption vary, but include bribery, extortion, cronyism, nepotism, patronage, graft, and embezzlement. While corruption may facilitate criminal enterprise such as drug trafficking, money laundering, and trafficking, it is not restricted to these organized crime activities. In some nations corruption is so common that it is expected when ordinary businesses or citizens interact with government officials. The end-point of political corruption is literally "rule by thieves."

What constitutes illegal corruption differs depending on the country or jurisdiction. Certain political funding practices that are legal in one place may illegal in another. In some countries, government officials have broad or not well defined powers, and the line between what is legal and illegal can be difficult to draw. Washington State uses this to their advantage to prevent disclosures that can lead to indictments. Double standards stack the bricks that shut you out of a fair compensation.

Bribery around the world is estimated at about $1 trillion (£494bn) and the burden of corruption falls disproportionately on the bottom billion people living in extreme poverty. "Wow, so the richer that you are the more likely your case will wing it through the system and you get the highest rewards and benefits while the poor who stand up for their rights to put up a good fight do not have a chance as they fall deeper into Poverty.

End of Chapter 6

Chapter 7
L&I Physicians

Be alarmed, without a doubt these physicians work for the Department of Labor and Industries and file the reports that gets them paid for their services. Your Claims Manager calls the shots and not your Doctors.

Injuries can range from damage so minor as to be hardly noticed, to that which is so severe that it causes death or prolonged disability. The size of the problem becomes apparent when it is realized that almost a quarter of all deaths in Europe and the US are caused by injury, particularly to children and young people (six times as many children die from injury than from cancer). In Britain, road traffic accidents are the main cause of death from injury, but in the US gunshot and knife wounds kill more people every two years than the total number of fatalities in the whole of the Vietnam War, and in young black males gunshots at home are the single greatest cause of death.

The pilot database has allowed the combination of the costs linked to individual ACC claims (which exclude hospital treatment) with the costs of the hospital treatment for that injury. The injuries identified in the pilot test had incurred costs of $171.2 million by the end of December 2002. Although only about 5 percent of all injuries identified in the pilot test were covered by ACC claims that involved entitlement payments, these injuries accounted for about 50 percent of the total costs of all injuries identified in the pilot as reported by December 2002. This proportion would be expected to increase over time, as some injuries, especially those in this group, will continue to incur costs for many.

It should be noted that the Department of Labor is currently undertaking a project to identify appropriate methods of estimating the costs of injury. Once recommendations have been made, it may be possible to incorporate these so that more comprehensive estimates of the cost of injury can be made.

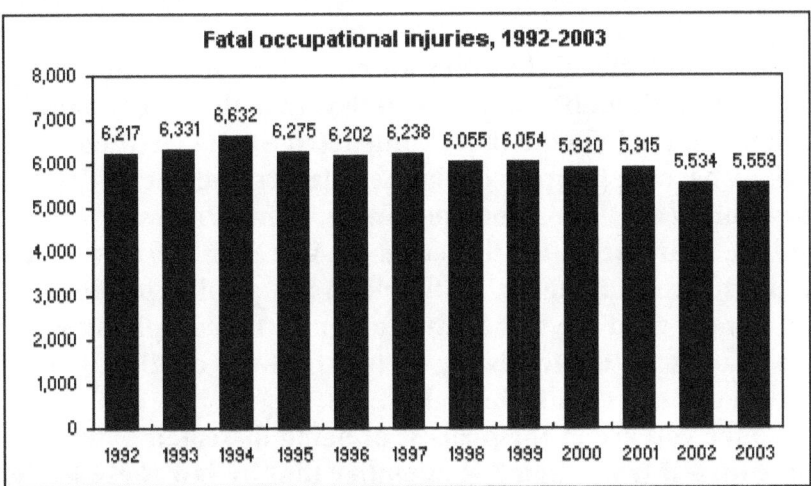

This chart does not include those persons that died from the trauma of being run through the wringer.

The Insurance Information Institute estimates that fraud accounts for 10 percent of the property/casualty insurance industry's incurred losses and loss adjustment expenses, or about $30 billion a year. Fraud may be committed at different points in the insurance transaction by different parties: applicants for insurance, policyholders, third-party claimants and professionals who provide services to claimants. Common frauds include "padding," or inflating actual claims; misrepresenting facts on an insurance application; submitting claims for injuries or damage that never occurred; and "staging" accidents. Prompted by the incidence of insurance fraud, about 40 states have set up 48 fraud bureaus (some bureaus have limited powers, and some states have more than one bureau to address fraud in different lines of insurance). These agencies have reported increases in referrals (tips about suspected fraud), cases opened, convictions and court-ordered restitution.

"Perhaps we should hear more about some of these persons getting busted? Some injuries will prevent you from working two hours

but for one hour you are at your best. Sometimes you can carry groceries and at other times you can barely get on your feet. With a camera following you around think how easy it is to edit which shots you are filming. Once you are injured on the job the first suspect is you."

  I interviewed at least a dozen care workers and specialist Physicians and learned that they all have the same complaint about Washington State Labor and Industries. In order to get paid for their work done on L&I clients these contracted State Certified L&I physicians become puppets of the Legislators and the Officers of Washington State Labor and Industries. Some Professionals go as far as sending their patients bills because L&I refuses to pay or take up to two years to sent payments. With only a few strokes of the pen this doctor can get paid the same day, go figure. By complying with the Claims Managers' demands for certain findings or dismissing medical objective evidence on a technicality.

  Once you are in the process of being dissected how can you defend yourself from them? Remember that by law these leaders are immune from prosecution for laziness, lying, incompetence, or being stupid. Can you believe that this is written into law, believe it. Yet there are laws passed that make the victim accountable for everything he or she do or say. Your Attorney can quit your case at any time for and reason. Attorneys use this law to keep their clients at bay while the State dissects the victim for information that can assist them in stopping your claim.

  It is unethical for your Attorneys to consult with your treatment specialists and doctors. I have seen them scheme together, all three, your attorney, L&I Claims Manager and your own doctor. There is no balance and justice lies in the hands of those living in mansions and playing golf as their people suffer. Ethical behavior can be defined by the dictionary or defined by your Legislators to suite there own budget needs and pocket books.

  What Happens to those persons with a 2% disability rating by your doctors and you are 100% disabled. I will tell you what happens. "You bend over and grin as you and or your family is booted into the street. My Attorney quit in the middle of my compensation settlement trial and left me hanging. This happens to thousands of claims because the injured worker has run out of money or will to carry on the fight. In my case, my lawyer offered me a $500,000.00 settlement if I pleaded insane and stopped writing books. It has been a hard life but this is my sixth book that I published after turning down my Attorney. All my books are distributed or in the distribution process.

State Facilities Detachment

This detachment provides security, protection and assistance to the Department of Labor & Industries Office in Tumwater as well as the State Archives Office. The investigation of criminal offenses, threats, trespassing and protection of precious state documents such as the original state constitution are among this unit's duties as well as providing detailed security assessments for state facilities.

What about all the files that get lost and information on microdots that vanish. If nobody can get into this facility then it must be the Staff losing documents and records vital for clients to get a fair hearing and judgments. These lost files are managed by both sides of your compensation claim so your case is decided by Attorneys before you ever have a chance to prove your case.

Our state's competitiveness standing on employment costs include more than just workers compensation. L&I should do everything possible to help make our state competitive. Employers don't look only at one segment of their bottom-line; they look at the total picture. Something that L&I refuses to do when considering the imposition of another tax increase on employers. When our economy is so fragile, employers cannot absorb this rate increase along with increases to health care, minimum wage, liability insurance and unemployment insurance along with regulatory increases of complying with the state ergonomics rule. Employers in our state cannot continue to absorb all of these costs while at the same time providing jobs....does anyone care what this is doing to me and my employees? Something has to give!

"There is no excuse for the lack of funds and for employers to be taxed. The Attorneys for the Washington State Legislators are paid hefty fees to maintain the secrecy and the persons involved in making major L&I decisions, monies vanish, lost forms and paperwork trails that lead

to nowhere constitute the reason behind the lack of funds to support Washington State Labor and Industries."

INS has shifted focus, halted field raids

This stoop labor, which begins at dawn and continues seven days a week through the asparagus season, is some of the hardest work in agriculture -- an arduous first foothold on the American economic ladder for undocumented Mexican workers.

Of the 54 workers laboring in this sun-baked field, perhaps 12 are in the United States legally, estimates foreman Juan Hernandez.

"Are we going to put all the white people out there with a bucket on their hip?" asks Hernandez, who came here legally in 1975, starting as an asparagus cutter. "I don't think so."

While the law doesn't allow it, U.S. immigration practices and economic realities have all but guaranteed it: Undocumented workers, an estimated 6 million of them, are a mainstay of industries across the United States.

"I ask you my readers; does this make a statement that can be ignored? It seems that there are those persons above the law and those who are subject to the laws of this great nation." And in Washington, where agriculture remains the dominant industry and a top employer, undocumented Mexicans comprise up to 70 percent of seasonal farm workers. Their low-wage labor allows the state's $1.2 billion tree-fruit industry to compete on the international market and gives Americans the lowest food prices in the world.

What doctors do these illegal immigrants see and who pays for their treatment? It makes for a formidable, if largely illegal, economic triad: In March, under pressure from growers and politicians, the Immigration and Naturalization Service (INS) quietly signaled a significant shift in national enforcement policy: That is where our monies go and I for one count all the homeless peoples in this great nation and how they could make the difference up in taking these non skilled labor jobs. San Francisco successfully operates such a program and I believe that it shows a great example of how Americans can have American jobs. It would generate the economy and fill the unemployment ranks along with giving these persons another chance for a decent life. Ask them, homeless will work for a living if they could find a job. Finding a job when you are living in the street is nearly impossible to accomplish with the Government aid and assistance offered to only Mexicans.

An Independent Medical Exam (IME) is a medical evaluation that may be requested by a claim manager or self-insured employer. The purpose of the examination is to establish clinical observations and conclusions about the worker's condition.

These evaluators check the dirt in your fingernails, judge your wear and appearance in general, they are there to prove for L&I that your injury is not severe or caused before the accident. Remember that the cards will always be stacked against you and you have to fight to win your compensation rights. You have to fight for your rights and ignore the way you are treated, like an animal or a lab rat.

High quality IMEs help protect the rights of workers and employers in Washington State by enabling accurate and even-handed industrial insurance benefit payment. IMEs should provide unbiased, accurate and comprehensive information and be carried out with dignity and respect for the worker. They are bought and paid for by the State.

That bipartisan immigration "reform" bill, crafted during secret negotiations led by President Bush, Sen. Edward Kennedy and Sen. John McCain, combines a Republican desire for cheap labor with a Democratic vision of cheap votes. The result is a stubborn refusal to halt illegal immigration, one of the most serious problems facing the United States. By granting legal status to millions of illegal immigrants, this legislative chimera would make securing our borders even harder than it is now.

The Senate bill essentially offers amnesty for illegal workers who show up to pay a $5,000 fee, promise to learn English, go back to visit their home countries, and then wait up to 13 years here for a green card. However, the real risk of being sent home is extremely low; only a fraction, for example, of the 600,000 illegal's who are convicted felons being held in state and federal prisons will ever be deported. Even with generous incentives, many illegal's will find it easier simply to maintain the status quo.

An international forum focusing on labor conditions in the Washington State Apple industry was convened in Yakima on August 8. Under the auspices of the North American Free Trade Agreement (NAFTA) the forum was one part of a complicated process arising from complaint filed in 1998 by progressive labor unions in Mexico.

The complaint alleges that conditions in Washington orchards violate labor standards mandated by the NAFTA side agreement on labor, the North American Agreement on Labor Cooperation (NAALC). The complaint could ultimately result in trade sanctions against Washington apples, including loss of export privileges. Mexico currently buys about 30% of Washington's exported apples.

"United States Government supports illegal activity if it is to their advantage. Nobody should be above our laws! "

The complaint (official title, Public Communication number 9802, filed with the Mexican Department of Labor) names violations of several of the eleven labor principles of the NAALC, including, the lack of legal protection for farm worker union organizing and collective bargaining, discrimination against migrant workers, a failure to effectively enforce state laws with respect to minimum labor standards and the protection of worker health and safety. In August of 1999, the Mexican government completed its review of the complaint and requested ministerial consultations. The August 8 forum was agreed to by the US and Mexico in May 2000.

Marking the first time that workers have had a chance to confront a US industry under NAFTA rules, the forum was designed for immigrant workers to put their concerns on record, speaking directly to industry and the authorities that enforce the labor laws.

We need laws in favor for Americans to get fair hearings instead of Attorneys so busy with their golf games that they laugh and joke amongst themselves during telephone conference hearings with your life falling apart before you, and your walls come tumbling down. These decision-makers forget that you are even there, what chance is there that they had ever studied your claim? They break you like a wild animal, as average citizens we are all expendable for the whole but who decides who represents the whole. Greedy and corrupt 89*politicians, that's who, who else?*

Speaking for our own laws, the somewhat defensive representatives from Washington State agencies by and large didn't have much to say about the elements of the complaint. They all claimed, by and large, to be enforcing the laws to the best of their budgets and mandate. As it is largely the sufficiency of that enforcement and of the agencies' budgets and mandates that is at issue in the complaint, there was little in the way of mitigation these agencies could offer. *Blatant noncompliance of Federal Laws means nothing to the State of Washington.*

Department of Labor and Industries officials professed shock at the accounts by injured workers of being denied benefits because they are in the country illegally. In truth, as insurance benefits, all workers pay into the system and are officially entitled to benefits, despite their undocumented status. The officials insisted it must have been misunderstandings, and rushed to take information from complaining workers.

The Dept. of Health has one pesticide inspector for the whole eastern side of the state (three on the west side). Workers' Compensation claims for pesticide exposure are routinely denied more often than most other types of claims because it is difficult to correlate the worker's injuries with a specific exposure. No documentation is kept, thus, no exposures can be documented.

If you see a conspiracy against your claim and voice your opinion to your Attorney he will in turn call your claims manager with you accusations. Your doctor falls into the budget and they have a life and families too. Most are not from America and do as they are expected to do by the State Authorities until before you know it own their own hospital. Never say conspiracy because you will be tagged as mentally ill.

NEW YORK (Reuters) - The U.S. National Labor Relations Board filed a formal complaint against the Washington Post Co, saying the publisher failed to bargain with its employee union over extra duties asked of staff, the union said on Thursday.

The labor relations board's general counsel concluded that the Post "repeatedly violated established federal labor law" starting in 2006 by asking employees to work on the company's radio broadcasts, according to a statement by the Newspaper Guild.

"I have to ask myself, is there not better places to spend hard earned American taxes then to target the only organizations that act as watch dogs for the public reporting the abuses of Labor and Industries. We have discussed issues far more urgent then what seems to be a civil action."

Facts that you cannot find: The most fraud cases are against persons such as Firemen and women, Police Department employees, construction workers per capita. I can see that persons are singled out, make the news, and then their history is erased even from Press books.

Productivity change in the nonfarm business sector, 1947-2006

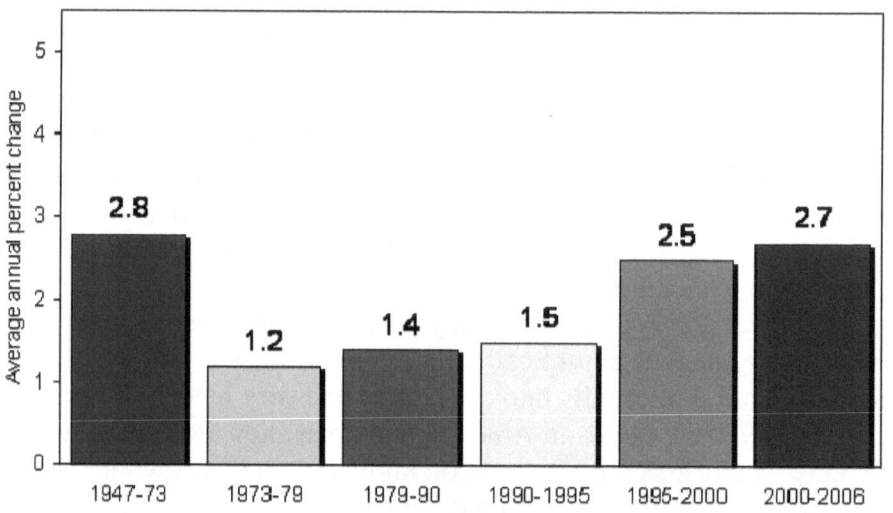

Productivity change in the manufacturing sector, 1987-2006

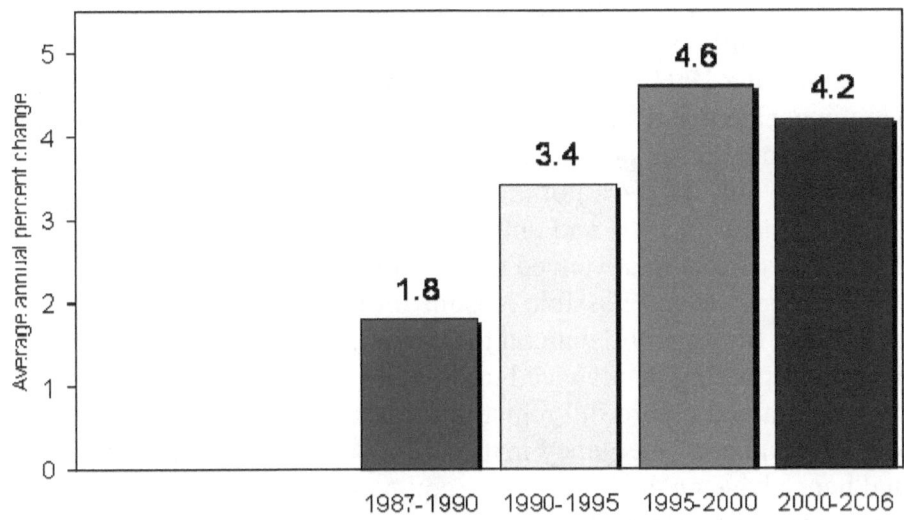

Since the Royal College of Surgeons reported on 1000 deaths from trauma in 1988 the upgrading of trauma care in Britain has been widely debated. Training in advanced trauma life support (ATLS) is seen by many people as a vital part of this upgrading process. Skinner, writing on behalf of the Royal College of Surgeons in 1993, stated that "all doctors involved in the initial resuscitation and subsequent management of patients with major injuries should possess a current ATLS provider certificate from the RCS." Senior house officers form the majority of the workforce staffing accident and emergency

departments. They should be trained in advanced trauma life support in accordance with the college's guidelines.

Thirteen major accident and emergency departments provide trauma care for the several million people who live in the Southwest. An audit was conducted in June 1994 to establish the proportion of senior house officers working in accident and emergency in the region who had a certificate in advanced trauma life support. The audit was repeated 12 months later. It was found that only 11 (16%) of the 68 senior house officers working in the 13 departments in 1994 and only nine (11%) of the 70 working there in 1995 had a certificate in advanced trauma life support.

There are several possible reasons for this lack of certification. The Royal College of Surgeons' data on the career stage at which doctors received their training in advanced trauma life support suggested that only 0.25% were trained before full registration. Most senior house officers work in accident and emergency in their first or second post registration job and hence have not had access to a course when they start their job. The problem is exacerbated because having passed a part 1 examination of a recognized college is a prerequisite for being allowed on to many courses. Many senior house officers are on the waiting list for courses while doing their accident and emergency attachments, but waiting times can be up to a year, and in a lot of cases trainees have moved on from accident and emergency before they receive their training. This is despite the expansion in the number of courses available.

The principles of advanced trauma life support help relatively inexperienced doctors to deal with complicated clinical situations in a controlled and structured way.[5] They thus improve the overall standard of patient care. Senior house officers working in accident and emergency should be trained in advanced trauma life support; a gold standard would be certification as a prerequisite for applications to work as a senior house officer in accident and emergency posts, or official training in advanced trauma life support could be built in to induction courses in accident and emergency. To achieve this, access to the courses needs to be improved. This has major implications in terms of resources.

We are conducting a national audit to record the numbers of senior house officers in Britain who have been trained in advanced trauma life support. It will be interesting to see if the figures from the south west reflect a more widespread problem.

A J Price, G Hughes

Certainly questions need to go answered, can we expect a fair shake, an objective look at job related injuries? There is no such thing as fair treatment. Many times, more often then not you are placed on a priority list in your Attorneys files. This determines the amount of time and effort that will be given to your compensation claim. Once you have an Attorney then you come to discover that he believes himself your god. You are not in the twilight zone you are in your Attorneys hands to do with as he pleases; right or wrong is not legally relative. This has become not only a Washington State issue but in many ways a global crisis.

Now we go to the Attorney' best friend in this game of who knows who power struggle, we cannot forget the D.O. No sir, which would be a fatal mistake if they want it to become one.

There is also a discrete need to drain the lower level of all the cash possible. Lower level such as physicians, Health Care workers, Therapy, etc.

Previous research has questioned the clinical qualifications and professional competence of physicians who work in correctional facilities. This article further explores these issues by analyzing social control mechanisms that are employed against prison physicians who (a) have been sued in state court by prisoners for medical malfeasance and malpractice, and (b) have had disciplinary action taken against their license to practice medicine. Physicians who were subject to suit are categorized by type of suit, medical complaint, plaintiff's injury, and disposition of the litigation. Drawing on previous research, the authors also classified physicians' rationalizations to prisoner litigation within Sykes and Matza's techniques of neutralization framework. Reporting that prison doctors have higher rates of disciplinary action taken on their license than physicians at large, the article uses the principle of less eligibility to question the ethics of restricting problem doctors to work exclusively in correctional facilities.

1. Employees should report all on-the-job injuries to their supervisor as soon as possible. Failure to report the injury the same day of occurrence may result in denial of the claim.

Failure to act at immediately will cost you the case whether or not you have all the objective evidence in the world. Judges will be to busy to look at your case and a no-name will close your case.

I would like to mention that these Professionals should have to follow the same standards and ethics as we must but they make their own laws. Now we will continue our way back to the D.O. I bet by now you are wondering who this person might be?

Neurology and Psychiatry
specialty practice

This doctor can do anything from get you a decent settlement to break you into pieces. This person can commit you, jail you, or overdose you. This is the doctor that both the Claims Manager and your Attorney press to produce findings for their cause. Working for L&I is bottom of the barrel for a Physician. Most Physicians would never take these cases on because of the heavy workloads, unpaid overtime, and they are lucky to get paid at all if they do not file the reports expected by the Claims Manager. .

The practice of neurology shall consist of and include that branch of osteopathic medical science which deals with the neuromuscular system, both normal and diseased. It includes all accepted therapies, assessments, and diagnostic studies.

The practice of psychiatry shall consist of and include that branch of osteopathic medicine which deals with disorders of the psyche of organic and functional nature. This includes all accepted therapies, assessments, and diagnostic studies.

The practice of child psychiatry is the specialty of psychiatry as defined above and as it relates specifically to the pediatric and adolescent age group. This includes all accepted therapies, assessments, and diagnostic studies.

The practice of child neurology is the specialty of neurology as defined above as it relates specifically to the pediatric and adolescent age group. This includes all accepted therapies, assessments, and diagnostic studies.

Requirements for certification

To be eligible to receive certification from the AOA through the American Osteopathic Board of Neurology and Psychiatry, the applicant must meet the following minimum requirements:

1. **The applicant must be a graduate of an AOA-accredited college of osteopathic medicine.**
2. **The applicant must be licensed to practice in the state or territory where his/her practice is conducted.**
3. **The applicant must be able to show evidence of conformity to the standards set forth in the Code of Ethics of the AOA.**
4. **The applicant must have been a member in good standing of the AOA or the Canadian Osteopathic Association for the two years immediately prior to the date of certification.**
5. **The applicant must have satisfactorily completed an AOA-approved internship.**
6. **A period of three years of AOA-approved training in neurology shall be required, after the required one year of internship.**
7. **One year of credit may be given for two (2) years in an AOA-approved residency training program as determined by this Board (i.e., Internal Medicine, Neurological Surgery).**
8. **A period of three years of AOA-approved training in psychiatry shall be required after the one year of internship.**
9. **A period of two (2) years of an AOA-approved training program in child neurology, at least two (2) years of AOA-approved residency training in general neurology; or one (1) year of general neurology and one (1) year of an AOA-approved residency training in pediatrics shall be required after the prerequisite one (1) year of internship. Each applicant for certification in child neurology must be certified by the Board in general neurology prior to applying for**

examination in child neurology.

10. **A period of four years of AOA-approved training program in child psychiatry (two (2) years child, two (2) years general) shall be required after the prerequisite one (1) year of internship. Each applicant for certification in child psychiatry must be certified by the Board in general psychiatry prior to applying for examination in child psychiatry.**

11. **Following satisfactory compliance with the prescribed requirements for examination, the applicant is required to pass appropriate examinations planned to evaluate an understanding of the scientific bases of the problems involved in neurology, psychiatry, child neurology, and/or child psychiatry; familiarity with the current advances in neurology, psychiatry, child neurology, and/or child psychiatry; possession of sound judgment and a high degree of skill in the diagnostic and therapeutic procedures involved in the practice of neurology, psychiatry, child neurology, and/or child psychiatry.**

Oral, written, and clinical examinations are conducted and required in the case of each applicant. Upon successful completion of the written examination, the applicant is eligible for the clinical and oral portion of the examination.

The members of this board shall review, if not perform, the grading of each written examination. The conduct of the clinical examination may be delegated to a committee of not fewer than two individuals maturely qualified in neurology, psychiatry, child neurology, and/or child psychiatry.

A full description of the method of conducting the examination is formulated in this Board's Regulations and Requirements, and provision for reexamination is made.

Applicants desiring examination for certification are required to file an application which shall set forth the applicant's qualifications for examination as stated in paragraphs 1 through 7 in Section 1 of this article. The procedure for filing applications is set forth in the Regulations and Requirements.

This person can declare that you do not know what you are saying or that you are delusional. Imagine that on your portfolio. In Book 2 we will give you actual legal proceedings carried out to kill your benefits (Forms Documents). This D.O. can declare that your condition was a pre-existing disability and you are railroaded out of your home and into the street.

Certainly you will have to conform to stay in compliance so you must take the medication that is prescribed. This makes it tough to get to the many appointments scheduled for you by L&I Physicians. If you miss one you can lose your compensation. Often the appointments are on the same day and hours apart. L&I working with the D.O. can make your life a chaotic hell. Never complain, then they might single you out. If you are Jewish keep it to yourself because in the Washington State system it will be held against you. It is best to keep your religious beliefs to yourself to be safe. In the eyes of these wealthy Attorneys you are scum digging for gold.

X-rays, cat-scans, MRI's do not have a chance against a D.O. because this person can manipulate the verdict. All your appointments are important and be sure to know there are hidden cameras most places you are required to be treated. Save your x-rays but the doctors will contend in a few years that they are old fractures, before your injury. Years pass as you wait to collect or collect as you are waiting. Time is on your Claims Managers side, bones heal, files get lost, witnesses move etc.

The End of Chapter 7

Chapter 8
Referrals

Referrals are important because you can request services from a different provider more capable in assisting in your recovery of a work-related injury.

Choosing a Primary Care Doctor

This is the most important choice you will make after a job-related injury. Certainly this Doctor will refer you to his partners who also own part of the Clinic or Clinics. Each highly schooled and apt in their profession and each bent on earning high profits. This question can never be answered by the scholars of our world, how do you define pain, what is pain and how will effect your daily routine?

A **primary care physician**, or **PCP**, is a physician who provides both the first contact for a person with an undiagnosed health concern as well as continuing care of varied medical conditions, not limited by cause, organ system, or diagnosis. A PCP generally does not specialize in the treatment of specific organ systems, such as neurology, cardiology, or pulmonology, nor perform surgery. The term "PCP" is most commonly used in the United States. A primary care physician can be described by training, skill and scope of practice, role in the health care system, and the usual setting in which care is delivered. Primary care physicians are declining in numbers in many developed countries.

This Physician will always try his or her best to help you the best way possible. Washington State holds many potential threats over these Doctors along with how, when and how much they get paid for there services. Good news, these Doctors do not get intimidated easily because they belong to their own realm of Power Organizations who carry great influence but when it comes to fighting the State it id a futile attempt ay best and Doctors lose their license to practice medicine. If I did not know better, Washington State is operated by lazy incompetent, and oh, you cannot sue them for lying so the law speaks in volumes. Basically as far as we know they decide cases by lottery. Physicians with L&I watching them closely, controlling profits, leaves a lot of initiative gestures.

Certain clinicians, most commonly those trained in family practice, general practice, pediatrics and internal medicine are referred to as primary care physicians. Some HMOs consider gynecologists as PCPs for the care of women, and have allowed certain subspecialists to assume PCP responsibilities for selected patient types, such as allergists caring for people with asthma and nephrologists acting as PCPs for patients on kidney dialysis. Some experts and groups have included nurse practitioners and physician assistants by broadening the term to primary care practitioners.

This is where the treatment begins for you and ends. Choose your Physicians well, if you do not want to go to a referred Doctor you can choose another or have them pay for a second opinion.

A set of skills and scope of practice may define a primary care physician, generally including basic diagnosis and non-surgical treatment of common illnesses and medical conditions. Diagnostic techniques include interviewing the patient to collect information on the present symptoms, prior medical history and other health details, followed by a physical examination. Many PCPs are trained in basic medical testing, such as interpreting results of blood or other patient samples, electrocardiograms, or x-rays. More complex and time-intensive diagnostic procedures are usually obtained by referral to specialists, due to either special training with a technology, or increased experience and patient volume that renders a risky procedure safer for the patient. [2] After collecting data, the PCP arrives at a differential diagnosis and, with the participation of the patient, formulates a plan including (if appropriate) components of further testing, specialist referral, medication, therapy, diet or life-style changes, patient education, and follow up results of treatment. Primary care physicians also counsel and educate patients on safe health behaviors, self-care skills and treatment options, and provide screening tests and immunizations.

Referrals come at you from everywhere, choose them well, research them first and then decide your next move. A primary care physician is usually the first medical practitioner contacted by a patient, due to factors such as ease of communication, accessible location, familiarity, and increasingly issues of cost and managed care requirements. Many health maintenance organizations position PCPs as "gatekeepers", who regulate access to more costly procedures or specialists. Ideally, the primary care physician acts on behalf of the patient to collaborate with referral specialists, coordinate the care given by varied organizations such as hospitals or rehabilitation clinics, act as a comprehensive repository for the patient's records, and provide long-term management of chronic conditions. Continuous care is particularly important for patients with medical conditions that encompass multiple organ systems and require prolonged treatment and monitoring, such as diabetes and hypertension.

This decision will be the most important decision you will have to make, once you are injured on the job this is your only move.

Perhaps referrals cut the path to the final judgment in your compensation case. L&I can be extremely forceful and use Attorneys as case managers. These aggressive movers and shakers record every word you say to them and if to are having a telephone conversation the claims manager types every word you say into your file. With the sophisticated and high tech age here I wonder why they do not record. They can write whatever they like but a recording on tape or disc never lies.

Referral: The recommendation of a medical or paramedical professional. If you get a referral to ophthalmology, for example, you are being sent to the eye doctor. In HMOs and other managed care schemes, a referral is usually necessary to see any practitioner or specialist other than your primary care physician (PCP), if you want the service to be covered. The referral is obtained from your PCP, who may require a telephone or office consultation first.

Most Americans between the ages of 22 and 65 spend 40 to 50 percent of waking hours at work. Every year millions of Americans suffer injuries and thousands experience deaths in our workplaces. Yet little effort has been made to estimate either the extent of these injuries, deaths, and diseases or their cost to the economy. Thus, important questions about workplace safety and the economic resources expended due to workplace health problems remain unanswered. In this study, we address these questions by presenting estimates of the incidence, prevalence, and costs of workplace-related injuries, illnesses, and deaths for the entire civilian workforce of the United States in 1992. We also consider controversies surrounding cost methodologies, estimate how these costs are distributed across occupations, consider who pays the costs, and address some policy issues.

Certainly there are people getting injured on the job every day and statistics are tough to find. Labor and Industries is a closed secret society of law-makers and lobbyists with agendas that only they know, along their private contributors.

Referrals go to the people that will look out for you but Labor and Industries dictates how far they can go with their testing and time. It is like being in a loop of one evaluation after another until L&I receive the findings they need. All other findings are dismissed and the best finding for the State is processed through the winding legal system.

More than 195,000 patients die needlessly every year in our hospitals from a series of complications directly related to poor nurse staffing, according to a study released in May 2004. The authors attributed the majority of these deaths to "failure to rescue" (which refers to nurses' failure to promptly assess and treat conditions that develop in a hospital), bedsores, postoperative sepsis and post-operative pulmonary embolisms. (HealthGrades, 2004)

A survey of patients found that nearly **half of recently hospitalized patients reported their care was compromised by inadequate RN-to-patient ratios,** and that the majority of those surveyed supported legislation to regulate ratios. (National Consumers League, 2004)

The Institute of Medicine of the National Academies of Science reports that **"nurse staffing levels affect patient outcomes and safety."** Insufficient monitoring of patients, caused by poor working conditions and the assignment of too few RNs, increases the likelihood of patient deaths and injuries at a time when avoidable medical errors kill up to 98,000 people in U.S. hospitals every year. (IOM, November 4, 2003)

Inadequate staffing precipitated one-fourth of all sentinel

events—unexpected occurrences that led to patient deaths, injuries, or permanent loss of function—reported to JCAHO, the Joint Commission on Accreditation of Hospital Organizations, the past five years. (JCAHO, August 7, 2002)

A New England Journal of Medicine study documented that **improved RN-to-patient ratios reduce rates of pneumonia, urinary infections, shock, cardiac arrest, gastrointestinal bleeding, and other adverse outcomes.** (NEJM, May 30, 2002)

Research in the Journal of the American Medical Association found that up to 20,000 patient deaths each year can be linked to preventable patient deaths. **For each additional patient assigned to an RN, the likelihood of death within 30 days increased by 7 percent.** Four additional patients increased the risk of death by 31 percent. (JAMA, October 22, 2002)

The Massachusetts Department of Public Health reports **medical errors and complaints at hospitals have increased by 76 percent in seven years.** (DPH Division of Health Care Quality, 2003)

Poorer hospital nurse staffing is associated with higher rates of urinary tract infections, postoperative infections, pneumonia, pressure ulcers and increased lengths of stay, while better nurse staffing is linked to improved patient outcomes, according to the Agency for Healthcare Research and Quality. (AHRQ report, 2001)

Two-thirds of bedside nurses in Massachusetts report knowing of patients, who suffered serious complications as a result of understaffing dying horrible deaths without hope.. (Opinion Dynamics Corp., 2003)

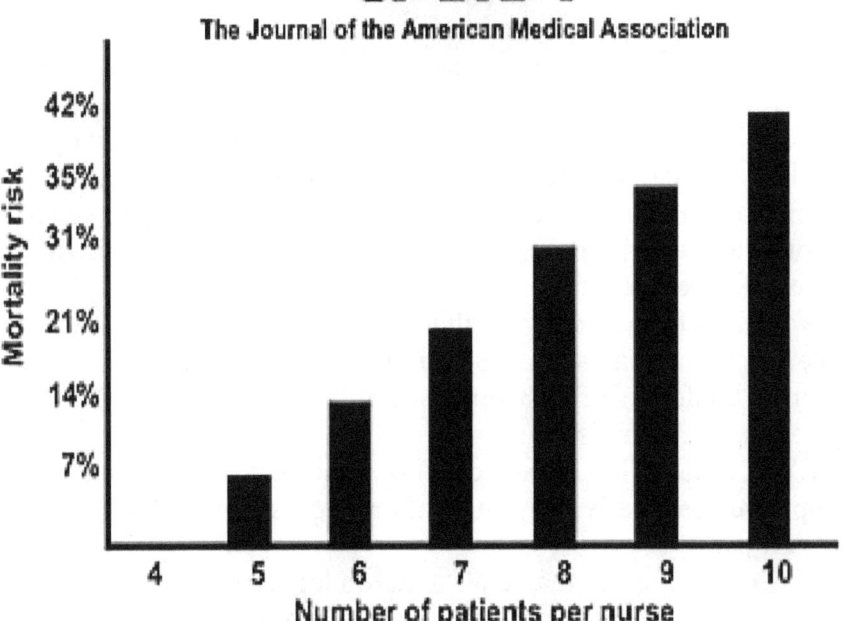

Each additional patient per nurse was associated with a 7 percent increase in mortality. The difference between four to six and four to eight patients per nurse would be accompanied by 14 and 31 percent increases in mortality.

A survey published in JAMA found that for every patient beyond four assigned to a nurse resulted in a 15 percent increase in job dissatisfaction and a 23 percent increase in burnout for nurses. (JAMA, 2003)

Referrals make or break your compensation case; you cannot fight a group of lawyers that say there is nothing wrong with your finger even if it is bleeding from a cut to the bone. It is a big joke for these people and they are not afraid to tell injured persons this because these people in power have a god complex fueled by greed.

If you want to fight and win there are several options available to you. You are an American and if you know how you can use their laws against them. I could have finished this affair; all they wanted me to do was stop writing, and publishing.

NEW YORK (CNNMoney.com) -- A lobsterman drowned off the New Hampshire coast early in August, after he got entangled in nets and dragged overboard.

A day or two before that a Washington logger was struck in the neck and killed by a log that had worked loose and rolled down a hillside.

In central California on August 5, a crop duster pilot crashed and died. **Fishermen** It was another tough year for fishermen in 2005; 48 died, up from 38 the year before. That made it the nation's most dangerous occupation in 2005, with a fatality rate of 118.4 per 100,000 - nearly 30 times higher than the rate of the average worker.

Loggers This group kept its tragic status as one of the most dangerous occupations by recording 80 deaths, a fatality rate of 90.2 per 100,000. That's an improvement from a year earlier, when there were 85 logging fatalities. Of the 339 construction workers who died, about 32 percent of them suffered fatal falls of a story or more.

You must take into account the unreported deaths in this chart,

Rank	Occupation	Death rate/100,000	Total deaths
1	Fishers and fishing workers	118.4	48
2	Logging workers	92.9	80
3	Aircraft pilots	66.9	81
4	Structural iron and steel workers	55.6	35
5	Refuse and recyclable material collectors	43.8	32
6	Farmers and ranchers	41.1	341
7	Electrical power line installers/repairers	32.7	36
8	Driver/sales workers and truck drivers	29.1	993
9	Miscellaneous agricultural workers	23.2	176
10	Construction laborers	22.7	339

persons that were expendable to their employers. We have covered the working man deaths overseas and the unreported deaths. The State will always downsize the figures and color the charts but the truth is, "every single American is expendable and these statistics will never be accurate.

Labor and Industries downplays these stats. Claiming that Job injury death rates are dropping, the good thing about numbers is that you can arrange them and form any conclusion you please, you can make something seem bad or good by the way you describe or report on its status. My point is this, all the deaths are not reported and many times the job injury death is blamed on another pre-existing condition or the fault of the victim. Remember that these leaders have hearts as black as the darkest night and the lofty feel of prosperity as most of their client's eek out a living, while others become homeless and disabled living in the streets of Seattle.

Imagine if we counted the injured and the dead from the Gulf war, I believe that these people should be counted and allowed the same benefits that a job retains. After all the military is called a job and treated as a job until you get injured. Then you are first the victim of a war and again the victim of Labor and Industries.

Such a complex system as Washington State Labor and Industries brings discrimination to the poor and great wealth for the favored. I investigated how this all worked and gotten a good look inside only to learn that they keep their mouths shut and act with confidence together. I can make conjectures that would be extremely close to the truth but believe that by the time you finish this series of five books you will draw the same conclusions as I have drawn.

January 30, 2006 - Based upon the latest national census of fatal occupational injuries from the Department of Labor's Bureau of Labor Statistics, workers who are required to climb cell towers and other communications structures throughout the country have been identified as having the most dangerous job in America.

Although tower climbers are one of the smallest specialized construction groups with approximately 8,700 employees, they had ten fatalities from workers falling from a tower in 2004, representing deaths per 100,000 workers. You get paid more for working heights

Most of these job accidents create injured workers, who then are referred to assorted medical facilities for treatment. Certainly, union workers get the best medical coverage and far better than the average worker considerations. Returning to work or reassigned to a job that suits their disability. Representation by your union gives you the best possible scenario on a skilled labor basis: to get the correct physicians and treatment quickly so that you may heal sooner. Where you work decides what happens to your life after a job accident.

Carefully choose which Physicians will treat your injury. Several interviews with some physicians proved that they would not bend or change their findings to get paid sooner. Unfortunately, these Doctors are dismissed by L&I and their reports and findings ignored. If it is possible, any way you can contrive a way to get one. These physicians will submit you to the right clinics for your injury and show compassion about your plight. I wish that I could publish their names to bestow honor to them but then they would be targeted by over-zealous L&I Investigators. L&I have the final say on who your care-givers will be. You still have means to get who you want to treat you. Book 2 will speak about this subject intensely giving tips that you can follow so that you do not go through the wringer again.

Camas, WA July 7, 2006 the following explains how to find the top specialists in a specific geographic area. There are many things to consider when looking for a top specialist in your area. First, its best you make sure they're board-certified in the specialty field pertaining to your medical needs. In addition, it's a good idea to make sure they have special expertise in the condition/procedure you desire. For specialists who are highly recognized by their patients and peers, their status can usually be obtained by conducting a solid search.

Forget the yellow pages; instead spend some time online browsing for a particular specialist in your area. A good idea is to make sure the specialist you find has been researched from a company who specializes in physician background reports or has rigorously reviewed the physician's profile.

Referrals - Finding a specialist who has special expertise in your conditions/surgical procedure, and with solid credentials is key. Use caution with any referral agencies who are free, accept fees from doctors, or who are connected with a hospital.

In this day and age, doctors are trained using advanced surgical technologies such as minimally invasive surgery, tele-surgery, robotic assisted surgery, and many others. With minimal incisions being made, it is said that within ten years, some of today's surgical procedures will be considered barbaric.

Like with any other service/product that's introduced to the market place, through trial and error it takes time to perfect the product. Certainly, robotic assisted surgery, since 2000, it's been off to a solid start. Many doctors agree that robotic assisted surgery has many promises and eventually will be the way most surgical procedures are conducted.

I hope that this chapter has shed a new light on referrals and the importance of getting the correct treatment for your injury. Remember that if you receive a job-related injury to find a Primary Care Doctor and get the proper treatment by know your referrals.

The End of Chapter 8

Chapter 9
Secret Files

Files, more files on top of files. Files gathered from every clinic you visit and every appointment you have along with x-rays. Enough x-rays to diagnose your injury easily MRI's cat-scans, and a host of tests, psychological and physical. Private files kept secretly for unmentionable reasons existing hidden and updated. Files sent to the Federal Government, journals and diaries and compiled statistics.

Power is distributed by who you know. Important decisions made by associates that play by their own rules following their own secret code of ethics. Men and women with inflated egos and the power of the pen and collaboration from their chain of command to appoint these persons to nothing less then Judges. "Judges with Doctrines, and Masters Degrees" asking you to connect the dots staring at your hands, noting if your fingernails are clean or not. Many of these files are on disc or microdots and unavailable to the general public. In reality only 2% of the U.S. population has no hidden files on them somewhere. Our Government likes every American accounted for which means . . . those persons who believe they are not noticed are wrong. They are only being ignored. Makes a person wonder which scenario is worse.

Secret files are truthful and accurate but never allowed into court and in many instances its existence vehemently denied.

On the night of Nov. 9, 1945, FBI counterespionage agents staked out a house on Keeler Street in the hills above the Campanile and gentle green slopes of the UC Berkeley campus.

As fog blew through the trees, the agents watched George Eltenton, a suspected spy for the Soviets, park his car and enter the house.

There are secrets and then there are secret files. Secrets change with the times but files can last forever. I believe that a person' privacy is sacred, guaranteed in the Constitution on the United States. Unless there is probable cause for it I see no need for secret files on private citizens yet,

L&I boasts about watching injured claimants, this brings home the point that once you have a job-related injury then you are a suspect first, injured worker last.

Indeed, there are several secret files on you, hundreds, and some have thousands. If you think big money is watching you then believe it because it is not paranoia. Government and big money are the same, they control the world and we should forgive them for neglecting their own citizens. I say hog wash, take care of the taxpayers and the American Public and then see what you can do to change the world.

The nerve of this private organizations, and clubs! They pass your files around like winos passing a bottle in the park. Power makes a body feel god-like and almighty. These people will warmly smile at you with frozen hearts and the best interests of their employers in mind. I believe that better control is needed and audits performed to keep our leaders honest. If we do not take this pre-emptive move then before you know it you will be sporting bar codes containing your medical and mischievous files for easy access.

Book 2 will display pages of journals and diaries given to us by the victims of Washington State. I am sure that you will find them quite interesting.

POLICE hold serious fears for the safety of secret informants following last week's theft of confidential documents from an unmarked police car.

This is a random example of can happen and occasionally will continue to happen and there is nothing we can do about it. There is no law against being sloppy. I have sent records and my own files to both L&I and SSA, both Agencies lost the files and it cost me thousands of dollars. They claimed that I should have made copies and I asked them why, only the originals count. There is no way to beat the system but there is a way to fight and win.

U.S. Says Press Can Be Prosecuted for Having Secret Files,

The Bush administration said that journalists can be prosecuted under current espionage laws for receiving and publishing classified information but that such a step "would raise legitimate and serious issues and would not be undertaken lightly," according to a court filing made public this week.

"My whole point about everything is that the people should have the final say about our future. Keeping us in the dark gives Government power, more power then they can handle. That is obvious is it not? If our journalists know about it then it was old news when they reported it, so what is the big deal? I will tell you the big deal is the secret files and the names written inside of them."

"There plainly is no exemption in the statutes for the press, let alone lobbyists like the defendants," Justice Department lawyers wrote in response to a motion filed last month seeking to dismiss charges against Steven J. Rosen and Keith Weissman, former lobbyists for the American Israel Public Affairs Committee (AIPAC).

We need to stop this senseless manipulation of our future, before this great mass of power and secrets implode and begin targeting imaginary enemies. While, allowing our enemies free access to cross our borders, who decides what a secret is, obviously it is the person with the most to lose.

Did you know?

Governments across Latin America have launched investigations after revelations that a US company is obtaining extensive personal data about millions of citizens in the region and selling it to the Bush administration.

More hidden secret files in vaults for what end? Americans need to know what our leaders are doing so that we know who to elect during elections. It is easy to pass the buck or find scapegoats but under the light a secret never should have been told in the first place. What country was the man from the pentagon telling secrets to Journalists?

You heard the story about a scorpion hitching a ride on the back of a turtle; remember what the turtle asked the scorpion half the way across the lake? Why did you sting me scorpion, now we will both die? The scorpion replied, because it is in my nature, I could not help myself.

We will end this chapter here to protect us from imagined secrets.

The End of Chapter 9

Chapter 10
How Long is the Wait

This is what will make you or break you. It is very common to be upset at your attorney after your personal injury lawsuit is filed because such a long time passes between the time the lawsuit is started and any settlement or trial. In most states, the other person's insurance company owes you no duty to settle quickly. Your case can be settled before trial or drag on long after the trial is over.

The insurance company knows you're in a hurry to settle your case, and uses this knowledge to try to get you to settle for less. Here is a partial list of some of the things that can happen to slow down your case:

Discovery:

This is the insurance company's opportunity to discover everything about you and the accident. You will get lots of written questions to answer under oath. You will have to produce documents and medical records, plus admit or deny specific written statements put to you.

You and your legal representative will need to gather up all the medical records, bills and other documentation of your injuries. Some of these must be obtained in a specific way to make them admissible at trial. This often takes time and capital.

Depositions:

You will be asked questions under oath, with a court reporter typing up every word you say. The insurance company's lawyer will ask you in great detail about your injuries, your medical history, the accident itself and your treatment. You will to be subjected to grilling over the smallest of details.

Motion Hearings:

The insurance company lawyers may have what feels like an

endless capacity to file motions and go to hearings on motions. Some of these motions are unimportant to you, but some may be critical to your case.

Many courts are forcing lawyers to mediate or arbitrate cases prior to trial. Some courts will not give you a trial date until you do so. Mediation is typically a settlement conference without the formalities of court. A neutral party will try to help the parties reach a middle ground. Its not usually binding meaning the parties are stuck with the result unless the parties reach an agreement and write up a settlement agreement.

Arbitration is a different breed. It is often a binding mini-trial of the case in front of an arbitrator or panel of judges who listen to an informal presentation of the matters involved in your case.

Trial

If your case does not settle, it must go to trial, where six or twelve strangers will decide what your injury is worth.

Trials are scheduled on the courts schedule, not the lawyer's schedule. Cases sometimes take years to be scheduled for trial, especially in some major urban areas. Having a case that is two or three years old before going to trial is not unusual. And once you have a trial, your case may not be over. There may be an appeal and further motions and hearings. *"Thus it could take twenty years or to the day you die for a settlement."*

Collection Issues:

You may also have difficulty collecting from the insurance company or the person responsible for your injury. The insurance lawyer will have to have a check or draft issued by the company. And before they send you money, you will be required to sign a release document and file some sort of dismissal motion. These things also delay payment. Once the money comes in, your lawyer will have to run the check through his or her trust account. If it's an out-of-state check, there will be another delay of a week to ten days before the funds are disbursed. And your lawyer will be deducting litigation expenses such as deposition fees, transcript fees, filing fees, service of process costs, medical records costs, costs involved in documenting medical bills, costs of hiring expert witnesses, costs of paying treating doctors to testify, subpoena charges, lawyers fees, and any legally-required medical bills or liens.

The average wait in a brfe LLC survey was seven years however some go as long as thirty years before an agreement is reached. I interviewed a couple at a church in Shelton, Washington who were married a few days before the job injury and nearly fifty years later their compensation claim was denied. Go figure?

Litigation can eat up a lot of time and money. Settlements after litigation can be very disappointing after spending years in battle. Sometimes its better to settle before trial for less than to go through the process and end up with a small settlement or perhaps a bad result at trial.

Independent Medical Exams, Peer Reviews, Independent Medical Reviews are paid for by the State of Washington, how independent can they possibly be?

L&I can wait you out; they can drag it on forever if they chose to do so. Then if they have a mind to do it, they can crush you. We are all expendable in their eyes.

From 1992 to 2000, there were 1,282 work-related deaths reported in New York State (excluding New York City). More than 90% of these fatalities involved men. On average, the construction and agriculture industries had the highest numbers of fatalities. Transportation-related accidents were the most common cause of death among both males and females. Nothing has changed but the numbers, they are higher now and ten times as many persons are out of work because of a job-related injury that has been denied by their claims managers. This number is an estimate; the true count must be much higher. It takes a conspiracy to maintain state budgets and I supposed if there was a better way then our leaders would find it. Sure, in-between naps perhaps, they like the way things are now.

Workers' compensation is a no-fault insurance program that is supposed to pay medical costs and partially reimburse the lost wages of workers who suffer job-related injuries or illnesses. In Washington, that insurance is provided through the nonprofit State Fund, or for some large businesses, through direct payment of claims (self-insurance).

Who funds the State Fund? The businesses that are not self-insured and their employees pay premiums into the fund to insure workers' claims. (About 70% of workers are covered under the State Fund.) In return, businesses receive not only insurance against these claims, but more importantly, immunity from lawsuits for damages resulting from workplace injury and illness.

Washington is the only state in the country where workers contribute to the cost of workers' compensation premiums. Washington workers contribute more than 26% of total premium cost. This means that employers in Washington get a particularly good deal on industrial insurance. Washington, in all of the recent objective studies (the 2004 Oregon Rate Study and the 1998 WA Industrial Insurance Performance Audit) is recognized as a low-cost state. The Oregon study doesn't even account for the 26% employee contribution, so the employer costs rank even lower.

You would think that because of worker contributions to L&I the people would have more to say about the way Washington State Labor and Industries operate and perform at the present time. In reality the people of Washington do not have a vote, or can persons voice their opinions without retribution by WSL&I Agents.

Every year in the Legislature there is pressure to reduce benefits from business interests seeking to lower their premiums. Labor, on the other hand, seeks to keep funding stable and maintain or increase the benefits for injured workers.

Why have L&I if the workers paid for the costs of insurance leaving the employer with a clean bill of health and pockets filled with loose change? I was hired as a employee after offering to sub contract the work and pay my own insurance Boomer decided that he wanted the full weight. Now perhaps I understand why. Being a Canadian Company Boomer had special incentives and State protection to work in Washington State. He had his friend the claims manager to handle things for him. He bragged about his parties and guns, reminding me of a cowboy taming the west. A real big shot and he had a right to be. You will be surprised at what finally happened to this $90,000,000.00 Project when you read book five of this series.

In addition, there also is pressure from the private insurance industry, which is excluded from the workers' compensation market, and sees a huge new potential for profit in industrial insurance. Several attempts have been made over the years to allow private insurers to tap into that market.

There is more then enough money going around, too bad little of this monies reaches resources that will help an injured worker.

The goal of our workers' compensation system is set forth in RCW 51.04.010: Sure and certain relief for workers, injured in their work, and their families and dependents. *Once it finds its way into the realm of Attorneys in Washington State these words mean nothing.* They are vacant words filled with promises and hope but in reality, these words should be followed to the letter of its laws and enforced. Persons with great influence are above these laws and protected by them. Only we can make the difference by insisting that once corruption is suspected in Government that we have it thoroughly investigated and prosecuted if it is deemed necessary to prove a point. The point being that the people should always be honestly informed and have the ability to monitor Washington State Labor and Industries.

The Washington State Labor Council believes all attempts to change our system should be judged by that standard: ***"Will changes promote sure and certain relief for injured workers, and provide fair compensation for the disability suffered by the worker?"***

Sure it would if there were not special interests groups involved in designing policies. This is my opinion, you can have yours too because we live and work in America.

Obviously Not "Will it save businesses money?" or "Will it allow insurance companies to make more money?"

It is all about making money and injured workers are easy prey for these beastly monopolies.

Here are the facts. Throughout the country, workers' compensation has been "deformed" so that injured workers have lost ground in all areas, from eligibility to level of compensation.

Washington, with its many problems, is viewed as a model of efficiency for the entire country. The 1998 performance audit found our state's system to be in the top 25% in benefits paid, and the bottom 25% in costs. Subsequent state-by-state studies consistently rank our state in the bottom third in terms of **workers' compensation costs and don't even account for employees' share of the premium or the Retrospective Rebate Program, which pays employers hundreds of millions of workers' compensation dollars in safety incentives.**

Millions of dollars freely given to those that oppose workers compensation entirely makes my skin crawl.

Some practices have developed within the Department of Labor and Industries (L&I) that cause great hardship and even cruelty to injured workers. While employers have received nearly $1 billion in dividends and refunds in recent years, too many injured workers are found employable at minimum wage and cut out of the system, or they are sent to "Independent Medical Exams" that are neither independent nor performed by practicing medical providers.

When an injured worker files a workers' compensation claim, L&I decides if the claim is compensable and what benefits, if any, are due to the worker. By statute, an employer or injured worker has 60 days to protest an L&I decision. (The main reason an employer would protest is because claims may affect its "experience rating," which may result in a higher premium.) If an employer or worker is dissatisfied with L&I's decision on the protest, they can appeal to the Board of Industrial Insurance Appeals.

The problem is this: when an employer protests an L&I decision finding an injured worker's claim compensable, the claim is put in abeyance and usually time-loss benefits cease. Because the protest resolution can take *months*, this creates an undue financial hardship for the injured worker and his or her family. Why do we have to suffer to increase the wealth of the guilty?

Similarly, appeals to the Board of Industrial Insurance Appeals suspend the worker's time-loss and medical benefits pending the decision. It is not uncommon for a board decision to take 18 months.

The solution seems simple. **Whatever L&I's initial decision is, it ought to stand** pending the next decision, whether it is a protest to L&I or an appeal to the Board. Organized labor supports this common sense approach.

Time goes on and money gets short for common things you need around the house. You have a tough time paying your bills and your children need a lot of things for school that costs money. Another day that you are expecting your compensation checks, on Wednesday every two weeks that comes in the mail on time.

You open your mailbox and instead of a check you get a letter that explains your benefits have been suspended because your employer protested your claim. You run into the house and tell your wife and she cries. Life is not what it used to be with your fourth operation on the way and your only income cut off. How do L&I expect you to drive to your appointments without car insurance or paying the loan on your car? Banks are calling, the landlord is waiting and your Attorney is on vacation. You call relatives and borrow more money to pay the bills and provide launch money for the children.

Unfortunately, in many cases, injured workers suffer an injury or illness that makes it impossible to return to their job of injury. L&I or the self-insured employers then begin a process that, in many cases, leads to an "employability" or "able to work" assessment.

If you know what you are facing and where it is coming from you can fight and win quickly. When asked for split second decisions, ask for a moment or two so you can think about it. You cannot trust your Attorney in Washington State because it is regulated and controlled by those that operate the system as a whole. This book and the others that will follow can give you the upper-hand because you can prepare for what is coming.

The problem is this: L&I adopted a standard in 1985 that defined "employability" or "able to work" as the ability to work at a job that pays at least the federal minimum wage. Since 1985, about 75,000 workers injured so severely that they could not return to their job of injury have been found "employable." Their benefits have been terminated and they have been left, in many cases, either unemployed or working at jobs with substantially less income than their wage at the time they were injured. They have received no vocational training, as they are ineligible once they are found "employable" at federal minimum wage. Workers who have spent years developing their skills are told they can be employed at a minimum wage job, regardless of what they were earning at the time they were injured.

You were earning $60,000.00 a year but you can work a labor job at minimum wages, yes sure, great idea for the employer but it clubbers the injured worker whom I like to refer to as the victim. Most of the time the medications injured workers are prescribed warns about driving and working with machinery yet they are classified as employable.

The solution is proposed in the 1998 Performance Audit. To quote, "The standard for employability as it relates to vocational rehabilitation benefits should be some portion of wages at the time of injury rather than the federal minimum wage."

I guess this is one of those laws that are chosen to be ignored. This means that every case settled in Washington was unfair therefore should be reassessed.

Labor has proposed a standard of 80% of wage of injury. A worker unable to return to their job of injury would be eligible for vocational retraining unless they were, in a vocational assessment, determined able to work at a job paying 80% or better of their wage of injury. I wonder who was receiving 5% on my compensation because I was getting 75%.

You can expect to go through dozens of evaluations before L&I find Evaluators that reach positive findings for Employers. Medical determinations in the industrial insurance system are central to the issues of eligibility for benefits, determination of ability to return to work, decisions about whether a worker has reached maximum medical improvement, and the level of permanent disability. Each of these decisions triggers certain benefits or loss of benefits for the worker, and these decisions are frequently the source of disagreement between the injured worker and the department or the self-insured employer.

There must be recognition that the medical provider who consistently treats the injured worker has the best sense of what is going on with the worker. If an Independent Medical Exam is required, it should be at a medical facility suitable for the examination, and in a location reasonably convenient for the worker. The examination must be conducted with due regard and respect for the privacy and dignity of the injured worker. The worker, at his or her own expense, should have the right to have a representative at the examination who, without interfering or obstructing the exam, can record the examination.

The worker's attending or treating provider should be given the first opportunity to conduct an examination or make a report on the medical issue in question. The treating provider should be able to make a consultation referral. There should be an effort to set up an agreed-to exam -- with the exam being agreed to by the worker and the state or employer (if self-insured). Only after these steps should an Independent Medical Exam is ordered.

Unfortunately this is seldom the case and these examinations are in conducted inside contained environments. Most times these sites are an hour or two from your home and no matter how injured you are there is no way to miss an evaluation and avoid noncompliance. You have nothing to say about these exams because you are not consulted about them beforehand by anybody. If you miss the exam your compensation checks will cease and medical bills will arrive in your mail. So how long before they settle with you is an easy answer. It is when your condition becomes stable and constant. Who decides this, they do.

In my final analysis, the workers' compensation system belongs to the workers it serves, not their employers... and certainly not to the insurance companies looking for a new way to make money.

According to OSHA figures, musculoskeletal disorders cost the nation up to $50 billion dollars a year, including both direct and indirect costs. Washington State's Department of Labor and Industries reported that some 50,000 workers in the state of Washington suffer from work-related musculoskeletal disorders annually, costing the state more than $411 million in medical treatment and partial wage replacement payments. This amount only accounts for the direct costs of Repetitive Stress Injuries. The indirect costs of musculoskeletal disorders are much more difficult to quantify. However, OSHA estimates that the cost to employers was $15 to $20 billion dollars in workers compensation costs and $45 to $60 billion dollars in indirect costs for 1995.

This proves my point that employers have too much control over their employees. It is a no win situation if you allow them to keep you off balance and rushing to your appointments. If you are stressed out and tell your doctor then you have a mental illness that will dog your steps to the end. Doctors can say that you are imaging the pain or lying about the pain. Watch out for kind, trusting, giving and persistent Doctors because they are using you in one way or another to further their careers or personal gains. Employers can push you into over-working and over-straining your bodies, they do not care about you, and all they think about is their

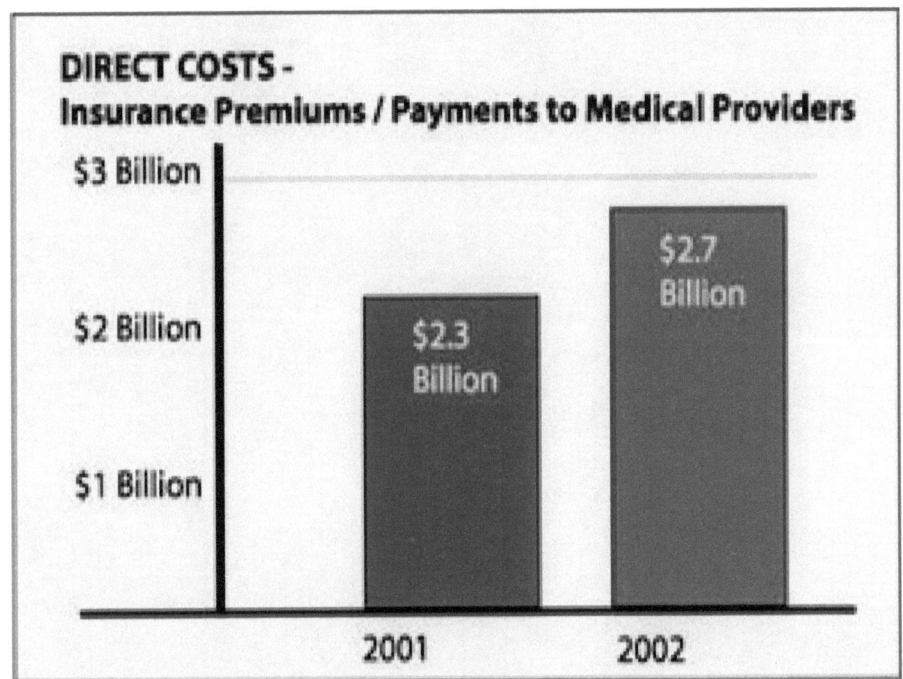

overhead in profits.

Big Business controls the State budget, these are old figures, imagine the costs for 2005-2008. We know that most of this money will not go to injured workers and you are learning where these monies do go. You have only a part of the whole picture but by the time you are finished with this series the whole picture will appear under a bright light.

The End of Book 1

Author Commentary

    This book is Dedicated to Troy Kohls of Madison, Wisconsin. A long time friend and partner it was Troy who came up with the idea to write this book in 2002.
    I was severely injured and unable to work. Early in life I studied physics and engineering and I owned my own construction Co when LAB Construction LLC in Seattle, Washington changed my life forever.
    Troy assisted me founding Bee Roses Feathers Entertainment and put a substantial amount of money funding brfe. Troy monitored me and knew that I was being put through the wringer. I was offered a mental evaluation and if I went along with the program. My Attorney promised to get me over $5000, 000.00 for an Award. I refused for the simple reason that I am not crazy and included in the deal was that I stop writing, stop publishing and keep my mouth shut. Troy and I decided that it was unethical and so we decided to push Bee Roses Feathers Entertainment. If I would have been labeled crazy then everything I write would mean nothing. I continued going through the wringer until my Attorney did some fancy work with the Social Security Department, then a couple months later he quit during the middle of my trial. Troy was always sending money, at times my compensation would stop for several months. Then I would receive it all at once. Every time my employer appealed an L&I decision my checks would stop until the review board would reinstate the compensation. My girlfriend became an alcoholic and we fought a lot over L&I and why it was taking so long to get a settlement. In the five years of collecting compensation I wrote over fifty books. Because of Troy Kohls I am not homeless and have all my books.
    This series of books my Attorney was infuriated about and threatened me privately. I am an American so I can tell it like it is. I have that right to express my opinion and state my views, and though the threats were concrete I will not be moved or swayed by a show of power. I distributed five books before pushing edits on this series.
    I wrote this series to help the hundred thousand or so persons

disabled and going through the wringer. To all Americans that want knowledge of Labor and Industries and how to meet them on an level platform. Certainly this series will make your time valuable and teach you how to make them play your game and not there game. Finances make a big difference; if you pay for your Attorney in cash then he works for you. If he gets a percentage of your take home compensation then he is for sale to the highest bidder, There are laws that change names of crimes into a procedure name and create a system where the money controls all Attorneys involved, and indeed. Legalize bribes by calling them fees or Attorney compensation. Many names and titles get changed or switched around like Departments, and if the need arises Claims Managers. After you read these books you will be prepared for the worse and get what you are entitled within two years without an Expensive lawyer.

Learn your rights now and watch for messy jobsites, over-bearing bosses, and unsafe equipment. Search for the First Aid Kit and if there is not one there then report it. You have the right to perform your work in a safe environment so you better make sure that it is safe before starting work every shift. Take my word for it when I say that the boss has more important things on his mind then your safety.

These books were written in the order that makes it easier to follow so you too can fight and win your Compensation Case.

Coming Soon

Smiling faces promising relief and showing compassion are the caregivers hardest to trust. Perhaps you have noticed with your own medical care that those persons to the point, taking care of business, not wasting time but performing their jobs dutifully, those who really do not have time for small talk are the professionals. They are polite but not overdoing it. The biggest asset is a care worker that is not playing head games and asking personal questions about you.

If they are digging then they are searching and what they could find is another pre-existing injury to add others to, eventually they will be able to explain away the work related injury with your pre-existing injury. What occurs here is that most of the blame for the injury falls on pre-existing injuries. What you tell warm smiling faces gets recorded and filed.

Never let down your guard because everybody including your Attorney searches for weaknesses in your character. I advise that the best thing to do is say as little as possible and research and write your questions down for a later date. Be alert; be sure that it is you're x-rays or other medical records that are being reviewed. Always ask for the results and have it in writing. If they refuse to give you your records and files then it means it is part of the investigation on you. Brfe investigation learned that these details are facts not fabrications. We can go into detail about the way this transpires, and describe the chain of command but that well is in Book 2, 'on sale this summer.' Remember that everything that you say can be held against you in the wringer. Stay alert and choose your care-givers well. Know your rights and never allow an Attorney to dismiss your rights. Once you are done reading my books you will no doubt be well capable of beating the State of Washington Labor and Industries and the Attorneys Behind it. I point is that you can fight and win, if you stand up for your rights.

I will only give you the laws that help you get on your way to a fair Court. I will not confuse you with the mumbo jumbo that they refer to as laws but in reality are not laws at all. All you need to know is the Federal and State laws and know in which courts to appeal your case or ask for a expedited solution to your injury and home situation. I will keep this series to the point and bar no punches. They will leave you to die if it puts a few grand into the pool, you are expendable, ask any worker at the counter at your local Labor and Industries Complex. They also encouraged me to write this book exposing this fiasco they call an Organization. You will know what you're facing and how to combat the flurry of psychological attacks on your home and person.

If it was up to our employers, persons do not get job injuries; they injure themselves on the job.

More Books by Kal Keller
Deadman Cove and the Xeno Project

The Xeno Project and Xeno Stars

Xeno Gods & Demons space and time

Six Chilling Nightmares

Blood Book 1 Walled City of the Dead

Washington State Labor & Industries & the Attorneys Behind It   How to Fight and Win

Labor & Industries Secret Files

Humiliation and depravation are harsh but successful weapons used against work-related injured and their families. Once a person loses there dignity, or have to fight to keep it alive L & I with the assistance of the claims manager and your own Attorney keep you ultimately struggling to keep your appoints. Now all my books are written by one finger because anchor bolts hold down my tendons in my right hand.

L & I Physicians found that my hand was 98% all good so it was stable in there eyes. They graded their own surgeries; Physical therapy reports were buried or covered up, shredded. I am sure they would tell the truth in court but you need to understand. Your Attorney cleanses you and uses you to the best of his Firm' interests, not yours.

I was earning $600.00 a week or more and now I receive 374.00 a month to live on. I have persevered up to now but I fear that disaster can happen soon. Objective evidence dismissed, Attorney quits during trial, I get 0 incomes for seven months, yes my good friends, it can happen to you.

Future books in this series will explore the numbers honestly conducting our own polls from peoples exiting L & I buildings every day.

Attorneys willing to stand up to the truth.

We have conducted these interviews in 2000-2003 which the results will be posted in book two. It is time that we started watching what they are doing because I promise you, that they are watching you whether you were injured or not.

I dare you to find recent statistics about the number of job related injuries in the last three years, or about lengthy injuries and disabilities anywhere through any resources. This information is kept secret from the public to give them time to cover-up corruption. What you do not know will not hurt you is Government policy, indeed. They know better and we do too. Americans should stand up and fight for their rights in any manner ethical or not. Attorneys get pay-offs from injured workers who are not injured but are operating their businesses with enormous profits to be handed out and hands greased. I infiltrated these places but know better then to expose them after series death threats and Attorney pressured me into surrender. Certainly I will write about them without using names so as to give my readers the best possible advantage to win their compensation case and be treated as people and not animals or criminals. I have no Felony record but it makes no difference about who you are but if you were injured on the job. You are kept blinded and brainwashed so when you do get injured on the job you are easy meat for the sharks. Try to disprove me; I dare you to try

Workers compensation systems vary from state to state. State statutes and court decisions control many aspects, including the handling of claims, the evaluation of impairment and settlement of disputes, the amount of benefits injured workers receive and the strategies used to control costs.

Strategies is just and another word for targeting, scheming, bribing, dropping expendable clients, spreading the money around, in this way the monies lost in transfers can be accounted and more persons can pass the buck.

Workers compensation costs are one of the many factors that influence businesses to expand or relocate in a state, generating jobs. When premiums rise sharply, legislators often call for reforms. The last round of widespread reform legislation started in the late 1980s, generally, the reforms enabled employers and insurers to better control medical care costs through coordination and oversight of the treatment plan and return-to-work process and to improve workplace safety. Some states are now approaching a crisis once again as new problems arises.

Reforms reinforce the wringer and in this manner eliminate a host of compensation claims.

I have spoken to several immigrant works in central valley; brfe acquired great insight on what is happening in the central valley in California.

Immigrant workers are pressured no to report their injuries. Some have stated plainly that if one employee causes a large compensation payoff then all members of that family would be replaced by eager youth waiting in line to get into the fields. It is apparent that losing a finger or other severe injuries are insignificant to employers. Immigrants, some illegal immigrants are capable of treating and caring for the injured on the job facilities without ever needing to report the accidents. Desperation is best of friends with our Government. To survive and become an American is worth risking your life and limbs, just ask any immigrant in the fields, if you can interview them alone you will learn about the sacrifices made and the monies saved by our government. Perhaps you believe that you are immune because of your job title, think again. You are as expendable as a migrant worker.

High demands and high pressured government mandates, funded by private interest groups, spending millions of dollars a year helping employers overcome the threat of costly expenditures.

You might ask yourself who you can turn for help, nobody. Social Services have their own wringers and they are all related to government Departments. From our studies California has the best workers compensation system in the United States; if you are injured at work then you will be compensated.

This fact only applies to the general population, falling short of meeting the needs of their employee's strongly encouraging immigrants not to report their injury.

I hope that you have learned how to begin the fight; in the next series you will learn how to protect your object evidence and be sure you file it at the top. Your Attorney might feel that it is not worth his time and effort.　　　Good Luck

131

Labor Industries
Secret Files

Book 2

Written by _____ Kal Keller

Cal's Realm of Nightmares
Art by Kal Keller
Standard Copyrights License
Non-Fiction
2008

All Illustrations   Created by Kal Keller

copyrighted **Cal's Realm of Nightmares**

In the chapters ahead of you we will focus on the processes and examine alternatives that are never mentioned by your Attorney but are within the laws of the State of Washington and certainly federally mandated actions that some States blatantly ignore. We will show you the paths that can appeal your case to the State Supreme Court or perhaps higher.

If you're like most people, you've been going to a doctor since you were born and perhaps didn't know if you were seeing a D.O. (osteopathic physician) or an M.D. (allopathic physician). You may not even be aware that there are only two groups fully licensed to practice medicine and surgery in the United States. The fact is both D.O.s and M.D.s are fully qualified physicians licensed to practice medicine, do surgery and prescribe medication. Is there any difference between these two kinds of doctors? Yes and no.

California has the best operating workers comp system in the United States. This is due to the attention and swift vital treatment in the best medical facilities is offered to the workforce. Each branch of medicine has its respective California licensing board. The Medical Board of California licenses medical doctors (M.D.s), investigates complaints, disciplines those who violate the law, conducts physician evaluations, and facilitates rehabilitation where appropriate. Both the Medical Board of California and the Osteopathic Medical Board are within the California Department of Consumer Affairs. Honest and sympathetic care saves money, California returns more workers to its workforce then any other state in our country. Washington State would do well to follow California's example.

The Medical Board of California is the State agency that licenses medical doctors, investigates complaints, disciplines those who violate the law, conducts physician evaluations, and facilitates rehabilitation where appropriate.

The Board performs similar functions for allied health care professions including registered dispensing opticians, spectacle lens dispensers, contact lens dispensers, licensed midwives, and research psychoanalysts. Everybody has a price or a way that they can be got, or extorted in one way or another. California enforces their laws equally;

unbiased law-enforcement within their own ranks, Job injuries can make or break a state such as Washington as California is decades ahead in reform and technologies.

This book will illustrate the progress of reform in Washington and give you the inside information you need to know about avoiding the wringer and guidelines set forth by your own Attorney.

We will show how Government Depts. work together covering-up their mistakes along with which golf courses are the best places to visit to overhear conversations among Attorneys about their clients.

Our investigations searched for the heart of this crisis and who controls it, we hope that you can understand that not all information we have learned can be disclosed in fear of retaliation and threats. You ever notice that your Attorney always will insist for private meetings, your word against his, an Officer of the Court. In order to get a fair deal you need to know the laws that keep your rights enforced. Unfortunately this burden is yours and we will show you how to keep you rights as major priorities and not the State the major priority for fair hearings and Judgments on your compensation case. The bottom line here is that there is more to the picture then meets the eyes.

We have decided to place these subjects in our books in this series. Expect Book 2, to bring you out of the dark while placing the guilty under a new light. We know who are behind the conspiracies but do not know how deep they go into Government.

Our investigations continue as we dig deeper into the facts unveiling new truths. Perhaps we should keep a better eye on our trusted Officials being sure that they stay ethical and keep us, the people first. It seems that once a body is powerful, wealthy, and influential then you become an insect in their eyes. We all have a right to our opinions whether they are liked or not, we have the right to tell the truth and ask for reforms, but they might not fancy this design.

Expect horrific circumstances and victimizations in situations you expect others might fall into, imagine if it happening to you, or you, or you.

The Washington State Board of Osteopathic Medicine and Surgery has immediately suspended the license of osteopathic physician Keith L. Hindman (OP00000771) for allegedly prescribing controlled substances inappropriately. This action, called a "summary suspension," means Hindman must immediately stop practicing as an osteopathic physician pending the outcome of a hearing. "If the state sees that you have lost your value to their cause then specific employees get targeted."

According to the statement of charges Hindman prescribed excessive quantities of controlled substances without sufficient medical justification and continued to prescribe despite signs of patients' prescription abuse. Hindman is accused of prescribing pain medication to patients without justifying a need in medical records. He allegedly continued to prescribe drugs when they were not effective, failed to document physical exams and failed to explore other treatment options.

The Washington State Board of Osteopathic Medicine and Surgery regulates osteopathic physicians and osteopathic physician assistants in Washington. (This means that they direct physicians to do as Washington state needs or demands in medical reports.)The program establishes, monitors, and enforces qualifications for licensing, consistent standards of practice, continuing competency mechanisms and discipline. Rules, policies and procedures promote the delivery of quality health care to state residents. What this means in a nutshell is that L & I have all the options. Whether it gives policies and procedures in the workers favor or the employers is a matter of opinion. Read these policies for yourself and learn that it allows these physicians leeway with immunity.

Any Physician in the United States can be charged with these same charges were they too be singled out as an example for a self pat on the back. Some persons must continue to receive the same pain-killers all of their lives, your doctor decides after many examinations and evaluations. In the end, it id the Government who decides, which side of the line your doctor is walking on, it is their call.

Most Doctors that do not treat L & I patients brag about it because they know that treatment is dictated by the State as are monies due for payment of services. Pharmaceutical companies make up the lost wages with incentives and bonuses to dispense their drugs. This interferes with your treatment as a patient from the handing-out of certain popular drugs, some yet untested on the general population. All of this stacks the cards against you with a doctor from L& I hard up for cash.

According to a new study, from the Center for Injury Research and Policy (CIRP) at Columbus Children's Hospital, the number of kids in America injured in nonfatal school bus accidents each year is more than double the estimates suggested in former studies, with motor vehicle crashes topping the list of injuries. Covering up accidents and changing statistic numbers assure votes for popular politicians.

An estimated 23.5 million children travel billions of miles on school buses in the United States each year. The CIRP study is the first to use a national sample to describe nonfatal school bus-related injuries to children and teenagers treated in hospital emergency departments across the country. Conveniently easy to cover up and save face, the responsibility for these injuries lies in poor roads construction and alcohol abuse.

According to the study, which was published in the November 06 issue of Pediatrics, from 2001 through 2003 there were an estimated 51,100 school bus-related injuries that resulted in treatment in an U.S. emergency department. That is about 17,000 injuries annually.

School bus-related injuries, one of the study's authors stated, "Our results indicate that they are more than three times more common than earlier estimates. In addition, the findings from this study indicate that traffic-related crashes are the leading means of nonfatal school bus-related injury for children in the U.S.

According to the study, the highest proportion of injuries occurred during the months of September and October with children aged 10 to 14 years old suffering the most injuries compared with all other age groups. Traffic-related accidents, where the child was injured as a passenger on a school bus as a result of a collision between the bus and another motor vehicle, topped the list of causes and accounted for 42 percent of the total injuries. Among all the patients, strains and sprains were the most commonly encountered injury. Remember that it is impossible to configure true values and assessment in these studies. Thus a sprain or strains can be a general objective description without mentioning hairline fractures among other conditions that follow these injuries. Continuing and severe side-effects from a sprain or strain, I have seen construction workers hands that were swollen and severely scarred that never complain in fear of losing their great paying jobs. Workers everywhere know the consequences of fighting the state. All employers' premiums into one giant pool called the state budget for Washington State Labor & Industries certainly makes the state the employer.

The authors emphasized that, since the data was collected from NEISS, only kids seen in a hospital ER after their accident were counted.

Children receiving chiropractic care after injuries, or ones that were treated by their parents, school nurses/doctors or pediatricians, were not integrated into the total injuries reported.

It is easy to make things appear better then they really are because it saves the State money. Book 3 will try to follow these monies trails and learn if it can all be accounted for.

Accidents at the workplace have been a huge and increasing problem for all American corporations since the industrial revolution when the formal working industry first started to take shape. The lives of countless workers have been either taken or forever scarred by accidents that could have been easily avoided by fundamental training in safety procedures.

Book 2 is going to expose the process and define explanations that seem to be rhetoric and not much help to an injured worker.

Chapter 11
"Doctors of Osteopathic Medicine"

Osteopathic medical schools emphasize training students to be primary care physicians.

- D.O.s practices a "whole person" approach to medicine. Instead of just treating specific symptoms or illnesses, they regard your body as integrated whole.
- Osteopathic physicians focus on preventive health care.
- D.O.s receive extra training in the musculoskeletal system -- your body's interconnected system of nerves, muscles and bones that make up two-thirds of its body mass. This training provides osteopathic physicians with a better understanding of the ways that an injury or illness in one part of your body can affect another.
- Osteopathic manipulative treatment (OMT) is incorporated in the training and practice of osteopathic physicians. With OMT, osteopathic physicians use their hands to diagnose injury and illness and to encourage your body's natural tendency toward good health. By combining all available medical procedures with OMT, D.O.s offer their patients the most comprehensive care available in medicine today.

Osteopathic medicine is a unique form of American medical care that was developed in 1874 by Dr. Andrew Taylor Still. Dr. Still was dissatisfied with the effectiveness of 19th Century medicine. He believed that many of the medications of his day were useless or even harmful. Dr. Still was one of the first in his time to study the attributes of good health so that he could better understand the process of disease.

Applicants to both D.O. and M.D. medical colleges typically have a four-year undergraduate degree with an emphasis on scientific courses. Both D.O.s and M.D.s complete four years of basic medical education.

- After medical school, both D.O.s and M.D.s can choose to practice in a specialty area of medicine such as surgery, family practice or psychiatry--after completing a residency program (typically two to six years of additional training).
- Both D.O.s and M.D.s must pass comparable state licensing exams.
- D.O.s and M.D.s both practice in fully accredited and licensed health care facilities.
- D.O.s receives extra training in the musculoskeletal system; your body's interconnected system of muscles and bones that make up two-thirds of the body's mass.

Washington State Dept of Labor and Industries (L&I) must approve examiners who perform independent medical examinations (IME) in Washington, Oregon, or Idaho. These examinations are for workers covered under Washington state workers' compensation. These are the doctors or specialists that make or break your compensation case.

An IME is a medical evaluation that documents the worker's condition. This helps L&I or self-insurer give appropriate assistance to the worker and make decisions on the claim. IMEs may decide whether the worker has reached their maximum benefit from treatments or if any permanent impairment remains. This goes back to the state and does not address the injury. Does not consider scar tissue, future degeneration, every time it rains your joints swell and your back aches. State of mind of the injured worker or future problems that materialize from the injury. These industry doctors evaluate their first impression they get about you and follow the agenda secretly sent to them on what decision to make and what rating to give. What can we do about this? There is much we can do to bring about changes for the good out of corrupt system. Book 5 will go into detail about the steps that we the people of America must take to reclaim our country from dishonest politicians.

- High-quality exams provide unbiased, accurate and medically sound information. Unbiased says who? This book is unbiased but you can't help shedding a tear or two for the persons that we interviewed.

    The insurer may request an IME. They may also arrange for one in response to a request or an issue raised by the attending doctor or the employer at the time of injury.

    Employment of physicians and surgeons is expected to grow faster than the average for all occupations. Job opportunities should be very good, especially for physicians and surgeons willing to practice in specialties—including family practice, internal medicine, and OB/GYN—or in rural and low-income areas where there is a perceived shortage of medical practitioners.

Demand for physicians' services is highly sensitive to changes in consumer preferences, health care reimbursement policies, and legislation, for example, if changes to health coverage result in consumers facing higher out-of-pocket costs, they may demand fewer physician services. Patients relying more on other health care providers; such as physician assistants, nurse practitioners, optometrists, and nurse anesthetists, also may temper demand for physician services. In addition, new technologies will increase physician productivity. These technologies include electronic medical records, test and prescription orders, billing, and scheduling.

    Knowing that your case can stretch into years, or a lifetime imagine how your compensation claim is affected by new laws. The D.O. is the person that can manipulate you the must. Conversions between doctors and your Attorney are commonplace yet it is unethical and unlawful to do so. The State starves out the doctor and the doctor becomes desperate to get reimbursed and paid for their services contact your Attorney and ask what they must do to get paid. At this point you have lost your case. In a matter of a year or sooner you will get a 1-4% disability whether you can work or not.

The End of Chapter 11
"Doctors of Osteopathic Medicine"

Chapter 12
Physical Therapy

Top 10 responsibilities   Importance

Plan, prepare and carry out individually designed programs of physical treatment to maintain, improve or restore physical functioning, alleviate pain and prevent physical dysfunction in patients.

94

Perform and document an initial exam, evaluating data to identify problems and determine a diagnosis prior to intervention.

92

Evaluate effects of treatment at various stages and adjust treatments to achieve maximum benefit.

90

Administer manual exercises, massage or traction to help relieve pain, increase patient strength, or decrease or prevent deformity or crippling.

90

Instruct patient and family in treatment procedures to be continued at home.

88

Confer with the patient, medical practitioners and appropriate others to plan, implement and assess the intervention program.

86

Review physician's referral and patient's medical records to help determine diagnosis and physical therapy treatment required.

84

Obtain patients' informed consent to proposed interventions.

83

Record prognosis, treatment, response, and progress in patient's chart or enter information into computer.

83

Discharge patient from physical therapy when goals or projected outcomes have been attained and provide for appropriate follow-up care or referrals.

Physical Therapists Assess, plan, organize, and participate in rehabilitative programs that improve mobility, relieve pain, increase strength, and decrease or prevent deformity of patients suffering from disease or injury.

Compiled ahead of you is important information on what to use to ease your pain. Doctors will not inform you about most of these aides so that you will be charged for clinic or hospital braces and other out-dated medical equipment at outrageous prices.

Elasto-Gel wraps are made of tough, flexible gel covered with a four way stretch material that allows for maximum conformity, heat transfer, and comfort. These versatile wraps can be used for both hot and cold therapy treatments. When used for cold therapy the wrap remains flexible at temperatures as low as -20 F and remains cold for up to 40 minutes. When used as a hot wrap it provides moist heat that quickly penetrates muscles and joints. The wrap can be heated in a microwave in less than 2 minutes and it retains the heat for up to a half hour.

Wrist pain from injury, surgery, arthritis, and similar disorders often responds well to heat therapy. By increasing the temperature in the hand & wrist area, heat therapy enhances blood circulation and helps to relax sore muscles, reducing stiffness and increasing mobility.

Just about anyone who has run for an extended period has suffered a lower-leg injury. A pulled calf muscle a strained soleus, a tight Achilles' tendon. Ralph Havens, a physical therapist at Mission Hills Physical Therapy, offers an unusual technique that has alleviated lower-leg pain for a number of patients. *"I have suffered the same injury, it came out of nowhere and the next day I was screaming in agony and continued for two months before Achilles' tendon was diagnosed. During the process of being treated by several doctors I was humiliated and accused of lying Morphine cid not ease the pain nothing worked."*

All you need to carry out Havens' program is a tennis ball and 7-15 minutes a day. The program is based on firmly pressing down on a tennis ball at 18 different locations on the bottom of your bare foot.

The first three spots are at the base of your toes. With the ball pressed against a wall, keep your heel and the ball of your foot on the floor. Push down for 10 seconds at each spot, wrapping your toes around the ball. You should press down pretty hard. As you move around your foot, some of the spots might hurt a bit initially, the pain, shouldn't be excruciating.

The next three spots are just behind the ball of your foot. From there, move to the middle of your foot, then to the back, just in front of your heel.

Next, turn your foot parallel to the wall. Hit the three spots on the inside edge of your foot. Again starting just below the ball of your foot, to the middle and then just in front of the heel. Finally, hit the same three spots on the outside of your foot. Again, make sure you apply the pressure for 10 seconds. "People say their whole leg feels lighter," says Havens, who completed the Boston Marathon in 2:51:52.

Cervical Spondylosis

A disorder that results from abnormal growth of the bones of the neck, (cervical vertebrae) and degeneration and mineral deposits in the cushions between the vertebrae (cervical disks). *"Injured on the job with a back injury complicates this existing condition that happens to all humans in time."*

Cervical Spondylosis results from chronic degeneration of the cushions between the neck vertebrae (cervical disks) and mineral deposits (calcification) in the disks. There may be abnormal growths or "spurs" on the vertebrae (the bones of the spine*). On the job stress and working with computers, sports, hanging drywall and construction occupations are just some of the causes for this injury or complicating existing degeneration of vertebrae.*

This causes gradual compression of one or more of the nerve roots, resulting in progressive pain and movement or sensation abnormalities that resemble herniated cervical disk but are usually less severe. The spinal cord may be compressed (spinal cord trauma) with resultant movement or sensation or function losses of the areas controlled at and below the level of compression.

Risks include old neck injury (which may have occurred several years previously). However, the disorder also occurs frequently in older people who have no history of neck injury. It is thought to result from natural degeneration of vertebrae resulting from aging. This affects everybody whether slightly or severely in their lifetimes.

Numerous cases are not preventable. 'Such as proper equipment and techniques when playing sports' might reduce the risk. Prevention of a neck injury is the best treatment.

The goal of treatment is relief of pain and prevention of permanent spinal column trauma and nerve root injury.

In mild cases, no treatment is required. Discomfort is minimal and often occurs only when triggered by specific head movements. Exercises to strengthen the neck may be optional treatment for those persons that suffer a traumatic job injury. Restriction of neck movement reduces pain. This is often accomplished with a cervical collar (neck brace). Intermittent neck traction may be suggested instead of, or in addition to, a cervical collar. This usually consists of a halter-like device placed on the head and neck and attached to pulleys and weights.

For severe cases, hospitalization with complete bed rest and traction for 1 or 2 weeks may be needed. Analgesics or muscle relaxants may help to reduce pain. Surgical decompression of the spinal cord in the neck may be recommended if there is significant loss of movement, sensation, or function. It may also be needed if pain is severe or if pain is unresponsive to other treatment. Surgical procedures may also include removal of abnormal bone growths, and stabilization of the neck with hardware or by fusion of the cervical vertebrae.

The outcome varies some cases are mild and never require treatment. Other cases are progressive and chronic. Some cases are severe. In a few cases, permanent disability results from compression of the spinal cord.

I suffered from a lower back injury in Sacramento California. *"Fortunately micro-laser surgery cured me, in fact my back is in better shape then it ever was in the past. California cured me with prompt care and quick medical testing. Before bone spurs formed and continuous back exercise taught to me by physical therapists located in Sacramento keep my back pain free."*

The End of Chapter 12

Chapter 13
Privileged Client Information

Attorney-client privilege encourages clients to reveal to their attorneys all pertinent information in legal matters by protecting such disclosures from discovery at trial. The privileged information, held strictly between the attorney and the client, might remain confidential as long as a court does not force disclosure. The privilege does not apply to communications between an attorney and a client made to further a fraud or crime. The responsibility for designating which information should remain confidential rests with the client. In its most common use, however, the attorney claims the privilege on behalf of the client in refusing to disclose to the court or any other party requested information about the client's case.

Privileged Client Information does not exist with the client. It is used by the law firms for their advantage, in the end, they are businesses and the Firm always comes first.

You become a number as does all your private information and files. These facts are not meant to harm you but remember that it has price tags and priorities attached to theses numbers that will affect you in one way or another.

Because attorney-client privilege often balances competing interests, it defies a rigid definition. However, one often-cited characterization was articulated in *United States v. United Shoe Machinery Corp.,* 89 F. Supp. 357 (D. Mass. 1950). The court expressed five requirements: first, the person asserting the privilege must be a client, or must have sought to become a client at the time of disclosure; second, the person connected to the communication must be acting as a lawyer; third, the communication must be between the lawyer and the client exclusively — no non-clients may be included in the communication; fourth, the communication must be for the purpose of securing a legal opinion, legal services, or assistance in some legal proceeding, and not for the purpose of committing a crime; fifth, the privilege may be claimed or waived by the client only (usually, as mentioned, through counsel).

"Why have these rules if they mean nothing? It is part of the wringer."

Sometimes, even when all five of the *United Shoe* requirements have been met, courts will still compel disclosure of the information sought. The courts base exceptions to the privilege on rule 501 of the Federal Rules of Evidence, which states that "the recognition of a privilege based on a confidential relationship ... should be determined on a case-by-case basis." In examining the privilege on a case-by-case basis, courts weigh the benefits to be gained by upholding the privilege (preserving the confidence between attorney and client) against the harms that may be caused if they deny it (the loss of information valuable to the opposing party).

The courts have declared that the fact of an attorney-client relationship itself need not always remain privileged information (*National Union Fire Insurance Co. of Pittsburgh v. Aetna Casualty & Surety Co.,* 384 F.2d 316 [5th Cir. 1967]); the privilege may be upheld, however, **if the very existence of an attorney-client relationship could prove incriminating to the client** (*In re Michaelson,* 511 F.2d 882 [9th Cir. 1975], *cert. denied,* 421 U.S. 978, 95 S. Ct. 1979, 44 L. Ed. 2d 469 [1975]). **Also, the attorney-client privilege does not always protect the client's name or the amount paid to an attorney** (*Wirtz v. Fowler,* 372 F.2d 315 [5th Cir. 1966]). **Further, the attorney's perception of the client's mental competency will not always is protected** (*United States v. Kendrick,* 331 F.2d 110 [4th Cir. 1964] *[holding that attorney's testimony that client was responsive, logical in conversation and reasoning, and understood the proceedings did not address confidential matters]).* "Says who?"

"You are assessed and given a value then you are listed in the proper group unless you make the difference fighting the system forcing your Attorneys to follow the law for your best interests, and not the Firms interests." You are groomed for failure. In general, exceptions to the attorney-client privilege can prove tricky to defense attorneys, who try to keep a client's potentially incriminating disclosures confidential.

One exception, however, is intended to protect attorneys: *Meyerhofer v. Empire Fire & Marine Insurance Co.,* 497 F.2d 1190 (2d Cir. 1974), *cert. denied,* 419 U.S. 998, 95 S. Ct. 314, 42 L. Ed. 2d 272 (1974), **held that an attorney may circumvent the privilege if revealing information would relieve her or him of accusations of wrongdoing.**

Now I am sure you are getting the point of this chapter that the only secrets that exist are between Attorneys while leaving you out of the network or circle of working Attorneys on your case.

A client is not always a person; a corporation can be a client and may have a right to the attorney-client privilege. The Supreme Court's decision in *Upjohn Co. v. United States,* 449 U.S. 383, 101 S. Ct. 677, 66 L. Ed. 2d 584 (1981**), ensured greater protection for confidential information between a corporation and its lawyers.** In the mid-1970s, Upjohn Company faced accusations of making questionable payments to officials of foreign governments in order to secure business from those governments. In response to those accusations, Upjohn authorized its corporate attorneys to conduct investigations of foreign payments. When the Internal Revenue Service (IRS) issued a summons for the investigative documents that Upjohn had left to its lawyers, Upjohn refused to comply with the request. Upjohn argued that the documents were privileged. The Supreme Court ruled in favor of Upjohn, and this decision became the standard for determining the nature of services either legal or business provided by the corporate attorney. *"Every American should have the same rights, we as Americans should band together and demand that our laws be enforced in favor of the people of America."* It seems that Judgments are decided politically and by the fairness of the facts.

By the early 1990s, the attorney-client privilege was narrowed by federal guidelines intended to combat money laundering, *(Always an excuse to remove more Rights from the American people).* The federal government, in conjunction with President George Bush's crackdown on drug trafficking (called the war on drugs), pressed an IRS policy that would hinder drug dealers and other criminals from disguising profits. The law required attorneys to disclose to the government any cash payment in excess of $10,000, and the name of the client making the payment (26 U.S.C.A. § 6050 I).

In *United States v. Leventhal,* 961 F.2d 936 (11th Cir. 1992), Robert Leventhal, an attorney in Florida, refused to disclose to the IRS the names of clients who had paid him over $10,000 in cash. Leventhal's clients wished to remain anonymous, and Leventhal argued that the attorney-client privilege gave them that right. Leventhal cited the Florida Rules of Professional Conduct, which require disclosure of confidential client information only in rare circumstances. The federal government sued Leventhal. The court ruled that disclosing the clients' identities revealed only the existence of an attorney-client relationship, a simple factual matter not within the scope of the privilege. Therefore, Leventhal had to reveal the sources of the payments.

The Sixth Circuit Court of Appeals followed *Leventhal* in *United States v. Ritchie,* 15 F.3d 592 (1994), *cert. denied,* ___ U.S. ___ , 115 S. Ct. 188, 130 L. Ed. 2d 121 (1994). Attorney Robert Ritchie had challenged the same IRS policy, but the court noted that Congress gave the IRS broad powers to ensure compliance with the tax code. Appeals court judge Alice M. Batchelder held that there was no ***"constitutionally protected liberty interest in spending large amounts of cash without having to account for it."*** We need more enforcement on this issue.

Attorneys have decried the federal government's position in such cases. But the attorney-client privilege remains useful as a defensive measure in more general circumstances. The privilege remains an exception to the general rule that individuals must testify to all facts within their knowledge. Rooted in ancient principles, it fosters trust within this important relationship and helps attorneys fully develop their clients' cases by encouraging complete disclosure of relevant information. "Who decides what is relevant? Everything is done in the states favor, you are never conferred with during decision making nor do you know when your privileged information is used, and by whom.

Under certain circumstances, information possessed by an attorney cannot be disclosed to others without the client's consent because of the attorney-client privilege or certain other legal concepts. The attorney-client privilege, which dates back to the reign of Elizabeth I, was originally based on the concept that an attorney should not be required to testify against the client and, thereby, violate a duty of loyalty owed to the client. At that time, it was the lawyer who held the privilege. Today, the privilege is held by the client; while it may be asserted by the lawyer on behalf of the client, only the client can waive the privilege. *"In Book three we will explore these circumstances."*

Generally, in order for the attorney-client privilege to apply, there must be an attorney-client relationship and the communication must be made by the client in confidence for the purpose of obtaining legal advice. It does not matter whether the information is communicated orally, in writing, or by nonverbal communication, such as nodding the head. *"Your Attorney can quit without warning you at any time so all privileged information belongs to the law firm you have a contract with."*

The privilege also applies to information provided by the attorney to the client. Not only must there be an attorney-client relationship, but the communication must be related to the seeking of legal advice. As a result, it might be concluded that communications do not fall within the scope of the attorney-client privilege based on the extent to which the client is seeking business advice or technical advice. Also, because the communications must be in confidence, if a third party not having a common interest is allowed to be present during the communications or if it is intended that the communications be delivered to a third party, the attorney-client privilege will not apply. *"This is another way to entrap you. My Attorneys and my Doctors had working relationships. By this I will clarify; one of my Physicians so desperately needed her money that she had me delivers notes to my attorney. Before long the two of them conversed on the phone exchanging information about me. All this information now was not privileged but used to manipulate my case in favor of the state."*

Some unusual questions regarding attorney-client privilege have arisen in connection with patent agents. Some courts have concluded that even though patent agents are not lawyers, they are lawfully engaging in conduct that causes them to act like lawyers; they have held that the privilege applies. In other cases, emphasis has been placed on the fact that the patent agent is primarily a conveyor of information intended ultimately to be disclosed to the public, and, as a result, the attorney-client privilege has not been applied.

Only the client has the power to waive the attorney-client privilege. ***"We have all ready established that in fact there is no such thing as attorney-client privilege."*** It is important to bear in mind that a waiver may occur even though the client does not intend to waive the privilege. For example, if the client carelessly allows the information to be disclosed to others, confidentiality will be lost, and a waiver will occur. The waiver may also result from failure to object to the demand for disclosure in litigation, unfortunately you are not notified about this motion made by your employer during litigation and you do not have to be notified by your attorney by it. Remember that you signed your rights over to your attorney and what you do not know can hurt you.. Once the privilege has been waived, it is treated as a waiver for all purposes.

Another factor that, in many instances, more broadly and more effectively prevents disclosure of information received from a client to others is the ethical obligation by the attorney to maintain client confidences. As a general legal ethics precept, an attorney is not allowed to reveal client confidences to others or use the same to the disadvantage of a client or for the benefit of himself/herself or someone else, ***"without obtaining consent from the client."*** This ethical obligation exists regardless of whether the attorney-client privilege or the work-product doctrine applies. However, there are some exceptions to this obligation that are recognized in many jurisdictions. In some jurisdictions, an attorney has the discretionary right to reveal confidential client information if such disclosure will prevent substantial physical harm to a third person. ***"Who makes this decision, and furthermore; can these scenarios' be created for an injured worker by circumstances of the injury. Surely in many cases these people would have never been in trouble before in their lives. Had they not gone through the wringer?"*** Other jurisdictions not only recognize the substantial physical harm exception, but also give an attorney the discretionary right to disclose confidential client information if disclosure is necessary to prevent substantial injury to the financial interests or property of third persons. Many jurisdictions have an ethical rule, applicable in litigation matters, that crafts it a mandatory requirement for an attorney to disclose confidential client information to a court when it is necessary in order to avoid assisting a criminal or fraudulent act by the client. *"Your attorney can use this against you, if he has a mind to invent this scenario then he will profit in ways that have been kept secret forever. We will explore these mute but well used advantages in book three."*

It is important that clients be aware; that unlike interactions wherein confidentiality agreements are relied on as a basis for avoiding undesired disclosure of information. **"The association with a lawyer is different."** The broad-based ethical requirements concerning confidentiality combined with the attorney-client privilege and work-product policy; offer substantial benefits to the client. It must be noted, however, that the scope of the confidentiality necessities whether they are based on precepts of legal ethics or not the attorney-client privilege or the work-product doctrine; will vary from jurisdiction to jurisdiction. It is important that you stay on top of your game by learning the laws in your jurisdictions.

It is recommended that clients question attorneys in their respective jurisdictions as to the scope of the confidentiality obligation. *"If you do not question your attorney, by law he is not compelled to outline the gist of your private information. Remember that your files all are under different policies and privileged information varies with enforcement. Laws create an atmosphere of complete attorney privilege immune to scrutiny. There are millions of words compiled in laws that protect attorneys. It is not your Attorney that must inform you of the unwritten policies but up to you to learn for yourself. Perhaps in the future brfe LLC will investigate labor & industries state to state. All we do is some book work and go to the right depts. asking the right questions. It is recommended by us that even if you have retained an attorney you learn that you have to fend for."*

The End of Chapter 13

brfe Entertainment

Many Employers forget who you are as they struggle to reach their goals or dreams of financial freedom. You can always be replaced at your position, at your job, so you are expendable. You were hired so your employer can profit and you earn a salary or wages. Employees are accountable on an hourly or daily basis; however employers can pass the blame to employees with little effort on their part. Power plays and sexual abuse on the jobsite are cleverly disguised with unrelated titles. Employers literally have the power of your life or death in their hands. My advice is to keep your personal life private especially from your employer.

Your Medicine

Chapter 14

Injured workers must be prepared to know well the prescribed drugs they are taking. Learn about the side-effects and how well they work with other drugs you are ingesting. Injured or wronged employees often trust the system for a fair shake. These people suffer the most because the state spends more money enforcing choice laws then they does assisting injured workers.

Wounded workers are expected to be as productive as they were before the injury. The harder you try the better case your employer has on you as slandering, fraud and you will be tagged, placed into a profile as you are added into a list. Medicine calms, numbs, kills pain, elevates, depresses, and with the right combination of drugs has a complacent effect on the patient. Over-use past this point will daze the patient and cause painful severe spasms. I supposed the saying goes like this; dumping salt on the wound. . .

Leading mental health charity Rethink today called for an end to the shameful practice of over-prescribing of mental health medicines, following the publication of a Healthcare Commission report into medicines management.

The Healthcare Commission has published a national report on medicines management that finds up to one in three people in hospital are prescribed more than maximum recommended doses. Forty two (out of 83) mental health trusts volunteered to take part in this review.

Rethink's chief executive Paul Jenkins said: "The Healthcare Commission has once again highlighted a shocking over-prescription of powerful medicines to people in hospital experiencing a mental health crisis.

"Up to one in three people are being prescribed above maximum

recommended doses of medicines that can have serious and long-term side-effects." As well as defying national regulations, this over-prescription actually delays successful discharge in many cases. *"Injured workers become confused or trance into a daze as they spin inside the wringer."*

Once mental illness is established and you are prescribed psychotic or other drugs of this type. Then you are doomed unless you give total control of your case to your attorney. If your attorney believes you will earn him a great profit then he will resolve your case. If you are not worth this attorney's time you will be handed over to labor & industries. You can guess the rest.

"The National Institute for Clinical Excellence issued statutory guidance as long ago as 2002 on the best use of medicines for the treatment of schizophrenia. It is shameful that so many trusts have failed to properly implement it four years on. Everyone has the right to the best evidence-based care, but it is unacceptable that people experiencing a mental health crisis can still be treated as second class citizens."

Substance abuse is a growing menace in the society. Anyone can be a victim of it, disregarding age, gender and ethnicity. Substance abuse can be broadly defined as the situation in which the use of a substance causes a detrimental effect on the physical and mental condition of an individual. Further, substance abuse can also have devastating effect on the financial, social and even legal standing in the society of a person.

Overprescribing drugs helps the state win their case and deny your claim. This is the bottom line; if you want to win keep your wits about you.

The 'substance' in substance abuse can be almost anything. It can be either legal or illegal. Even the non prescribed use of prescriptive medicines has and can be termed as substance abuse. In cases of substance abuse, injections, inhaling and oral usage of the substance is common. However, sniffing and smoking of the said substance is also seen in some cases.

"Doctors have a lot of leeway; they have your life in their hands along with prescription drugs. Perhaps the most common way of

substance abuse is the non prescribed use of prescribed medicines." Simply put, an overdose of sleeping pills prescribed by a doctor is substance abuse. Alternately, taking any substance into the body in any other way than as prescribed by the doctor is substance abuse.

"Stress and pressure from your employer and your claims manager can lead some persons to commit suicide."

Certainly a prescription drug vendor or salesperson would disagree with this following assessment...

When prescription drugs are taken correctly, they are safe. Taking too much or taking them when they are not needed is drug abuse. Abusing drugs can be dangerous. People can become addicted to prescription medicines the same way people are addicted to illegal drugs. People who are addicted to any kind of drugs need treatment. The more of these drugs you get prescribed the larger the kickbacks will be from the pharmaceutical companies for the Doctors.

Medicine is everything, it determines what you are as far as labor and industries go, they base all their final findings and judgments by your prescription history.

Easily be accomplished through over prescribing drugs or consuming the wrong drugs. Changing the direction and focus on your compensation case can be standard operating procedure with labor and industries. Overzealous salespersons and doctors to turn a large profit place aside the needs of the patient to accomplish this goal.

"I know this to be a fact because I saw the said actions with me own eyes. Yep, sure enough I said appointments cancelled to meet with drug vendors to receive free drugs and earned kickbacks. I write the truth not as I know it but calling them as I saw and see them."

Drug rehab clinics should be set up for free to be utilized by all patients. Many times you will have prescriptions from several Doctors and the mixture could be fatal in the long run of the wringer. This will prevent Attorneys from sending you to their physicians who work on contract thus compromising your treatment. Attorneys trade favors and clients as if they were drafting rookies in the NFL. Compensation are sacrificed for higher claims and easy runs for choice clients while others like perhaps you will be extracted from the system, wrung out, case closed with minimal if any resolutions on your compensation case. You can appeal the decision and have three years to do so. This would be the time to take your case to the highest court. Yea . . .

Now you have been marked because at this point of the game you will not be able to find a law firm to take your case. You have been marked by the State and the Bar Association. Drugs and your prescriptions along with surgeon evaluations had determined you to be a liar and a crybaby. *"Where do you go from here?"*

You go to your computer and turn it on. Then you need to search for compensation Attorneys who will work with you online and telephone to represent yourself. Once you do this labor and industries see you under a new light and will begin making special considerations and recognitions.

We will use a fictional name to tell a true story. I hope that this will prove to be a good example of what could happen if you are prescribed the wrong medications.

Ralph hurt his back on the first day of the job never reporting his injury. It was painful and Ralph began drinking a lot of beer after work to kill the pain. This injury happened ten years ago and Ralph is a foreman now but his back has gotten worst, a lot worse.

Finally Ralph visited a Doctor and filed a claim. Ralph collected compensation for six months and all was well until the checks stopped. The last evaluation Ralph attended claimed it was an old injury unrelated to his job. Ralph was fired and now suffers from a herniated disc. Falling into debt and living on the edge. His back injury prevents Ralph from employment and he has no money to pursue his closed case further so his wife moves in with her mother. Ralph is now living in a house with an eviction notice on the door. The bank repossessed Ralph' truck while he was sleeping and he did not have the money for the electric bill.

Ralph stared at his boots and work clothes neatly stacked next to his tool belts and boxes as he designed a hangman's noose out of one-inch hemp rope.

Ralph was desperate and in agony, his back was getting worse and in a short time he knew that he would become homeless so he had made his mind up to kill himself.

Two days later a friend found Ralphs body hanging in the center of his living room with his shadow covering his tools. Ralph was pronounced dead an hour later, he managed to stay alive after he hung himself but finally died from medical complications.

Ralph should have been covered for his injury but before his case became objective he was wrung out of the system.

My question is why did not the doctors see this coming? Why did his Attorney or labor and industries allow Ralph to see a physiatrist when he requested for one. Why did everybody look the other way as this man slowly died from mental illness he contracted from his life being torn apart by the system that was supposed to protect him? This story was told to me by a county coroner and we shared a moment of silence in sadness for another victim of rubber-band laws.

There are many stories and some are sadder then Ralphs. Families suffer from an injury to a loved one, and it is a roll of the dice if you are worth their trouble to be properly attentive and give you a hundred percent for your compensation case to rule in your favor.

If you speak up for yourself then they say you are rambling, if you try to impress them more they claim you are yelling, unruly, and need psychiatric care. (You must be crazy if you think they are wrong).

Medicines you consume label who you are but you do not have to go with the program. Sorry, yes you do or you become non-compliant and your case is closed. You can protest, be sure it is in writing and you keep a copy for yourself. Now you will be prescribed drugs to discredit your testimony and to keep you off balance as the system takes over your life.

The best way to be sure that the medication you are taking is the one you need is by searching the internet. Be alert and watch for the vendors, be sure that your Doctor is medicating your health condition and not their pocketbooks

This situation is not a bad thing if it were not abused but many times greed over-rides ethics and consumes goodwill. Lobbyists are working hard full-time on their toes pushing more litigation to widen the laws and create an atmosphere for vendors of prescription drugs. There are more untested drugs vended then people know. Some of these drugs we have dubbed as Xeno drugs. These new series of medications are explorations into the future of medicine that are highly controversial among religions and political figures the world over. This is my opinion; it would seem that animal DNA should stay in animals and out of human.

Psychiatric Medicines

Prozac is an important indicator that L & I is going to use a D.O. to gain your trust, evaluate you, profile and categorize you for L & I. This person will at first be beneficial to your health and compensation claim. Then your Doctor will be harassed by L & I to improve reports and determine that the patient is faking their condition. At first your Doctor refuses and gives objective evaluations, then L & I stops payments to the Doctor your own luck changes for the worse. She increases your dosage and asks you to try another drug that she or he believes will alleviate your pain. Your Doctor tries to hold out and gives you the support you need. The payments for services are now three years late and your Doctor caves in and writes the reports that will collapse your compensation case, cut your benefits and send you on a slew of evaluations, one after another.

Soon you are taking sleeping pills, muscle relaxers, pain-killers, mood elevators and high blood pressure pills.

The D.O. will eventually declare you out of your mind or having a pre-existing injury not job related. Remember that your D.O. can prescribe any medication, more prescriptions then a regular PHD so this person controls the outcome of your compensation case. If you refuse twice you are in noncompliance, if you miss two appointments or are late, same thing. L & I can see that you are making all your appointments on time therefore judging you able-bodied for some jobs. Your D.O will be the only person in the wringer that can get you the benefits you deserve. Surgeons grade their own surgery, Physical therapy reports are ignored and you are guilty of fraud if you step on the wrong toes.

Damages to your body and reparation should be an easy process but the more attorneys on the job the better for the state. The Attorneys that has huge advertisements in the yellow pages is the attorneys to avoid.

"Muscle Relaxers and other medicines which reduce swelling."

Manna from heaven for tendon injuries, Celebrex is the drug among the injured in the know: It works better then vicodon and keeps working. I can only take one every other day but it works. Celebrex may have side-effects for some people or complicate an existing condition like an ulcer or other malady. .

Swelling is the force behind pain. Inflammation, Puffiness, Distension, Growths or unwanted bumps all are concerns that can be dealt with easily using drugs such as Celebrex and over the counter drugs like Advil.

Spasms are uncontrollable movements of tendons or muscles, I know what an inward twisting spasm feels like and the pain freezes you into place. I have not found a completely effective drug yet for these spasms but medicine for restless leg syndrome seems to keep the spasms in tow.

"If you do not look out for yourself do not expect the courts to do it for you."

Yes sir, muscle relaxers can prevent surgeries of the future and bring quick relief of you tendon or muscle pain. Soreness, throbbing, tenderness, stinging, smarting, pain that never goes away, eases a bit at times but is always present.. Then there is more pain that is not compensated or considered at your hearings in court.

In the L & I community grief, sorrow, anguish, agony are not considered but encouraged.

You might say that you would never lose your self composure but could you weather; nuisance, drags in your compensation case, pests like letters that come from nowhere with deadlines and conditions from L & I.

Compassion is a weakness; demand your rights and those laws be applied to your case search for comparisons with other court cases in the law library.

Sympathy and other human traits are hard to find once you get out of a lobby in an L & I building. Kindness, Consideration, Empathy are not written into policy but you will find discomfort in the Coldness.

You must be alert and choose your words carefully when questioned by a claims manager and know that every word you say is recorded.

Life goes on after you win or lose your fight and you must be prepared with a plan.

If suddenly they diagnosed you with what they call arthritis it is damage from your job injury and somewhat like arthritis but completely different. I thought that it was pretty slick that physicians can miss diagnose your injury and get away with it because it is somewhat like the condition they diagnosed in another case or so.

If L & I can get out of paying for conditions of the future resulting from your injury they will nip it in the bud quickly. After a few years they clarify your injury as an old injury implying that it occurred after the industrial accident. Do not believe that your attorney will cover your ass because he is too busy covering his own.

Clonazepam works to relieve the shakes, and controls spasms. Celebrex controls the pain and retextures your tendons and muscles.

Nexium will coat your stomach and treat reflex disease. Levaquin 750 MG will return your immune system if you are healing from a severe injury and catch a cold or the flu, or even an infection. Some drugs reduce or weaken your immune system, ask your pharmacist what drugs these are.

You start with the original injury and by the time you get through the wringer your hair is grey and you are a bundle of nerves. There is no way to avoid this unless you get on the right meds quickly and are left alone to heal. You do not have to be a micro-biologist to know that the healing process has never changed and never will change. You need care, and peace and quiet to heal properly without constant attacks by the Government upsetting you and keeping you off balance. By the time you are through the wringer you forget what are new and which old injuries are the job injuries, pretty slick if you ask me.

Medicine, Medication, Remedies, Drugs, all control your world so the best advise is this; less prescriptions you have the better your compensation case will go. Celebrex-like drugs are the answer to tendon, back, and muscle pains, it will at the least ease your pains.

The End of Chapter 14

Job injury ready to happen on a cluttered jobsite in Seattle

Chapter 15
Focus Your Time Objectively

Limit Your Time to the evidence that proves your claim as legitimate and objective. Be sure to get the correct x-rays and the proper equipment to display the findings of these x-rays. Do not hand them to your attorney because you will never see them again. I was shocked to see the law firm that worked for me make objective evidence vanish. Attorneys can get vindictive and get away with it. Everything you get on your own, collecting physical therapy records on your own time is a waste of time to hand over to your attorney. Use the objective files you collect and a record of all the drugs you have taken throughout treatments of your injury during appeals.

     Washington law does not allow for punitive damages in civil cases. This makes it a less attractive venue for major tort damage litigation. It also means they do not care about your suffering and blame you for it. This is an issue your employer beats before the cards are stacked and stays immune to shady treatment of your compensation case. They can push your buttons all day long, they can say you are ranting and raving and use it against you. They can say you are inventing conspiracies and send you to a shrink.

     Most injured workers receive workers' compensation benefits through L&I am Insurance Services Division. The benefits provide compensation for on-the-job accidents and occupational diseases. Payments to workers are made from the State Fund, the employee- and employer-funded premium pool maintained by Insurance Services. Workers not covered by the State Fund may work for self-insured employers -- businesses large enough to qualify to provide their own workers' compensation coverage. Even then, Insurance Services regulates and certifies their coverage.

"The employee contributes into the state fund but the employers get all the breaks. Perhaps this bill should be footed only by the employer and the state, there seems to be no reasons to tax the employee for the wringer that are made of dead-end policies."

The Washington Industrial Safety and Health Act (WISHA) of 1973 give L& I the primary responsibility for overseeing workplace safety. The WISHA division of L&I sets standards and conducts inspections of worksites for compliance with state laws and regulations. Most L&I rules are done by public comment. However, WISHA has the ability to institute emergency rules for 120 days if it thinks they are required. Fear not these employer watchers. I have visited twenty jobsites and only Union jobs met these requirements. Canadian and overnight LLCs were never inspected to show up on the jobsite until they were called by the boss.

A new study shows that day laborers on street corners and in hiring halls make up less than 1 percent of the work force, and that most are in the country illegally. WISHA overlooks and ignores high-profile jobsites and gives WTO jobs a walk on easy street. Employees suffer from improper tools, cluttered jobsites and little supervision. Illegal aliens cut down millions of trees stealing them in plain view without any trouble from Authorities or WISHA. Hundreds of trucks are hauling away our trees and destroying our lands and the ozone layer unheeded by local or Federal Authorities in Washington State. I would guess that these figures given to the public are blatant lies and misinformation.

The numbers of people who stand on street corners looking for work make up 0.02 percent of the state's total work force, according to the study by the Public Policy Institute of California, a San Francisco-based private research organization. Another blatant lie, you can go and count them now, there are thousands upon thousands of these workers in California and Nevada.

One out of every five workers injured on the job last year -- some 200,000 Californians and 5,000 on the North Coast -- are mired in a workers compensation maze of confusion, delays and litigation that will last an average of almost seven years.

And every year for the last five years, the wait has gotten longer.

The average time it takes to resolve a disputed claim in the Redwood Empire has risen 23 percent since 1992, or 6Ö months, according to an analysis of 26,400 cases. These figures are subject to error and manipulation of the facts presented as they please.

At every turn, most participants agree, there will be unexpected delays, the checks that don't arrive on time, the medical bills that aren't paid, the days it takes to get a return call from a claims adjuster, the one out of every four court hearings that are continued or rescheduled months later, the hours spent in depositions, the weeks it takes to schedule appointments with forensic doctors to resolve medical disputes, the trips to insurers' doctors for second opinions. You wish! What depositions my attorneys attended or defended will never be known. Saying that delays are only three years is injustice because you can count on it going for ten years if you suffered a severe injury.

Delays can start from the minute a worker files a claim . . . since an insurer has 90 days to decide whether a claim is legitimate. Meanwhile, some companies are trying to get the grace period raised from three months to six months. This will triple the delays and double the time it takes to settle. Time is on your employers' side.

Delay has become endemic to workers compensation. A 1995 study by the insurance industry found that insurers delayed accepting 43 percent of permanent injury claims. First off, it is against the laws of this great nation to deny these claims and begets a socialist atmosphere.

Workers who need brief medical care and don't miss much work fare pretty well and get counted twice for the statistics. But a worker who has a more serious or permanent injury will get caught in a slow-motion marathon that keeps many workers in limbo, unable to plan for the future, unable to get on with their lives.

"What do they expect us to do, how do they think we can survive, and last but not least, what nerve they have to treat American citizens whom some are veterans as if we did not make the grade for a fair shake of the dice."

Delays have gotten worse since the State Legislature restructured the system in 1993, experts say. That's because new laws made the process more complex and because employers got the right to challenge claims adjusters who don't thoroughly examine a claim.

"Your employer uses the state to continue the claim until you go broke, die from your injury, go insane, or stop trying to fight them because you are too sick and worn out to care."

"The employer community won the reform war, and they successfully modified the system in a major way, so it is not user friendly any more," Santa Rosa workers' attorney Michael Wall, 1997 president of the Redwood Empire chapter of the California Applicants' Attorneys Association.

Losing a war means losing it all, your chips are gone, and you are at the mercy of lawyers. I can think of better places to be. Each attorney is an interest group of one.

All we can do at this point and rally for our rights. After only the second book of this series you can see for yourself the injustice that produces such great suffering. I am sure that most of you reading this book has had a loved run injured on the job, and how did your compensation take place, was it easy or did you settle for the judgment far below the costs of your own health and financial losses. This process would only cost a fraction of what it does now if the rules were enforced on both sides of the table.

Insurers place a large share of the blame for delays on the state Division of Workers' Compensation, which they say takes too long to judge disputes and rate permanent disabilities. Insurers also say the agency does a poor job of helping workers navigate the system.

In so much as to give you confusing information and asking for the same files or objective proof that they seemed to have lost once again. They act majestic and all-powerful but if you spy on them during their free time you learn that they are insensitive and aloof. They could not care any less how your case turns out because all they watch are the profits and easy monies.

Injured workers are easy to set up for a fall, millions of dollars are wasted each year searching and inventing injured workers committing fraud against the system. While all this time tens of thousands of trees are being exploited illegally by illegal aliens. If this branch of the Government would have to account for all the millions, billions spent in this program there would be no way to accomplish this feat accurately.

Insurers also blame a system that is too complex and subjective, a system that the state Legislature has changed so many times in the past eight years no one knows how it works.

"Are we supposed to sit back and relax as our elected Officials blow away our hard earned taxes, I do not believe so?"

We have to be accountable or we are fined or go to jail. Our elected Officials seem to decide by not deciding, creating laws that protect Government from Americans? I have traveled the world and seen enough of the world to know that Government trends are destroying our middle class citizens and doling out wealth to the vain and law-making class of Officials. I demand that the people behind the hardships and death associated with Government policies be investigated and then prosecuted and the good separated from the corrupt.

The State Labor Code, which is the bible of workers compensation, is 1,000 pages long. For related case law, the index alone runs to nearly 2,000 pages, said Edward Woodward, president of the California Workers' Compensation Institute, the research arm of the insurance industry.

Some worker advocates believe, however, that the delays are a calculated strategy by insurers to hold on to their money as long as they can, so they can invest it. *They also believe insurers use delays to force workers to settle cheaply.*

"Economic duress is one of the biggest tools insurance companies use to make the worker settle," said Santa Rosa worker attorney William Ferchland.

"There are insurers who as a matter of practice will contest virtually every claim," said James Ellenberger, assistant director of the AFL-CIO Department of Occupational Safety and Health in Washington. *"I've talked to hundreds of people who say that this is not an unusual practice."*

The Bottom Line Doctors say the long and difficult workers compensation process can seriously impede recovery.

I did not patrol the border and risk my life for this country to watch it get raped by our trusted public officials. I remember the days when there was personal pride and honor in doing well for the people of America but now it is big business like ATT and others like them that carelessly dictate policies to our elected officials. Lobbyists give for free that a person needs to work for a lifetime to achieve; we cannot allow this abuse of the American people to continue. We must demand that our rights be adhered to and that justice be served fairly to one and all.

"Many of the workers I see are extremely upset. They feel anger and helplessness, and that adds to the pain. It's so adversarial that it substantially impairs the treating physician's chance to help them," said Dr. Allen Gruber, a Santa Rosa pain specialist at North Bay Pain Care.

"I have been shocked that the system is geared so much to enforcement. It's almost like a police system. A large part of the resources seem to be devoted to ferreting out malingerers."

Increasingly, doctors are finding themselves caught up in the same web of delays that snares their patients.

Who can you blame? Doctors have families and bills; they earn a living as everybody else has to do. This makes them vulnerable to claims managers who insist on certain findings and reports. They know that it is one or the other that has to suffer and it will not be them you can count on that. You must take the fall so that they can get paid. A professional assessment needed to show that you are evaluated as 2% disabled from your work injury. Another tactic is to call you a gold-digger with old injuries, before your work injury. After so many years your bones heal incorrectly but this issue is ignored and you are angry but helpless and lost in the system. You can blame human nature . . . I guess.

Late payments to doctors have become such a problem that this year, the California Society of Industrial Medicine and Surgery asked the state Division of Workers' Compensation to intervene. The pressure is on the Doctors as the heat begins to fry them. The more you complain the longer it will take to receive their payments for services given. Late payments are the warnings that the reports were in favor of the injured worker and that L & I signs their checks. It is a struggle walking the ethical line trying to please everybody. Doctors are victims as much as the patients. We will do a study in book five of the number of Doctors that lost their license to practice because of an L & I investigation. I believe that the results will be fascinating.

Insurers "receive millions of dollars of interest-free money from providers in the form of float, the group wrote the state agency. It must be nice, free money off the sweat and blood of the working person.

All monies should be accounted for and traced to be sure that it never went into the wrong hands. Float money never gets a return; it buys yachts and huge expensive homes in the best areas of any city. Great examples are Gig Harbor Washington and Lake Geneva, Wisconsin.

These trends will continue as attorneys control more of our civically governed system. Attorneys will draw the line on what is politically correct and our national fiscal budget. Powerful attorneys in LA and Chicago follow agendas empowering attorneys as powerful officers of the court.

Instead of watching cable TV search on the computer for the right choices to make. Do not trust your attorney to watch out for you because the Firms interests always come first and pressure from L & I claims managers can get heavy even on your attorney. Attorneys take on more clients then they can work through the courts so the elimination process begins with your own attorney. It can be you that is eliminated.

Free money for attorneys and private secretive corporations is not acceptable to us, we are the American people thought to be dumb about politics. We are not stupid and we know what is going on. Government diligently strives to make Americans feel mute. We are not deaf and dumb and when the American people have had enough of lies and misdirection we will stand out fighting for our rights as they are taken from us on a daily basis. I believe that Government should share with the people their master plans and see what we say about it.

Reforms that accomplish nothing for the worker, everything for the employer and little for the employee is creating a rift in the American way. So many think tanks, so many law-makers, 98% attorneys believe that these reforms are the best there is. Is it not time now to express ourselves, perhaps reform policies by the vote of the nation as a whole. Allow Americans to know more, bringing us into the loop, explaining why these long-term decisions and laws have been made?

Late payments to doctors often boomerang on injured workers, because doctors become reluctant to treat them. There is more then reluctance, there can be blame and expendability of the patient.

Late, delayed, behind schedule, Overdue, Tardy, and deferred are a few ways to describe L & I non-compliance and intimidation of Doctors. Friendly Doctors can cut both ways depending on how long they have worked with the state. Do not forget that if you are late for two Doctor Appointments you can be in non-compliance. If everybody followed the rules and laws the system would work. This is difficult to accomplish because these reforms and laws contradict each other so erase one-another leaving L & I Judges to make final decisions, or Claims managers. Each delay in your case counts against you, never forget this and live by it during your fight to win.

Just because L & I are late does not mean that you cannot pay the Doctor yourself if you have the money to do so this Doctor can win your case for you. You can always fight fire with fire if you are fighting for principles and not awards but you must likely than not will get both.

Use you time objectively and stay informed because at some point, one-fifth of injured workers, half of all workers with a temporary disability and almost all workers with a permanent disability, will throw up their hands in frustration and go to court.

Not me, I did not bother because suddenly all of my own records of past proceedings were unavailable to me, forbidden and belonging to the lawyers that quit in the middle of the trial. A judged openly joked with the DA as I listened. I guess they already had me pegged.

My attorney threatened me with his tone of voice as he said; ***"Do not write or call us and you are forbidden to enter our office."*** Barred from my own records and the findings and decisions made by my attorneys.

On the North Coast last year, it took workers about two years to reach that point. Always think and act objectively as you choose your words well during interviews.

The court set up to untangle these disputes is a special court called a Workers' Compensation Appeals Board. Workers' Compensation Appeals Board will be dissected in Book Five of this series.

The End of Chapter 15

Chapter 16
Threats and Warnings

Have you ever felt intimidated or threatened by your attorney or an officer of the court that was not warranted? Threats can work both ways and they do not have to be intended as threats and are. There are many circumstances where an idea becomes a threat, or a change in your vocation. You can become a threat by demanding certain rights be employed to your compensation case. There are many reasons that you can be considered a threat. There are more reasons that you will feel threatened or forewarned, a good attorney can spook you and give you a late warning about an upcoming Evaluation catching you off your toes and unprepared.

First you need to order x-rays, then MRI's, Doctor reports specifically requested for this evaluation and whatever other files, financial statements, *"whatnot."*

"Do you know when a hostile evaluation can become obvious?"

Warning

It takes awhile before you find the building because parking is hard to find. You enter the building from an alley and walk into a converted medical evaluation clinic. You say good morning and the secretary ignores you. Then you ask if you are at the right office for your appointment? She glares at you as if you were a stupid animal as she hands you a clip board and tells you to fill out all the forms. During this time and the whole while you are at the evaluation you are on video. It takes you a while to fill out all the forms.

I am sure you get the idea; the Doctor is serious and completely observant of your every move. Your evaluation was over before it began. Torturous schedules and examinations can give you the shakes after a few runs around the block. I supposed to get the big picture you have to experience it. Now you have the book with the laws that protect you, focus on these laws, and be persistent about your actions being objective and polite.

L & I wants to see you angry, ranting and raving, being generally offensive on video. The warning here is

1. Keep a straight mind and a cool head during situations staged by L & I.
2. Ignore corruption but keep a normal, take notes.
3. Keep your opinions to yourself.
4. Attend all court hearings; demand that you be present because it is your right to be at the Hearings. Take notes.
5. Never show all your cards to your attorney.
6. Read everything you sign carefully.

Threats

Threats come in all different shapes and sizes. Threats, Intimidation, Pressure, Fear, Terrorization, Coercion, are present during the wringer and it can cause intense headaches.

Domination of you and your compensation claim belongs to your claims manager and your attorney.

Cruelty is used in many different forms such as; repression, conquest or breaking your spirit, subjugation, and being told that you are beaten.

Overwhelmed by the odds against you there is no choice but to be content with what you get or you will not get anything at all.

Beleaguered and Inundated, weighed down by the many appointments and a severe injury that hinders your progress is a set-up.

I consider this situation a treat, an unspoken threat by somebody in power. Circumstances are staged or created; it is an old military tactic that work well on injured workers collecting workers compensation. Bullying is a corporate art.

Coercion comes in many ways the most powerful of which is your worker compensation check that comes every other week. Duress is used as a tool using paperwork, forms to fill out, deadlines, Proper Operating Procedures.

Roving down a transcendently ridiculous, awe-inspiring road to nowhere, you complain to your attorney. You are threatened by an Officer of the Court and what is there that you can do? You are having flashbacks from the war and are accused of terrorist threats by your own attorney unless you shut up and stay out of sight. The whole process is nothing less than a fiasco that creates an atmosphere of pain. Two snapped tendons shoot pain up his body as the injured worker stands alone, stunned from the wringer.

List of threats

1. Loss of your compensation check.
2. Return to work and face your boss on unequal terms.
3. Fraud.
4. Video surveillance.
5. Attorney will threaten to quit.
6. Claims manager using stalling tactics or direct threats to close your case.
7. Attorneys earn more commissions on three to six month delays of compensation checks that get paid to injured worker after said timeframe.
8. The threat of all the staff in a law firm becoming hostile toward you because you are demanding your rights as an injured worker.
9. Threat of losing your home.
10. Threat of complicating your injury because of the strenuous evaluations you attended and continues attending.

After working in the system for a few years the state employee gets desensitized to human suffering. Godlike demeanors replace humble servants and it becomes a dog eat dog civilization attitude. You learn to keep away from the big dogs because you were bitten before. Threats can be denied by anybody giving them in the L & I network of operations. It is amazing that a person can place a family into homelessness by the numbers and live with it. In fact these persons are rewarded and promoted up the ladder where the sky is green. The L & I experience dehumanizes its employees or they end up at the funny farm.

Threats abound, all forms of threats. Some threats can be quite deadly if you are caught in the wrong situation at the wrong place and wrong time.

Warnings

You will be warned several times to get in line before you get the threats.

11. Do not speak with a claims manager.
12. Do not speak about your religious beliefs to your attorney.
13. Remember that you can ask for an expedited emergency advance from your settlement at any time during your case, even if your attorney tells you that you cannot.
14. Make all your appointments.
15. Never be late, try to be fifteen minutes early.
16. File civil suits, these law suits will bring attention to your case and help your injury case. It also will thin out labor and industries to give you a fair and decent award with medical benefits. We will get into this more in Book five.
17. Keep a photographic history of your injury and do not tell or show your attorney about these photographs.
18. Keep a log of all your appointments and the way you were treated from the time you walked through the door and exited after it was over.
19. Always stay cheerful even if you are down.
20. Keep your family informed and get them involved in your

compensation case. They can write letters to politicians, go with you to appointments, see you through the hard times and most important of all; witness at Evaluations.

My books have solutions for long-term problems along with good common sense.

Top Ten List of threats

1. If you cooperate with an investigation against the company you are fired.

2. If you report an injury it better be a broken bone or you get fired.

3. Report jobsite for lack of safety equipment you get fired.

4. Disagree with your own attorney threaten to quit your case.

5. Claims manager threatens to close your case.

6. Doctor threatens to hurt your cause if you do not pay her or his outstanding bill.

7. Take away your medicine or stop paying for it if you do not go along with the program.

8. If you defy me I will put you in jail, I am an Officer of the Court.

9. "If you do not stop writing your book I quit." Said to me by my lawyer and yes he did quit and I am publishing my seventh book.

10. I will have your car towed if you pasrk in my space again; claims manager or attorney.

Chapter 17
Employers and their Rights

An employer must always have a good, legal reason to fire an employee. However there are so many reasons to fire an employee it would take volumes to record. You can get fired because he does not like your smile, he can fire you for driving a purple car, and he can fire you for any reason he wants to elect to get the job done.

Your employer is required to give you severance pay if you get laid off. First they try to make you quit. Then they give you the worse tasks or bury you in the basement. If you are still around and you convince L & I to stand by your side you might receive severance pay. Special circumstances apply to each individual case showing that there is a way around every L & I law.

Anti-age discrimination laws apply to all employers. My nephew is a good example here.

Bruce worked at Burger King in Walworth, Wisconsin. The Manager abuses drugs with the minors working there. My nephew refused to take part in these activities and was banished from the group. Employees were mean to him and the manager tried to seduce him and this was Burger King. Now Bruce suffers an unknown ailment that can be severe after he was fired from Burger King, go figure.

Answers: All of these statements are false.

So what rights do workers have? What laws protect you when your employer fires or lays you off?

Most private-sector workers in the U.S. are employed "at will" by their employers. This means that either the employer or the worker can end the employment at any time, for any reason that is not illegal. What illegal is depends on where you live.

Say that your boss fires you, so that he can hire his brother instead. Your firing has nothing to do with your age, a disability, or your race, religion, or sex. Firing you is not against the law.

Laws forbid only specific actions that employers cannot take against employees. If employers take other actions against you, even if those actions are unfair, they are not illegal.

This means that if they ostracized you then you have to live with it. It also means that they can be rude and assign you the worse tasks on the job all of the time. My nephew learned about this at age 16 and my guess was contaminated by solvents or other chemicals on the job. Perhaps Bruce was the recipient of a practical joke of poor taste and toxic waste?

Children are exploited on jobsites globally but who would have thought the America was becoming more like a third world country than a modernized state. Walworth is regulated and controlled by a few chosen and fixed decision-makers. My nephew does not have a chance for compensation because Burger King pays the County and State for protection.

Children should be protected but if you glance at Walworth county rap sheet you will find scores of high-school dropouts and a controlled society of those who have and those who have not. I supposed that you can go through the drive up at Burger Kind in Walworth and buy a sack of weed with your shake and whopper if you know the manager.

Employment at will does not cover all employees. Some groups of workers are not considered to be employed at will. The law protects them more. Their employers must have a "just cause" for firing them. Examples of just cause are disobeying company rules or bad job performance.

Government employees

Civil service laws protect local, state, or federal government employees. Such laws usually say that your employer can only fire you for specific, "good cause" reasons. Your employer cannot fire you in order to hire a relative. The difference here is you never here them complain and there is good reasons behind this. They are well taken care of more then 50% of the time but some experience the wringer. Expensive long-term health care and large awards for severe injuries are contested on a regular basis, but these injured workers know better than to complain.

Employees with contracts

Workers with formal, written employment contracts can be let go only under a provision spelled out in the contract. Most union members have this kind of employment contract. Some executive-level employees do, too.

"Smart way to go, a lot of advantages and certain benefits for the times you need it."

Employees in certain States

If you live in Montana, Puerto Rico, or the Virgin Islands, your state limits the employers' rights to fire workers. Employers can only fire workers who are not on probation for good cause. This should be applied nationwide because it is just and fair.

Not all state policies are bad, some states do look out for the workers and enforce all of there laws. They can accomplish this because the laws in these states benefit both the employer and employee. No long agendas and no conspiracies against the people of the state. Policies made simple going through few hands and everything answerable, held responsible or accounted for. I am sure that attorneys do not live in these states to become millionaires through L & I. They would starve.

Employees returning from military service

If you return to your job after uniformed military service, your employer must have a good-cause reason to fire you for a certain time after your return. The Uniformed Services Employment and Reemployment Rights Act (USSERA) protect you.

Employers are Crybabies

Sometimes it seems employers don't have any rights. It is true, employers lose over 70% of all wrongful termination cases brought to court (source: (Public information. collected randomly) Over the past 7 years, the average wrongful termination award has been $536,927 with the greatest award being $28,040,000! This is according to Jury Verdict Research. I can see that this is a costly problem and proves my point that people mimic the powerful and try to get something for nothing. Ha

Ridiculous, paying out so much monies for one case. Pitiful, administrative overviews and supervision of the programs non-existent accounting of cases and losses of data contribute to this problem. People that get fired for wrongful destruction of property or willful crimes on the jobsite should be prosecuted to the fullest extent of the law. Those persons late for work on a regular basis or missing numerous days should be considered absconded.

Some workers go job to job to different states and file claims on the same injuries. These persons are the small minority of injured workers with the brightest light shone on them.

You can see, you want to stay out of court if possible. If you go to court, there's a good chance you'll lose and get a big financial penalty. For small businesses, losing a wrongful termination suit could mean bankruptcy or your former employee owning a large part of your business.

"This is the scam that has been tried three times with my company, brfe LLC Inc and has taken up a lot of our time and money." We fought and won but the threats linger as we hear nothing from these stalkers. One man is a hostile out-process from brfe and undermines everything we do, sooner or later the law will catch up with Stephen and he will go to jail. He is a part of ATT and infiltrated our company destroying everything in his wake. Stephen spying for ATT and getting caught, who knows perhaps one day I will own a piece of ATT.

So why are the cards stacked against you? Let me give you three reasons. This is what brings down the employer so more focus should be allotted to correct this crisis, but the main issue is long term workers compensation. I do not care who pays as long as it is not me. This attitude prevails with employers.

First, the jury is sympathetic with the terminated employee. Like all of us, every jury member has had an employer screw them around. Few cases reach a jury. He or she may have even been a victim of a layoff or firing. Therefore, it's the jury's chance to help the little guy even the score.

So, even when your case against the employee is airtight, you may still lose in court. I know this isn't comforting, but it's a fact you're going to have to live with. Your best course of action is to stay out of court, or have no employees, only owners working in the company.

Here are some shrewd or smart actions an employer can take to squash you. 1. You do this by writing a separation agreement with a release of claims and convincing the employee to sign it.

2. The supervisor often fires the employee without satisfactory documentation. You should know this rule:

"If it's not written down, the jury isn't going to believe you."

This means you have to build a case against the employee before you fire him. **"Oh no . . . no such thing like a conspiracy."** To build a good case, you must prove you warned the employee about the bad behavior and performance. Then you must show you gave him or her chances to improve. After 3 chances, you're justified in firing the problem employee. (For gross misconduct you can often fire for a first instance, but there are exceptions.)

By following this procedure, even a hostile jury must admit your treatment of the employee was fair.

3. Employers often lose wrongful termination suits because they fire for illegal and, frankly, stupid reasons... or at least the employee's attorney can make it look that way. For example, you should never fire a woman because she's pregnant (illegal) or because she likes NASCAR racing (stupid). The jury is going to frown on the illegal reason and feel sympathy on the stupid reason. Either way, you'll likely have to pay a $536,927 jury award.

So what should you accomplish?

Since this is your most powerful move to terminate your problem quickly you must get prepared to present objective relative evidence to show cause. You must attack the employee coyly but using everything you have including any costs paid out for damages.

If your employer fires you before you are aware of your injury you have three years to file a claim whether you are working there or not. The employer must realize the termination of the employee to save himself from further litigation.

Only fire for a legitimate reason

These are 1) **poor performance, 2) repeated minor misconduct, 3) gross misconduct and 4) business economics.** If you stick with these, your case will be much stronger and your chance of losing will be reduced dramatically. Most employers will not take the time to follow through so much of the blame lies there.

As the gap widens between the rich and poor in Los Angeles County, unskilled and other low-income workers find themselves increasingly marginalized in jobs that fail to comply with basic wage and safety regulations. These laws, governing minimum wage, overtime and safety conditions, protect workers regardless of their immigration status. Nevertheless, abuse abounds in numerous Southern California industries where recent immigrants from Mexico, Central America, and Asia are routinely exploited. A U.S. Department of Labor survey found that 67% of garment shops in Los Angeles violate minimum wage and overtime laws. As a result, workers lose over $80 million each year in unpaid wages.

Big business is immune to scrutiny, mostly because it pays big taxes.

We are the United States of America, by God. Titles get taxed if they have a mind to do it, singling out politically controlling the vote is all part of the big picture.

Accomplishing nothing for the people and returning us to an age long gone. America is in trouble with its domestic policies as the homeless cuddle in the streets. Veterans wearing uniforms are begging in the streets of San Francisco wearing web gear unable to find a job. Take a good look at America and realize that if our national crisis is not corrected, including Social Security, AFDC, welfare, immigration policies, veteran rights, and justice doled out equally to all. We are guaranteed these rights and we should hang onto them if need be with our lives. Let us repair our own nation before we try and change the world.

A right is the power or privilege to which one is justly entitled or a thing to which one has a just claim. Rights serve as rules of interaction between people, and, as such, they place constraints upon the actions of individuals or groups.

L&I will pay for the first medical appointment and an ambulance, if needed. **Workers may choose their doctor.**

If you have a good idea of what your injury is then go to that specialist so that he becomes your primary care provider. Choose the best facility possible, research the Doctors and then go there for your first visit.

If you do this then you have taken the first step for an easy ride on the wringer. This is the best move an injured worker can make because these doctors live by their reputations and are not afraid of L & I.

Document what caused the injury, talk with your employee and verify all information in the L&I accident report you will receive. Of course these forms can be judicial and biased but these are the reports that L & I researches. Go ahead if you have complaints of malingering then by all means add that in. Try and blame incompetence and laziness for the injury on your injured employee. He will never see this form anyways so be specific.

Make sure that you explain the injury so that it does not implicate you, the employer. Create an atmosphere in your report that the accident could have been prevented by the employee before the injury.

Go into detail about the first aid your offered and your quick response to the accident. Mention that the employee seemed to be hung over in a night of drinking. Your report can make the difference in the long run.

If you have any work available, get the doctor's approval. **Employees usually recover more quickly when they remain on the job.**
Plus you will be able to watch the injured employee and show that the person is able to work. Getting control of the employee is imperative for you as the employer to litigate your objections and appeals.

Available work can be anything and you can video the injured worker to use against this person. Give tasks that stress or have repetition and endurance. Number one; be sure to try your utmost best to return this employee to work. Get on him so this person feels isolated and hated by other employees. Remember that any work means anything.

The big shove The Early Return to Work

(ERTW) program ensures that providers, workers, employers and L&I work together and act quickly to assist injured workers return to work.

This will assure that your injured worker can return to a lesser paying job if one can be provided or found by the employee. Nobody follows the wage laws anyways so if your employee was earning twenty dollars an hour working for you but cannot do your work any longer then this employee can work sweeping out Quickie Mart for minimum wage pay or whatever other jobs are available. Under the right circumstances L & I Doctors are quick to authorize the employee to return to work.

Early Return To Work is designed to meet the needs of employers. Work is good therapy, even if it is in the mud up to your knees in wet concrete.

Employers and L&I work together and act quickly to assist injured workers find a place in life even if it means a lower standard of life then this injured employee has lived and is accustomed to. The good of the many overrides the success of one; injured workers dishearten and concern fellow workers at the workplace. Working together malignant workers can be weeded out of the system.

Washington injured workers benefits and responsibilities do not change if they live outside Washington State.

Shower the injured worker with paperwork and schedule meetings that lead to objective hearings. Research the laws in the state the injured worker is living and try to use them to your best advantage.

Controlling claim costs

Disability benefits have a much greater effect on your rates than medical bills alone.

This is why it is important for the employer to prove that you are worth less then you claim. There are several ways to do this with numbers, dates, and lost files.

First go after your employee's tax records and work history. Be sure to send employees detailed forms with every job that they ever had. Then run this information past social security and search for misinformation and lies. Prove that they should be valued at minimum wage scale because the money earned in a lifetime does not match the compensation being awarded now.

Once you have the tax statements of earnings be sure to examine closely the amount of taxes the injured worker paid out in his lifetime. Now you as the employer can play this out and limit your costs paying out workers compensation checks. This practice is outlawed but practiced openly just the same. Employers receive a lot of leeway; never forget this rule and you can cut your costs with little effort on your part. All you do is having the state do all the work.

Keep in touch with your Employee, Doctor and Claim Manager.

Employee

Is the injured employee willing to return to work? Hire an investigator and see for yourself if the employee is faking the work injury. If he is not faking it but chops wood for the fire, drives constantly, active in sports or a slew of other tasks that will show that the injured worker is not as injured as claimed or altogether faking the injury completely.

Call your employee and write down every the employee says. Be polite and concerned but do not take abuse from the injured employee. If there are threats then record them along with the time, date, and length of the telephone call.

Physicians

Every injured worker has a Primary Care Doctor and this person is the Doctor you want to get answers and if need be use arguments to get the employee back to work.

Convince the primary care doctor that you are being scammed, that this injured employee injured thyself for the free money. Stay updated on the employees conditions like any surgeries needed or therapies.

Remember to be positive and have a concerning attitude. Try and be helpful in any way you can but never slander yourself or speak poorly of the employee. Act as if you are the victim and then you become the victim. Always tip the scales to your favor when golden opportunities appear. Never meet with an employee alone, bring along a witness but if you have the extra cash. Donate monies to the clinic that the Primary Doctor belongs to.

Claim Manager

Invite him or her to dinner for a meeting and choose a good restaurant. Be professional and choose your words well.

Ask your Claim manager what the chances are that the employee has a legitimate case and then work with the claim manager to resolve the issues and eventually close the case. Work with the claim manager to overwhelm your injured employee.

Do not be afraid to ask for legal advice from the claim manager. The claim manager's controls the state workers budget.

Create a feeling of mutual trust and never disagree with a claim manager because he is on your side of the fence. Your claim manager will guide the wringer and squeeze the employee until the injured employee has lost the will to argue or fight.

Play some golf and ask the claim manager along, who knows the defense attorney might be there and you can get inside information after a few drinks. There are many ways to solve issues so never panic just asks the claim manager.

It's required! L&I offer consultation and safety checklists for businesses.

I have owned three businesses and the most they do is send you flyers to post on the jobsite and some you post and some you do not. Workers steel from the job things such as first aid kits and assorted medicines to tools and pencils, pens so it is a difficult task to meet any guidelines.

There are free services available and optional for employers, I encourage you to attend.

Moving jobs, construction jobs, many jobs move quickly from one jobsite to another so it is impossible to meet all the safety guidelines. I suggest you have the basics to protect yourself from an accusation. You should always provide these safety measures to your employees.

1). Well stocked industrial first aid kit.

2). Telephone

3). Never have only one person on the jobsite.

4). Never alter tools for special uses. Do not customize haphazardly such as installing the wrong handle on a hammer. Example; Five-pound hammer installed with a 16 OZ. handle, tools such as these are the causes of most hand injuries on the jobsite.

5). Keep Emergency phone numbers on the wall of your office.

6). Keep a clean jobsite.

These rules are standard operating procedure in most big corporations but there still are a few that lack these basic commonsense rules.

If these basic rules were enforced on the employers then this act alone with cut the injury rates in half or better.

L&I developed the <u>Employee Wallet Cards</u> to be a quick reference for employees to help them know what to do if they experience a work-related injury. They're designed to be easy for employers to complete and distribute.

Few employers use these cards because they claim the card encourages job related injuries. This is not enforced nor is it applied on most jobsites.

New laws would have to be emplacing to have these cards available in foreign languages.

Learn about this project and how you could participate in the next phase of the project.

If anything make it seem you are interested but cannot find the time for the meetings. It will be noted that your tried to participate.

Order or print project-specific forms and publications, these are not listed in the department's forms and publications database.

Know the form or publication you need?

If you are the first doctor to diagnose a worker for an occupational injury or disease, you are responsible for reporting this to L&I or the self-insured employer.

"What a joke, the employer does everything in his power to make this problem go away. The last thing he wants is for you to see a doctor because then he can accuse you of injuring yourself at home. These rules are a far cry to being realized in the workplace. If you ask for permission to see a doctor nine out of ten employees are denied by the employer. Doctors can only act once they examine the injured worker."

Now you are seeing both sides and know why it seems impossible to report an injury. Injuries get laughed off, walked off, and iced but rarely are reported to a Doctor.

This game is not fair but profitable to Ten-thousand people. Too bad these people are not the injured workers.

To initiate the claim, for your patient, fill out and send the Report of Industrial Injury or Occupational Disease (ROA) to L&I or the self-insured employer. The ROA is also known as the 'accident report'.

Now you have this information make good use of your objective time.

The End of Chapter 17

Chapter 18.
Objective Medical Evidence

    Evaluating the intensity and persistence of your symptoms, such as pain, and determining the extent to which your symptoms limit your capability for work General. When the medical signs or laboratory findings show that you have a medically determinable injury(s) that could reasonably be expected to produce your symptoms, such as pain, we must then assess the greatness and persistence of your symptoms so that we can determine how your symptoms limit your capacity for work. In evaluating the greatness and persistence of your symptoms, we consider all of the available evidence, including your history, the signs and laboratory findings, and statements from you, your treating or nontreating source, or other persons about how your symptoms affect you.

    They also consider the medical opinions of your treating source and other medical opinions as explained in explain further how we evaluate the intensity and persistence of your symptoms and how we conclude the extent to which your symptoms limit your capacity for work, when the medical signs or laboratory findings show that you have a medically determinable marring(s) that could reasonably be expected to produce your symptoms, such as pain.

    Will all this truly be a reality or just some parts of it? There is more importance placed on some evaluations compared to others and the findings are not related. Certainly they take opinions into consideration from others around you if those statements help the employer. They do not tell you the whole picture only narrate scenes in their policies.

    Doctors need to make judgments and I watched how they did it. These professionals are trained in behavior studies and human behavior. I must admit that having clean fingernails and well trimmed hair, wearing a suit; all do not make a difference in the final count. Doctors play God for a long enough time the begin believing they are gods. Hearts harden and certain malice shadows their characters.

Distant eyes observe every finger moves, twitch, perspiration, and heartbeat, skin color, pupils, fidgeting, and your eye movements. You have no idea that these physicians are trained to discredit you so they selectively choose the objective evidence that will be presented in court. Certainly it is going to lean against the injured worker.

I chose my own words for describing facts, facts are exactly what I exposed with words that give you a broader look at how to fight in this game of what not. Why beat around the bush, say and print what you think and not what they expect to hear from you.

Everything that I write you can see for yourself.

Consideration of objective medical evidence

Objective medical evidence is evidence obtained from the application of medically acceptable clinical and laboratory diagnostic techniques, such as evidence of reduced joint motion, muscle spasm, sensory deficit or motor disruption. All of these symptoms can be objectively explained and used against you.

Objective medical evidence of this type is a useful indicator to assist us in making reasonable conclusions about the intensity and persistence of your symptoms and the effect those symptoms, such as pain, may have on your ability to work. *"They find conclusive evidence of a degenerative disease, they always do."* We must always attempt to obtain objective medical evidence and, when it is obtained, we will consider it in reaching a conclusion as to whether you are disabled. However, we will not reject your statements about the intensity and persistence of your pain or other symptoms or about the effect your symptoms have on your ability to work solely because the available objective medical evidence does not substantiate your statements.

Consideration of other evidence.

Since symptoms sometimes suggest a greater severity of impairment than can be shown by objective medical evidence alone, we will carefully consider any other information you may submit about your symptoms. The information that you, your treating or no treating source, or other persons provide about your pain or other symptoms (e.g., what may precipitate or aggravate your symptoms, what medications, treatments or other methods you use to alleviate them, and how the symptoms may affect your pattern of daily living) is also an important indicator of the intensity and persistence of your symptoms. Because symptoms, such as pain, are subjective and difficult to quantify, any symptom-related functional limitations and restrictions which you, your treating or no treating source, or other persons report, which can reasonably be accepted as consistent with the objective medical evidence and other evidence, will be taken into account as explained in paragraph of this section in reaching a conclusion as to whether you are disabled.

We will consider all of the evidence presented, including information about your prior work record, your statements about your symptoms, evidence submitted by your treating or no treating source, and observations by our employees and other persons. Section 404.1527 explains in detail how we consider and weigh treating source and other medical opinions about the nature and severity of your impairment(s) and any related symptoms, such as pain. Factors relevant to your symptoms, such as pain, which we will consider include:

"Quite strict, adhered to by the word, interrupted by expects paid for by lobbyists. Other evidence is the majority of the evidence they use to evaluate your case."

---

1. Your daily activities; we have warned you in previous chapters about this part of the evaluation or wringer. The best way is to stay out of there sight but this can be a difficult task.

Remember that if you have physical therapy, and evaluations along with appointments for specialist Doctors. All of these appointments can make your day hectic and exhausting. Feel like a day at work and L & I makes record that you are able to drive and make all your appointments on time.

This shows that you can push yourself hard to make your appointments, and vocational meetings. Then you should be working. Imagine all this power used to bring into disrepute your injury and your complaints of pain. The amusing question that they ask is put your pain on a scale of one to ten. Then they calculate whether you lied. Then you are asked to write your daily activities down, and you are lost at what to write. This is part of the wringer.

2. The location, duration, frequency, and intensity of your pain or other symptoms; You must be sure to keep a detailed report on these events.

a. Give a copy to your attorney, therapist, and Doctors

b. Note any witnesses in public places and at home where other people witnesses you in severe pain.

c. List all the tasks you are unable to perform because of your injury and if it is getting worse.

d. Give locations dates and time of day for the pain and when the pain is worse.

e. Turn in your reports on a monthly or weekly basis.

f. Elect not to rate your pain, instead of 1-10 circles severe or write it besides the rating.

g. Add into the reports each time you complained about your pain and to whom.

h. Note tasks that others need to perform for you because of your injury.

i. Note added injuries suffered from being severely injured.

Example; Falling down causing an injury at home because of your work-related injury.

3. Precipitating and aggravating factors;

    a. Impulsive, Give rise to, Abrupt, Rapid, Sudden, and Bring on, impetuous are all words to describe this terminology.

    b. Impulsive describes precipitating; words used with so many definitions throw the play into the hands on claim managers.

    c. Rapid, Swift, Sudden, are words to describe an injury for a worker, choose the words that you utilize to express yourself vigilantly lest your own words be used against you.

    d. Go into great detail using a recording ledger or log to stay on top of questions asked of you at a later date. Your answers will be compared for truthfulness.

    e. Driving can aggravate your injury and arriving at your appointments on time.

    f. infuriating annoying frustrating maddening irritating are aggravating factors to an injury.

4. the type, dosage, success, and side effects of any medication you take or have taken to alleviate your pain or other symptoms;

    a. Medications change as does your treatments.

    b. Keep an accurate record of changes in your medications along with reason, date, and doctor who changed your medication.

    c. Times you were given medications at clinic and hospitals and prescribing doctors.

    d. Most of these records get lost; you will have your own records using this formula.

    e. Alleviation of your pain is important to write into your notes.

    f. Improvement in your condition must be written down accurately and in a timely manner.

    g. Side-effects, the aftermaths of treatments and medications can be good or bad, be sure to keep a record of each medication you are prescribed by a Doctor and the effects it had on your body.

5. Treatment, other than medication, you receive or have received for relief of your pain or other symptoms;

    a. Marijuana is a medicine used by over half the population of this country. It works for pain and relieves side-effects from mixing medications. Labor and Industries does not support this medicine and will not authorize payment for Doctors or prescriptions for Marijuana.

    b. Marijuana has been proven to alleviate pain and reduce stress.

    c. Medical herbs and potions on the market promise miracles. I advise that you ask your Doctor first before mixing these heath aids with your medications. It might cause a side-effect?

    d. Chiropractic medicine is optional and many patients claim to be helpful. I advise anybody to refrain from using this treatment because many times it will make your injury worse.

    e. Whatever other drugs or treatments you might be taking you better let your Doctor know about it.

    f. Record drugs you consume such as Nyquil and other over the counter drugs.

    g. Aspirin can affect many prescriptions and medications, be sure you use care while taking aspirin.

6. Any measures you use or have used to relieve your pain or other symptoms (e.g., lying flat on your back, standing for 15 to 20 minutes every hour, sleeping on a board, etc.); and

7. Other factors concerning your functional limitations and restrictions due to pain or other symptoms

    a. Relief, there are many ways to ease the pain but good mental health is the best medicine.

    b. Assistance help from relatives perhaps?

    c. Support from your church or friends?

    d. Special aids like braces or back, foot supports?

e. Respite, perhaps in a late compensation check owed for six months arrives in your mail?

A. Limitations   limits to your income

a. Boundaries, do you feel as if life suddenly has boundaries?

b. You cannot walk on your own, perhaps you cannot bend over, are these creating boundaries that you do not cross in fear of not being able to get back on your feet.

c. It is easy to become a burden while a person is disabled from a severe work related injury. Mention this to your Doctors and the hardships they create.

d. There is a limit, you can only walk so far and then must sit down.

e. Confined to a certain area because of your injury.

f. Is there a maximum value in your life.

g. Have you lost your freedom to enjoy life because of the hundreds of commitments to labor and industries and your attorney.

All of these factor into your case, you are the one that must let this information be known in court. Do not count on your attorney to do it for you.

Truth comes in many flavors and all of it is truth. It depends on how objective you are and how you present your objective evidence in court. First problem is getting the objective evidence entered as material evidence in court. The truth hurts but that is all that matters, ya.

B. Restrictions

a. Restraints, limitations, restrictions, are words associated with your medicines. With some you cannot go into the sunlight, with others certain vitamins must be avoided and the list goes on.

b. Be sure to keep a written list in your log book remembering to add any new ails that appear from your work-related injury.

c. Control over your life, are you so restricted that you need to depend on others to control your life; Examples

d. Cook your food.

e. Drive you around.
f. Pay your bills.
g. Manage your home life.
h. Does everybody seem to have power over you?

In my opinion there is no true means to measure the losses taken by workers injured on the job. There is no quick cure for this system until the people of America learn the truths in this book and others like it. It is a regular job to collect compensation and the state knows this so you will always be disadvantaged.
Medical Objective evidence can be used for you or against you.

8. How we determine the extent to which symptoms, such as pain, affect your capacity to perform basic work activities.

In determining the extent to which your symptoms, such as pain, affect your capacity to perform basic work activities, we consider all of the available evidence described in paragraphs through of this section. We will consider your statements about the intensity, persistence, and limiting effects of your symptoms, and we will evaluate your statements in relation to the objective medical evidence and other evidence, in reaching a conclusion as to whether you are disabled. *"They go through all this trouble to go through a process where most of your objective evidence is not submitted by your attorney or denied as objective evidence by the court. The reporting Doctor with the findings will be dismissed from the facts, erased from the files. The paragraphs that they speak of are all rhetoric, not enforced and budget minded decisions."*
We will consider whether there are any inconsistencies in the evidence and the extent to which there are any conflicts between your statements and the rest of the evidence, including your history, the signs and laboratory findings, and statements by your treating or nontreating

source or other persons about how your symptoms affect you. Your symptoms, including pain, will be determined to diminish your capacity for basic work activities to the extent that your alleged functional limitations and restrictions due to symptoms, such as pain, can reasonably be accepted as consistent with the objective medical evidence and other evidence.

"I was told by my powerful state attorneys that pain was not considered for compensation." Who are we to believe?

Consideration of symptoms in the disability
Determination Process

We follow a set order of steps to determine whether you are disabled. If you are not doing substantial gainful activity, we consider your symptoms, such as pain, to evaluate whether you have a severe physical or mental impairment(s), and at each of the remaining steps in the process. We also consider your symptoms, such as pain, at the appropriate steps in our review when we consider whether your disability continues. Explaining the procedure we follow in reviewing whether your disability continues. *"My point is that they will never rule against labor and industries certified Doctors. I have seen it with my own eyes, hard to believe but true as the silver dollar. Psychological trauma occurring during the overwhelming demands by L & I to keep your claim open. Watching families torn apart, alcoholism invading discarded, desperate families in need of help. It is time that these persons made the headlines; we have enough stories in our own back yard that need revealing."*

Need to establish a severe medically determinable impairment(s). Your symptoms, such as pain, fatigue, shortness of breath, weakness, or nervousness, are considered in making a determination as to whether your impairment or combination of impairment(s) is severe. *"There are other considerations that should be mentioned but have been dismissed. Internal bleeding, spasms, poor bone healing, damaged tendons, the list continues."*

Decision whether the Listing of Impairments is met.

Some listed impairments include symptoms usually associated with those impairments as criteria. Generally, when a symptom is one of the criteria in a listing, it is only necessary that the symptom be present in combination with the other criteria. It is not necessary, unless the listing specifically states otherwise, to provide information about the intensity, persistence, or limiting effects of the symptom as long as all other findings required by the specific listing are present.

"This gives a lot of leeway but to whom?"

Decision whether the Listing of Impairments is medically equaled.

If your impairment is not the same as a listed impairment, we must determine whether your impairment(s) is medically equivalent to a listed impairment. How we make this determination. Under we will consider medical equivalence based on all evidence in your case record about your impairment(s) and its effects on you that is relevant to this finding. In considering whether your symptoms, signs, and laboratory findings are medically equal to the symptoms, signs, and laboratory findings of a listed impairment, we will look to see whether your symptoms, signs, and laboratory findings are at least equal in severity to the listed criteria. However, we will not substitute your allegations of pain or other symptoms for a missing or deficient sign or laboratory finding to raise the severity of your impairment(s) to that of a listed impairment. If the symptoms, signs, and laboratory findings of your impairment(s) are equivalent in severity to those of a listed impairment, we will find you disabled. If it does not, we will consider the impact of your symptoms on your residual functional capacity.

"Significant cause can be all the above but there is a big glitch in

this design and that is elementary. I was the walking dead with blood pressure maxing 180 on the bottom, my doctor always told me to go to the emergency room but I said what the use is the effort. The problem has been diagnosed as poor blood circulation because of crushed vessels and nerves in my hand. I was in agonizing pain my hand red and black swelled and sore. The pain raised my blood pressure and this fact was never considered during medical evaluations."

Impact of symptoms (including pain) on residual functional capacity.

If you have a medically determinable severe physical or mental impairment(s), but your impairment(s) does not meet or equal an impairment listed in appendix 1 of this subpart, we will consider the impact of your impairment(s) and any related symptoms, including pain, on your residual functional capacity.

"This in a nutshell means nothing will be done, this issue will become mute."

That paragraph is some pretty fancy double-talk. Boy, they must think we are dense, perhaps they believe Americans are to busy to be smart and staying busy keeps Americans unaware of what is happening right under their noses.

"I beg to differ."

Remarkable Objective Medical Evidence

Example; 40 year old construction worker with history of left knee problems felt excruciating knee pain upon dismounting a rail car ladder 12-18 inches off the ground. Although continuing that shift, he sought medical treatment from his treating physician, who diagnosed a medial meniscal tear with ongoing patellar tendinitis of the left knee. The treating physician, a board certified orthopedic surgeon with a one-year fellowship in arthroscopy and sports medicine, treats 400-500 knee conditions annually. Claimant continued to work until he experienced increased left knee pain while shoveling snow approximately five weeks later. His treating physician took him off work and recommended prompt arthroscopic surgery. Claimant filed two claims, one relating to the ladder dismounting and the second relating to shoveling. He had also filed an occupational disease claim the prior year relating to his left knee problem.

The insurer denied all claims, relying on an IME opinion from an orthopedic surgeon whose credentials regarding knee conditions, if any, were not established and not inquired into by the insurer. In addition, although the IME physician believed claimant suffered from a knee condition which was 50% occupationally related, the insurer denied the OD claim in its entirety. Even after the treating physician challenged the insurer's position and recommended another IME with an expert in knee conditions and arthroscopic surgery, the insurer maintained its denial of all claims and did nothing further to investigate. The insurer also disregarded a warning from an RN case manager that if claimant *"doesn't receive treatment, I worry that he may not be able to do the lightest duty alternative job."*

Evidence: Exhibits:
Objection in Pretrial Order.

Where counsel failed to note objections to exhibits in Pretrial Order as required by ARM 24.5.318, exhibits admitted despite objections voiced at trial.

Trust your own judgment and stick by your guns. You need to respond to all mail you receive and be prepared to present what is asked of you in one day notice.

The End of Chapter 18

Chapter 19
Presenting Objective Evidence

Presenting Objective Medical Evidence goes through a winding process before it is accepted as objective evidence.

I had hired my own private Doctor known as the best hand surgeon in Washington and with his high tech dives and through testing this Doctor found striking remarkable objective evidence. These findings were ignored by L & I and my attorneys refused to present this crucial evidence to the court. I was not following the program, I wanted an opinion from other than a L & I board certified Doctor.

These are the steps to follow to be sure that your objective evidence goes to court and that you get a ruling on your disability.

1. Always try and go to the Doctors of your choice. Many Doctors are certified by L & I but are independent and unusual for them to see an L & I patient.

2. You have a right to choose your own doctors and for second opinions. Choose a Doctor described in #1.

3. Petition L & I to pay these Doctors for there expert services.

4. Send this new objective evidence to all your doctors and your Congressman for your District. Keep record of the dates and times copies were sent of these findings.

5. Be sure that your attorney is aware of objective medical evidence but keep originals with you, only send copies.

6. Seek Doctors until you get objective evidence on you work related injury.

Chosen Medical Object Evidence.

1. Medical Evidence proving that your injury is minimal mandated into objective evidence to use in court against you.

Having to choose between objective evidence diagnoses from

different doctors and radiologists makes all the difference in the world winning or losing your compensation case. We are not much better then the Nazis if you think about it. A family can be broken and homeless in the streets because of a wrongly made decision by the appeals board; people will walk by and not see them or joke about it. Where are our politicians leading us? Do they not know by now that there is no such thing as a super nation or a master or super race or peoples, it is about time that our leaders learned that the object of humanity is to achieve peace..

Yet, the corruption and lustful attitude continues among our leaders, they are always finding a way to give you accurate misinformation. Honest persons have no choice but to go with the flow if they want to stay in politics, and regular persons are afraid to voice their opinions. Corporations such as ATT create their own policies that make ineffective state laws.

Conspiracies

Yes you must be insane or off balance to believe that there is a conspiracy against you. Our own research of public information leaves no doubt the yes, there are conspiracies, and they are categorized. It will always be difficult and nearly impossible for an injured worker to present medical objective evidence. It all has to be approved by L & I own board of experts before your Doctor's findings can be evaluated. First we must define conspiracy so that you as the injured worker understands its implications on you workers compensation case.

Conspiracy; plot, scheme, plan, idea, proposal, design, ruse, and diagram, are all important in its definition of conspiracy.

The conspiracy is in place the moment you get injured. It is automatic set to run on auto-pilot. Designed to lead you into the wringer and down into hell what is called litigation.

Systems set up to win, as if a General of the Army created the scenario. Methods of findings are dictated by labor and industries, the only reason some persons receive justice is to balance the odds. We are fortunate that we have labor and industries at all with all the L & I money that is diverted to Congress, or the Pentagon to use for war projects or invading your privacy.

I learned that the only way to present objective medical evidence is in person, in court, by you.

What happens to Medical Objective Evidence?

1. Denied by Labor and Industry Physicians.

2. Review and discuss your objective evidence with your caregivers excluding your Attorney.

3. Once your Attorney learns about it he will notify L & I with your detailed information.

4. Surprises are good when presenting remarkable medical objective evidence in court, ask for a jury trial.

5. Play your attorney; do not allow them to play you.

6. Your Attorney refuses to acknowledge it because he has a different scheme on things in your case. The firm is trying to get you a higher paying disability.

7. Under pressure from the state Doctors can repute there previous statements or evaluations.

8. It gets filed in some files.

9. L & I labels your objective evidence as confirmed or not confirmed.

10. It gets buried as other evidence arises in the coming weeks.

11. Eventually if your attorney kept care of the evidence it will be filled as evidence in court.
    a. It can be denied by the court as not reverent.
    b. deferential, not with procedure of the court.
    c. reverential; obscured and ridiculous evidence, based on facts, not reverent to the case.

12. The court decides these arguments.

13. There is too many things that can unexpectedly go wrong with your remarkable objective evidence. The Doctor that can most easily dismiss this evidence is your D.O. This Doctor has all the power and not enough education to make there findings credible.

14. With volumes of medical evidence it is your job to locate and store remarkable objective evidence. Your attorney does not have the staff, the time, or the will to keep track of your compensation case without your help.

15. Relevant; **Pertinent, Applicable, Related, Appropriate, Significant, Important.**

16. Use these words to describe objective evidence.

Presenting Remarkable Objective Medical Evidence

Protect your paperwork and stay in close contact with your Doctor that gave you this evidence. Go for more testing, follow through. You will find that many tests you had taken in the past showed false readings when improperly set. This is why you must see a Doctor that has nothing to lose one way or the other.

Trying to get fair treatment from labor and industries is like a chess game and your opponent has two queens. There is no one method to present your remarkable evidence, there are many different ways to accomplish this and the more of them you utilize the better chance there is for this remarkable evidence to be accepted as objective evidence.

Remember that all the evidence in the world will not do you a lick of good if your attorney decides to quit.

In summary, there is nothing you can do if you anger the wrong persons in these Chain of events.

Applicable in Labor Industries terms means to get where you need to be in a hurry. Without the hassles of being waylaid. You have the right to be treated for your injury in the best possible way available. Everything is significant that happens to you while you are an injured worker with an open compensation case. You have to arrange all the facts so it benefits your cause in court, this means listing in order of events. All the medical objective evidence in the world will not assist you in your case if it is not Applicable.

Fifty-million Americans have no control what happens to monies they earned. It is garnished for this or for that, taxes take a big chunk, Social Security takes its share and whatever is remaining belongs to you. Every day new laws are passed targeted to gain control of the working man. Once our checks are controlled completely by cards imagine the possibilities. It would be like a child in an abandoned candy store.

Washington State soon will have tax tags on license plates and every mile you drive will be taxed. Labor and Industries is following suit with powerful networks of decision-makers that control policies deciding who are expendable, in the order they are. Corruption has overwhelmed our country and the sky is the limit.

What is the worry right? You are doing well and this issue does not concern you. Oh well, here is some food for thought.

The war on terrorism is escalating and global warming is destroying our planet. Our Government takes money from where-ever it can if it is in a desperate way. How important are you? It can be any Federal Department that hits you like a typhoon. Take into mind that there never is a warning and mistakes happen. One error can destroy a thousand lives on a normal processing error. Numbers are carried in lots to be processed, with the wrong key pressed they go to a different bin other then it was destined for. When this happens you can be wrongfully rewarded or ripped apart at the seams with intense investigations. Labor and Industries plays a major role during disasters and evidently terrorist attacks. Do you now see how everything is linked together and that if we do not do something now to stop the widespread of corruption by over-zealous attorneys and law-makers.

Remarkable Objective Medical Evidence is what your Claim Manager says it is.

The best you can do to win your case is to read these books. You can have your attorney disprove this book and claim it is invalid. Be sure to ask for objective evidence because nothing in this book can be disproved. This series of five books will keep your attorney honest or he will quit once he knows you know the system. In this case you are better off getting a lawyer someplace else, before you are tossed into the wringer and buried in the cards. There are ethical, honest attorneys available but you have to choose well being sure that they do not have more clients then they can handle.

I interviewed a lady who had been collecting workers compensation for thirty-five years. We will call her Miss Johnson.

Miss Johnson is now nearly seventy years old and finally received a large Compensation Award. She had told me about her wringer and that it took her youth and life away from her. In a final conclusion Miss Johnson said she was glad that her claim finally settled and had great praise for her attorney. As she praised her attorney her teary eyes told a story of bitterness and defeat.

Miss Johnson endured the wringer for over three decades and finally won her case. Her attorney earned 1.2 million dollars from the total of this compensation case. Her attorney could have settled years ago for a lesser amount of money but elected to drag this woman through the wringer for years to come. Miss Johnson lived in a shelter once to survive; she lost her life for the greed of attorneys.

The Firm profited on long-term income and monies through litigation dragging this case out for its longest duration.

Choosing your attorney correctly is the only way to properly present your medical objective evidence. If it is remarkable is argued in court if you have chosen an ethical attorney. Unfortunately these attorneys live modestly because L & I decides who to work with and if an attorney is ethical. That attorney becomes a liability not an asset.

The best way to retain an attorney is by visiting the office and speaking with clients. Clients say a lot they there are not supposed to say. Are these clients generally positive or negative at the law firm they hired or retained? Visit the attorney and meet with him, then hang around for an hour reading magazines and observing the attorneys and clients. If you do this a few times chances are that you will retain your own attorney and this attorney will be ethical. It is the rule of thumb that history repeats itself.

Objective medical evidence can be defined in many ways. One of the ways Labor and Industries neglects to mention is; meeting clients that invade your privacy or drag you into something that could cost you your life.

How might this happen, you ask?

Attorneys drag out compensation cases and the injured worker uses all savings, sells everything of value and Joe is waiting to be evicted.

This person is sitting beside you in the waiting room. He seems like a nice fellow and says his name is Joe. You exchange pleasantries and Joe asks you if you would like to have dinner on him, his treat and you say yes, sure, why not. You have over an hour to wait for your attorney to see you and get well acquainted with Joe.

Joe had some bad breaks and made some stupid mistakes. He was working on the side earning two-thousand dollars a week paying his attorney for protection a total of five-hundred dollars a week. During this time Joe is receiving $3000.00 compensation checks from labor and industries. Everything was going great for Joe but after seven years he was recognized by a Claim Manager not his own, while driving past him as he was framing a house. Disaster hit Joe hard and he was fortunate to have stayed out of jail. Today his case was closed and Joe was busted, nothing of his own to speak of because the state had taken all he had. Joe felt as if he had nothing to lose.

Fortunately Joe has an old Chevy station wagon and you limp, slowly but surely to the elevator and then down into the enclosed parking lot reserved for that building. Your back has nearly completely disabled you from a work related injury and after a year labor and industries claim manager had not authorized an MRI for your back. Joe assists you and before long you are at Denny's and having their daily special. You can see the truck from the booth Joe had chosen to have dinner.

Note; this is a true story that the attorneys at the law firm were not held accountable.

You get to like the guy and the two of you laugh after dinner at one of Joes jokes. Joe tells you that he was evicted and had to pack his belongings tonight and leave the house. Joe tells a long tale of lies and gains your sympathy and trust.

You feel bad and ask Joe if he is married. Joe tells you that his girlfriend is at the house waiting to be picked up. Then Joe mentioned that although they had no place to go, he had to take what he could and live in the car until he gotten his settlement. Of course there was no settlement to be had; in fact Joe knew he was lucky staying out of jail. He knew enough to keep his mouth shut about his attorney. Who was there for Joe to trust? Once you are in the wringer a couple of years you become weary of who you can trust. Joe shakes hands with you and rises from his seat to leave.

You think for a moment and then stop Joe dead in his tracks. "Hey Joe, why don't you and your girlfriend can stay at my house if you want until you get on your feet."

"Are you sure it will be okay?" Joe acts disinterested.

"No problem Joe, I have a spare bedroom and a guest room." You have no idea what you have gotten yourself into as you ride along with Joe to his house.

So far all goes well and two injured workers are teaming together because of necessity. You like the idea of help around the house and the extra income. You plan to charge the couple only fifty dollars a week but will soon be unpleasantly surprised.

Joe's girlfriend is high and drunk and the house is a mess. You help Joe load his truck and notice two rifles, the 22cal. did not bother you but when you noticed the assault weapon it made your skin crawl but it was to late to back out now. Sissy sat between the two men as Joe drove away from his house.

Joe stopped at the 7-11 to get some more beer and some food for the night. You did not protest even though you do not drink alcohol. Your back felt as if hot coals were burning into ash and your head ached. Watching out the window you see the first raindrops of the spring splatter on the windshield you realize that you made a big mistake allowing Joe into your home. Joe begins acting bossy and his sense of humor gone. Joe grabbed a beer from the fridge and tossed it to his girlfriend across the living room. Sissy missed the catch and the beer bottle lay broken atop a dresser. "Ooops," yelped Sissy.

"You might want to ask yourself why me?"

Because you were at the wrong place at the wrong time with a man feeling victimized by an attorney in the Firm you retained. Once the attorneys are finished shredding your life they set you free in the world with threats that if you wrote, called, or visited the office again you will be arrested and taken to jail. This is called the "attorney shank" you are displaced and left on your own.

Joe was victimized and now he is victimizing you. Joe wastes no time building a meth lab in his bathroom and soon all types of hoodlums begin frequenting your home. You feel trapped.

In a matter of months Joe files his compensation through a loophole his new attorney found in the system. Joe is elated and pays for the attorney services out of his own pocket. Joe goes back to work and money rolls into the house.

You live out of your bedroom avoiding the crowd of misfits that are now regulars, some even staying at the house for days at a time. ***"What can you do?"***

Your compensation checks are challenged by your employer and it will be months before it can be restored. You begin to borrow monies from Joe to pay your mortgage and other bills. Somehow your attorney had learned that Joe was staying at your house and was threatening to quit. Two weeks later your attorney quits your case. Given referrals to attorneys for various reasons also turning you down. You begin drinking and the gang at your house drops meth in your beer.

You are on a rollercoaster ride now, and getting farther into debt, Joe is doing well. Money goes a long way in Washington where there are the rich and the poor. There is not much of a middle class anymore so you work for a living if you can find a job; the pay scale is low and many employers abusive in the use of employees. Today you received a letter that said you were scheduled for a MRI and knew soon you would get your pay for the last six months.

Thirty years old and you can barely walk you have a big problem. Your attorney had a change of heart and suddenly everything looked great, except. Joe and his friends had taken over his home and you have no clue as to how to get him and his pals out. Sometimes you get some odd looks from strangers that come to the house.

You decide to go to the police but cannot find the time alone to do it. Walking is out of the question and surgery has been approved after the results of the MRI were examined by L & I Board of Physicians.

Your attorney has been busy setting you up with the Police. The unreported extra income was Fraud, Drug manufacturing was a long sentence, and a host of other indictments followed. You have no idea that in two weeks your house is marked to be raided sitting in the waiting room of your attorney's office.

Will objective medical evidence save you from prosecution of these indictments? You be the Judge.

The End of Chapter 19

Chapter Twenty
Child Labor

Alarmingly more and more parents is neglecting their children because both parents are working jobs to pay the bills. Some or many are sending there children to work for several reasons.

1. Job makes a great and affordable babysitter.

2. Parents need extra money.

3. Child wants a job.

4. Gives parents time alone.

5. Gives child hands on experience of working for a living.

6. Parents do not care.

7. Family business.

8. Peer pressure.

9. Cheaper than military school.

10. Vocational Training

Children learn first hand about drugs at most jobsites. Bad habits can be acquired and child abuse hidden. Yet there is little being done to prevent these behaviors so problems escalate and children are victimized.

Top Ten list of employer abuse violating Child Labor Laws.

1. **Overwork employee.**

2. **Unsafe working environment.**

3. **Child Abuse.**

4. **Drug abuse.**

5. **Alcohol abuse.**

6. **Peer abuse.**

7. **Ostracize the employee.**

8. **Inadequate water or shelter from the weather.**

9. **Toxic fumes.**

10. **Sharp instrument accidents, poor maintenance.**

Brfe LLC interviewed 100 child laborers and found that in our survey three out of five children have experienced at least three on the list of the top ten. Every child laborer has experienced at least one of these severe violations on the jobsite.

The number one complaint was being overworked. We selected

our group from various places of employment and the list above name the most often committed abuses to the least abuses on the jobsite as stated by the children.

    1. Most exposure to child abuse and drug and alcohol abuse is fast food restaurants.

    2. Overworking child labor mostly on construction sites and fruit pickers and field workers.

    3. Public Service jobs and fast food restaurants the employee. It can happen on any or most jobs.

    4. Peer abuse usually is initiated by the employer. Vocational jobs and community jobs can be extremely stressful, and this ties in with ostracizing a person for not fitting in. Civil Rights violations can also be broken.

    5. Unsafe working environments can be any jobsite whether indoors or out in the weather.

    6. All jobsites that use chemical solvents or cleaners bought commercially. Some of these products are untested and extremely toxic without the proper safety gloves and respirator. These cans or bottles come with white labels and the directions must be followed to the letter. There must be ventilation, air, and fans. Most employers do not know that these chemicals are toxic or do not care.

    I suffered from an injury such as this and filed a claim against Manpower but it was quickly dismissed. Every so often my hands bubble with blisters and itch horribly. Aloe seems to work for this condition. Who knows what blood disease I could have contracted if I did not open the doors and windows against the instructions of my employer. Nothing happened because I could still continue to work. I easily could have died if I had listened to the instructions from my employer. It seems that prospective buyers were examining the house as it was constructed and the boss did not want the buyers to smell the fumes. Employees are expendable if it makes employers money.

Silver gallon cans with white labels are the most dangerous but you can find these products in spray cans and other containers as well.

7. Sharp instrument accidents, poor maintenance is the most common violation. Poor supervision of employees during busy hours at restaurants and lack of updates for tools and programs in factories causes these injuries. I had a cut from a mill in a factory to the bone. My hand slipped of a wrench as I was tightening a bolt and my hand flew into a razor sharp mill. I received stitches, went back to work the same day. One of the owners slipped a condom over my finger and sent me back to the line running a drill press. A zigzag scar remains on my finger from one joint to the next, it is an ugly scar that resulted from production being moved up and working at unreasonable speeds. Mistakes and accidents happen.

8. Inadequate water or shelter from the weather causes many injuries that are never reported.

This is a bigger problem then you might think. Many times there is not enough water to go around or you drink unfiltered water from a hose.

Working means being aware of your surroundings, it is up to the Supervisor to make sure that this is done. Picking up tools and storing them once an employee is finished using the tool is not enforced therefore tools and cords and on other jobs you can have slippery floors, chemicals without caps or lids. Weather can complicate matters worse with rain causing electrical hazards and lightning bolts that kill instantly. Most employers bring their workers out of the rain, how many know the proper procedures to do this safely? Children get caught in dangerous jobs and do not complain. Many do not know that they are working with hazardous chemicals.

Where are the inspectors, and I will tell you through working with them that if you know the right inspectors you can pass anything through.

Inspectors and other Government Officials can be bought. Almost everybody has a price and private circles to authorize work that would otherwise be denied. Some will not bother to inspect and take the employers report to design their own. There are many ways to get around the rules but there is no way to keep our children safe on the jobsite, on any jobsite.

9. Alcohol abuse: Your child does not have to drink alcohol to be exposed to the effects of it.
      a. Watching the boss drinking all day long or watching the crew drinking a cooler of beer.
      b. A child laborer can have easy access to alcohol and sneak it home to drink later.
      c. Teenagers are at a clumsy age in there life.
      d. Co-workers can be a bad influence.
      e. Drinking is part of the working persons ritual. Your child will be influenced by this fact.
      f. Drinking on the jobsite after work is a common practice.
      g. Drinking is an outlet Children love to show off.

Alcoholism is the major crisis facing America today. On the road to disaster Americans are drinking more, every year it shows that another rise in statistics display more accidents, domestic abuse, murders, car accidents and a huge jump in alcohol related boat accidents.

All alcohol should be banned from the job and strictly enforced. This act would save labor industries millions of dollars every year. If we take care of the violations there would be more than enough monies for injured workers to get a fair shake, or game.

Americans need to vent their disappointments by electing new leaders. We need to channel our efforts to better the lives of Americans and allow strangers in far off lands to make their own way. We need to mind our own business and take care of issues here at home before our workforce dies in the war and aliens take all the open opportunities in our great country. We will become the strangers in our own land and we the people have little voice in politics to change this fact. People will not be Americans holding corporate power and deciding policies.

 10. Drug abuse: There are many different types of drug abuse at the workplace.

  a. Ever notice when your boss has a red face and is intolerant of little things and always screaming. This is a possible cause of high blood pressure. Either your employer refuses to get on high blood pressure medicine or does not take them as he is supposed to perhaps missing doses here and there. This kind of behavior can traumatize a child.

  b. Co-workers sometimes take drugs to help them work. Vicodon is a popular favorite. Co-workers at times come to work with a hangover from a late night party and are hazardous to children.

  c. Drinking and smoking dope at lunch is a popular favorite for 20% of the U.S. workforce. Temptations are always there at the workplace.

  d. Workers sometimes take drugs for pain bought in the streets because of a lack of proper healthcare for employees at some jobs. These workers are more likely to cause an accident that a child could be injured. More likely than not, injured children on the job are fired the same day.

  e. At most work sites drug dealers frequently sell drugs.

  f. The safest job for a child is lawn care and gardening.

Child Labor Law Enforcement

Enforcement of these laws depends on what District your child works. First the child has to report the injury. Children can be intimidated not to report the injury or they will not report it on their own mind.

Child laborers often have romantic feelings toward their boss. This makes it easy to be taken advantage of by a man or woman in her 20's or 30's in ages. This cannot be stopped but it can be enforced so that children are not molested by adult employers. Imagine your first love affair was with the manager of Burger King who two weeks later fired you. This scenario happens more then you think. Power is exploiting parsons without power, to do your will.

We will explore child labor laws in book four. We will analyze the laws paragraph by paragraph exposing the benefits and the disadvantages of these laws. At the present time two more surveys are being taken, one in Walworth County, Wisconsin and another survey in Salinas California, where child labor is a part of life.

We will dissect all the laws and explain what these laws (that can be interpreted several ways) affect your child' life. Our children are our future, now is a bad time to let them down.

Divide the laws that benefit the working child and expose the laws that hinder treatment for a job related injury. study the basics and if they have improved in enforcement in the past ten years, twenty years and thirty years. Break down the true intent of these laws, and cut apart excuses why they are not enforced. Dismember the misinformation and show that the employer can make a child disappear as easily if not easier then an adult injured worker.

Different methods are utilized for the two age groups but these laws work for labor industries and social security and not the injured worker. Examine the facts and calling them as we see them.

Scrutinizing every law and the persons behind these laws will give **We the People** good insight on where to cast our votes in the next elections.

Now, while we have a chance.

Now we must examine corporations, huge corporations worth billions of dollars and their lobbyists in Washington D.C. the effect they have on child labor laws

1. Corporations, with thousands, tens of thousands of employees get employer benefits not afforded to smaller businesses.

2. Benefits,

3. Reimbursement,

4. Payback,

5. Remuneration,

6. Settlement,

These items above leads to profit for the attorneys. Attorneys goals to the Firm, loyalty is concrete and secrecy total.

       A. Profit
       B. Earnings
       C. Return
       D. Gain
       E. Turnover
       F. Yield
       G. Revenue
       H. Losses
        I. Wages

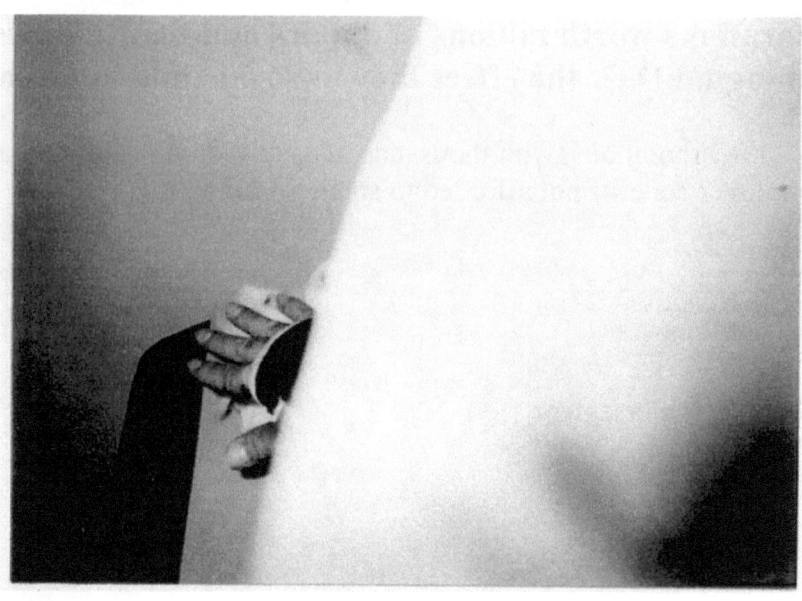

This is supposed to be normal after surgery, what it truly is remarkable objective evidence of a botched surgery. Once labor and industries and the Doctors turn to denial, or refusing to believe what they see. You are walking on thin ice and one way or another they will eliminate your workers compensation claim.

Child labor injuries are not much different; they can blame toxic poisoning on anything. They can say it happened before the child became employed. They can say it happened in his or hers father's garage at home. It cannot be pin-pointed because labor and industries can take weeks to investigate the scene of the accident.

In this way the employer has time to get rid of or dispose of the toxic chemicals he bought from a warehouse cheap with cleaning stock from Home Depot. A child is easy to discredit and community pressure is on the employer's side.

    Much such type of accidents occurs on jobsites. Brfe news is investigating Burger King in Walworth, Wisconsin. It is difficult to investigate huge mega corporations but not impossible. This investigation has been going on for nearly a year and two managers. 1/31/08 is today's date and it has been an interesting day indeed.

    An investigator tried to buy drugs and before the transaction was completed they backed out of the sale. The manager has a new policy of selling drugs to her employees who then sell the drugs for her. For reasons unknown the manager backed out of the sale for reasons idiopathic.

    Children that work at Burger King can order ecstasy with a whopper and a shake. Accidents happen in this situation and children cannot report injuries because of illegal drugs in their bodies.

    Is it the child's fault that he or she was introduced to drugs at the jobsite? Is it the child' fault when under severe peer pressure at work this child begins using drugs? Whose fault is it when one of these children has a severe accident? The employer can say it was not their fault because the kid was using drugs. Labor Industries supposedly clears the employer and rehabs the child, should they take an interest to do so. These children working at Burger King in Walworth, Wisconsin are accidents waiting to happen and the manager selling bags of marijuana for thirty dollars makes it affordable for these kids to get high. In my opinion the fault lies in the State for ignoring this situation in Walworth, Wisconsin.

    This makes slaves from Child Labor and I do not like it, do you? If I know about it and most folks in Walworth know about it what good it does to report it. It makes you a snitch, so these children in many ways are held hostage by the boss.

    Imagine a child, you see a child nothing more. It does not matter if the child is 12 or 17 years old. A child can be manipulated by an adult.

Stronger guidelines and strict enforcements of child labor laws should be enforced. I intend to have these laws enforced, for the safety of my nephews, nieces, grandchildren and the attitude these kids will have about Government protecting them. Parents cannot control there children while their children are at work or their part time job.

We must trust in our laws because we have been taught since children that without laws there is anarchy. What if we have laws that are selectively enforced? All Americans know this is a true fact and accept it as such staying mum. Politics control the enforcement of laws. Some laws are needed now but not in our best interests next year, mandates are set. America has always been a uniformed set of laws that never changed.

Our leaders have made a mockery of our laws by giving leeway for labor and industries to deny soldiers benefits from workers compensation. I know what it is like to transverse the darkness so thick that you can not see your hand in front of your face with the enemy searching for you. Searching for trip wires and staying aware for an ambush. Not enough water and dirt in everything including your nuclear biological gear and your firearms. Without being shot and without a scratch these soldiers that return from combat deserve the best America has to offer, including VA benefits and Workers compensation. Many of our soldiers are children 17 or 18 years of age.

Selectively choosing which laws to enforce and on who.

1. Enforce all fraud laws against the injured worker.

2. Enforce compliance without recourse for the injured worker.

3. Injured worker is bound by attorney client privilege but attorneys give out information using good judgment.

4. Enforce employer rights laws.

5. Enforce compliance of injured worker to program.

The End of Chapter 20

225
Chapter 21
Breaking Your Will
to Fight

This was a couple days before I finished building the forms, installing them, and laboring all the while staying ahead of the ironworkers.

I was laying out the timber for the backing at this phase and spacing the width for the footer. I knew that this job was sloppy excavation and the specks were incorrect so I had to do a lot of digging.

"In order to play the game you need to know the rules. In order to win the game you have to read between the lines. Once you're at this point, you can choose your own way to win. This book provides the tools with which you can win your compensation case because you know what to expect. If you know what to expect then you can prepare for it and devise your own strategies."

While asking on a daily basis if I could see a doctor the boss said no. I continued to go to work and in two days this next photographs will display the work I completed with no or part-time help. I gave a 100% because they could not afford to lose me. I was getting ready for the pour on Christmas Eve. Finally, after working half a day I was told to see a Doctor.

The picture above was taken during a storm but you can still see the clutter of steel and timber lying about. Holes and mud, I had pumped the holes for girders before snapping this photograph. The photo on this next page clearly shows the dangers of working on a job filled with hazards and the foreman and ownership unfriendly to each other.

Illustrating the need for organization of these organizations, "If politicians think it unimportant to vote on some issues because they do not have the time to research them they should lose our votes.

I did not notice any child labor on the jobs I visited other then my jobsite. I did see a couple of close calls but they were supervisors. you should never allow your children to search for jobs at hidden and isolated construction sites. "Ask John Gacey about hiring teenagers were he alive now."

Sending your child to work means checking on this child at the job on a regular basis and seeing the safety policies and observe the ones being followed. Speak with the employer and determine the type of influence this employer will beget on your child. If you would not work for this employer then chances are that this employment would produce a negative effect on your child.

See the disorder, mess, the clutter to walk on, atop, over or trip on. The pour was the next day on Christmas Eve.

Just me and the iron workers gotten this far, with my hand crushed I completed bracing the west side of these Simon forms. I feel like writing a song a song about it. Play it on the guitar by a roaring fire as a sing-along under a bridge for the homeless who lost their means to survive to labor and industries. Engineers and other professionals along with skilled labor living on welfare, and food stamps while staying out of the rain beneath a bridge. Makes me wonder if perhaps a good part of this country is becoming third world living.

Fifty-million dollars was lost in this project, makes you wonder where it all went. Perhaps to some attorneys in Gig Harbor or some other rich and exclusive resort filled with million dollar homes.

You're Will to Fight

This is your most important asset. The system allows you to take your case to the Supreme courts. So you're will to fight this compensation case to the end and receive a decision in your favor can be done in almost any workers compensation case.

Book 1 is filled with facts and idealisms being fed to the public. It is an introduction to books 2-5. Book five takes you through the appeals process and the means to reach the highest courts, after reading these books you can litigate your workers compensation on your own.

You must hold your ground and stick like glue to your principles. There are organizations that will help you for free and the self-help centers at the court house.

Your husband, boyfriend, or vise-versa has gotten a job to help pay the bills. She loves her job and makes friends working there. Then you see the changes in her once she begins to have an affair.

You can easily be overrun by your feelings. Many terrible events occur in your life during the wringer that will scar you forever. It will affect your life as if it were the injury itself.

Nothingness, things happen so fast that your life is being torn apart. There is no way to prevent unexpected events directly related to your injury suffered on the job. You feel that there is no way to control your destiny, persons who know you are seeing you as a burden now. You do not feel angry or sad; at this point in your mind you feel nothingness.

Emptiness, once you lived a life filled with activity and joy. Now you are worried and frustrated most of the time trying to keep up with the paperwork and appointments. You feel as if you are losing or lost everything you love, you feel empty.

Nonexistence, Your case that you appealed has been postponed by your attorney. It has been years and your friends and some loved-ones are beginning to blame you. You are late paying bills and your check coming this Friday is the last check until the appeal is heard by the court.

Another compensation case took your time in court because your attorney was bound to earn more profit from the caseload. He knew that your checks would stop for three months but did not consider the consequences causing your hardships by his actions.

You call your employer and plead with him explaining that your surgery is next month. You continue to stress that you're living on the edge and plead with your employer to retract his argument and allow the compensation checks to continue.

The employer yells at you and tells you he is against the surgery and believes that you are faking your shoulder injury.

You call your attorney and his secretary tells you he is at court, not available, with a client or home sick. You feel that you are ignored, that you do not exist, that you have been placed on the shelf.

Void, you are waiting for your appeal to be ruled as you wait for days, weeks, two months go by and your attorney has not called you. Passing through another phase of the wringer you have time to think deeply living alone in your big house. Suicide has been on your mind and the only reason to had not killed yourself is because of your love for your beloved pet. Passing through the void is where most persons lose their wills to continue the fight and settle for whatever they can get. If you pass through the void and still have the fight to win attitude you will be glad when you're back pay and workers compensation comes on the Friday of the fourth month since you had received your last workers compensation check.

Oblivion, Checks are on time and the cost of living increase gave you another fifty dollars every two weeks, time drags as you wait for physical therapy to begin after you recovered from surgery. You pay your bills and with the help of your shoulder brace you can drive your car again. You are living alone but at least life is bearable. Many things can occur during this time period that can hurt your chances to win your case. This is another way to keep you off-balance. .

Forgetfulness, Documents get mixed up, accidently lost as you neglect to keep track anymore. Because you believe that your attorney is taking care of your affairs. Driving begins to irate your shoulder and by the time you arrive at physical therapy your shoulder had turned red and puffy. During this time be sure to save every letter you get from labor industries and your attorney. Read then because some with deadlines need to be signed and returned.

Stupor, Your attorney office calls you and sets an appointment for you to have a private meeting with him at the Firm. Daydreaming after your meeting with your attorney you feel elated crossing the street, almost getting hit by a car. Your attorney had given you a pep talk filled with promises and reassurances that all is going well.

State of unconsciousness, Wool-gathering, you relax your defenses. Your attorney and labor industries have you right where they want you. This is the time you are ripe for the picking, in season for the kill. Comfortable and back in the saddle again you forget that your employer is fighting you every minute, every inch of the way to victory.

Dream, You begin dreaming about your settlement. Under a spell-like trance your attorney calls you with more good news that you won another appeal for more back pay.

The Act of Breaking Your Will

Breaking your will to fight; by now you can see how easy it can be for attorneys to wring as much revenue from your compensation as possible. What you are left with is irrelevant to the Firms involved and their combined goals. Here is a general process that weakens you and in the end can defeat you and break your will.

Shatter, Shatter you ideas and beliefs that justice prevails and protects the honest person. Only the best liars win their compensation cases and if you are not lying then your attorney is. They shatter your trust in the system and the right to fair judgments.

Fracture, your support system and wear out your welcome. Your body soul and will are fractured as you struggle to make all your appointments. Your way of life and your family ties have fractured almost beyond repair. Desperately you try to fit all the pieces back into your life.

Destroy all objective evidence with panels of L & I Doctors. Discredit tax information. Ask you for original documents that you had given labor industries in the past and they have on micro fish is cruel. Asking you for records of every job you ever had in your life. They bring into evidence your past and are swayed by opinions of persons sought out to bring into disrepute your believability. Search all your records humanly possible looking for anything to close you out. Destroying your self worth and telling you what you are worth is at the least dehumanizing. Shame, disgrace, and dishonor you. Breaking your spirit with good news one month and bad news the next tends to give you mood swings. This gives L & I the advantage. **(I have watched what this process does to people).**

Ruin

   a. Question, Your claims manager begins to question everything about your compensation case. You are asked to produce a more detailed work history and implications that you are further injuring yourself, complicating an injury to continue receiving compensation checks. Your integrity is brought into question as is your honesty so experts research your life. Your attorney questions you for the truth, using entrapping questions you leave feeling insulted and depressed.

   b. Unbelieving,
Doctors refuse to believe your claims of pain. Your employer believes that you can go beck to work, if not at his job then at another job with lower pay and lighter work.

   c. Incredulity,
Cynicism, a look of uncertainty, disbelief and sarcasm directed at you by your claims manager and your attorneys. You have been placed on the expendable list of injured workers destined to have their cases closed. Pessimism reeks from your attorney about your case and you are dubbed a troublemaker. You are hanging by a string or so it seems that you are. Officials during private hearings openly laugh and joke, seemingly as if you are an ant. Do not think that you are not, at any time and with a thousand means available to them; you become expendable when they decide that you are. With your reputation and reliability shattered you are a hollow shell.

   d. Suspicion, you become spooked and feel cornered. All your plans for your future have been ruined, crushed, and you are devastated and traumatized by the events of the last year. You are a broken person submitting yourself to defeat. This is when you lose your will to continue the fight. You are paranoid and wary, skeptical about trusting anybody again and blaming yourself for being stupid. (This is the ideal result condition for an injured worker collecting workers compensation).

If you only broken a bone or lost a digit on you hand or foot you will be treated with respect and dealt fairly with quickly. However if your injury is a back, neck, wrist, knee, or other long term serve injury you are put through the wringer. This way labor and industries can move the numbers around on graphs and scales giving itself glory.

I could write these books with the same promising rhetoric as some other writers do but that would be denying the truth. I can write this book proclaiming myself an expert and I would be on the money. Surely all my investigations, announcing myself as a reporter there was a lot that everybody wanted me to hear and they all want changes. State and Federal government workers have made themselves vocal. Perhaps they never thought that I truly would finish my study and write these books. All the workers at a major labor industries building in a non specified location wished me luck and said they could barely wait to buy the book. This was in 2003, now five years later I blow the whistle on illegitimate procedures used to process your compensation claim. I write this book as an honest American.

Will these books do any good? Of course they will, changes and fair treatment for everybody, employers and employees would make every one happier as they find new lines of communication working together to solve these problems. These books will hopefully stop government from dictating whether the employer or employer should have the overwhelming advantages. Both should be on the same level of importance.

I owned a construction company with 60 employees. I paid up to forty dollars an hour for professional carpenters that showed up at the job late and without hardhats or tools. These workers were not suited for the job. The job was dangerous and only experienced workers should have been sent to me, not persons that do not know the front of the ladder from the back or to use the claw end of the hammer to pound a nail or the head of the hammer. Labor Force inc is notorious for going after the money, reporting wages in a way for their advantage and beat 98% of there worker compensation cases. This too can be explained and understood if I take the time to explain the series of concepts but I can say this. There is a way around everything if you search hard enough and grease the right palms.

You cannot have an employee do a task that the worker is not qualified for.

This lust for cold cash goes to Federal jobs, to Depts. and all the way to major corporate employers. Free for those in the know easy, money, for the elite attorneys and officials in the proper secret chain of command, going to kickbacks of all sorts back to corporations. Money does not change people, government changes people. Certainly one can count on people taking so much before they begin to blow off steam. Americans are passive but if you piss us off then beware big bad wolf.

We have a Congress frightened of wolves but ready to go to war at a moments notice. Corruption should not be tolerated but the argument to this is that it takes corruption to govern. Without corruption there only would be truth and where would we be then?

In a better place if you asked me we would regain our respect as an ethical and civil nation and become the world leader we should be. Careers are made and lost through association. An honest man or woman is compromised every second of the hour. We would be in a better place if the done as we preached, if America was for Americans, solely for the people of America then life would be better for everyone. .

You can not let on that you are moved by the attacks from your employer and L & I. You must stand your ground and choose your words carefully. If you believe in god or some other religion grow strong in your faith. Do not let your employer using the government as a weapon break you will to continue to fight for your rights.

The law is on your side but the cards are stacked against you by your employer as your rights seem mute. Not even your attorney can guarantee your rights, only you can.

You need to build a wall of insensitivity around you that blocks out all negative influence and focus on following the plan in these books. Thoughtlessness inattentiveness coldness, all feelings that shoot at you constantly as you spiral through the wringer. Keep your self-composure and believe in yourself and your own ethical values. Write your congressmen or women, write the Governor, send objective medical evidence to the dept of heath and welfare in Washington D.C. Be active and confident knowing what to expect and your own way to deal with it using this book.

There should not be a fight for your rights to fair treatment because it is guaranteed in our laws. Yet only the laws that benefit the state are vigorously enforced. Faking their injuries strongly signifying that more law enforcement is needed, fraud department targeting slothful workers trying to cheat the state by faking injuries or making them worse then they in reality are. Soon there will be so many police under so many officials that all of our rights will be given on an as needed application.

If the state manages to break your will to fight and win then it will scar you forever. You will always be dependant on others and at this point in the game you will have acquired an environmental mental illness. This means that the wringer had caused you to have a mental illness. There should be by all rights medical treatment and compensation for this work-related severe disability but there never was and there is none now. We hope that our future generations of children will have the foresight that we lack to create laws that protect American workers and having them enforced.

Once God was severed from the state it was replaced with corrupted ethics. Whether you believe in god or not you must admit that the idea of god kept our great nation ethical and honorable, now our honor as a nation has reached rock bottom. What respect America commanded in the past has been replaced with hatred and jealousy.

It is time that we as a people demand that our mandates be followed to the letter of the law and that laws be amended to provide a safety-net for the injured worker.

A supernatural being is what we need to fix the mess we are in. We still live by old taboos and preconceived notions not decided by the people. Should we be afraid to speak our minds, of course we can say what we want because we are Americans; but in reality can we?

We have not addressed the children of injured workers and the effects the wringer has on them. Children are not dumb and know more about what is happening that parents believe. Foregone conclusions made by labor industries passes on to the children of injured workers. They feel the hopelessness and suffer for books, school supplies, and basic needs including nourishment.

Money gets tight and parents fight all night long into the next day. The children undergo changes, and get lost in their own worlds trying to shut out their parents. Do you agree that there should be a labor industries heath and services center for these children? I hope you concur with us and see the need as a crisis and not an issue.

Labor & industries and domestic violence go hand in hand together. Ask Child Services or Welfare Officials and they will concur with me.

These are advantages to your employer who keeps a weathered eye on you. Perhaps once you were friends with your employers but now you are treated as if you are a stranger. Indeed, we need more graphs showing statistics that matter. My interviews were conducted fairly and I was surprised the L & I lower workers in offices complained about there employer in this case being labor industries of Washington State and California. The game is tilted in favor of your employer for the present and as many reasons Congress will say they are the best for America I have twice as many reasons why it is bad for America and good for foreign invaders taking jobs and businesses over from Americans fighting in the wars. Turn the game around and give yourself the advantage by knowing what is around every corner and finding your way to meet the obstacle head on.

Take account the ethical events that occurred before our time . . .

"And Jonathan, Saul's son, had a son that was lame of his feet. He was five years old when the tidings came of Saul and Jonathan out of Jez-re-el, and his nurse took him up, and fled; and it came to pass, as she made haste to flee, that he fell, and became lame. And his name was Me-phib'-o-sheth."

This is an injury that occurred thousands of years ago. Let us venture into those times and see what happened next.

"So Me-phib'-o-sheth dwelt in Jerusalem; for he did eat continually at the King's table; and was lame on both his feet."

It is a good thing that Me-phib'-o-sheth did not have to go through the wringer.

I guess that you have to know somebody to have proper ethics applied to your compensation case. Me-phib'-o-sheth knew the right people in the right places to get relief for his disability. We can compare labor and industries to King David who allowed mercy and compensation for Me-phib'-o-sheth. However this is not the case because labor and industries is not king David but more akin to Lucifer if you compare their aggressive policies to discredit and destroy severely injured workers.

Me-phib'-o-sheth represents injured workers and Americans in general; and King David should represent our government but since god was severed from state in America our godly ethics have been replaced with man created corruption.

I feel betrayed, do you?

Writing is not considered employment by labor industries and provides no vocational training for liberal arts. I do not believe in the devil but if there are devils we voted for them, that is why they are in office.

However they will teach you how to stack shelves in supermarkets or the proper way to push a broom.

It will be up to you to keep your chin up and your spirits high. Stay with the program but be prepared to use the information provided in this book so that your ride in the wringer will be a short one. Remember that by the letter of the law they must pay you the amount you were earning at the time of your injury. Vocational training and back to work incentives work along this same law. This law is blatantly ignored and abused by attorneys. Please do not allow this to happen to you. Demand that the laws be followed even if you must take it to the U.S. Supreme court. If that is what it takes to be treated fairly.

Once your employer breaks your will he wins the game. You can be at the finish line ready to collect you reward when the walls come tumbling down. You have to stay on your toes whether they are broken or not you have to be waiting for it. You cannot be surprised by disaster if you see it coming. These books show and explain the laws and gives feedback on what the best move is. There are so many situations and varieties of injuries that these books will at least give you a foot to stand on.

You can bet your last dollar that enough people begin using this book there will be changes made and hundreds or thousands of unneeded L & I associated contractors and workers will go through our wringer created for them and the festering infection called corruption. This book lays it out for the average reader to use to their advantage, in-between these pages are examples and advice that show that you have to stand up for your rights because nobody else will do it for you.

The End of Chapter 21

Conclusions
Going over the main points

We have explored and examined both sides of this issue. Our teams of investigators are reporting new findings to me as I write this book.

1. As soon as your injury occurs go to the Doctor whether your boss threatens to fire you or not.

2. Choose your own primary care Doctor that will be the first Doctor that treats your injury.

3. The Doctor Office that you choose to be treated has the proper worker compensation forms for you to fill out. Your Primary care Doctor is responsible for filing the claim with labor & industries.

4. Do not be intimidated to return to work if your injury prevents certain movements by you body.

5. It is best for you to fight now than later. Be sure that if you received a severe injury the Doctor records this information.

6. Take a note book and record the objective evidence the Doctor discovers during your examination.

7. Record times, how long before treatment and the length of time this treatment needed.

8. Begin writing a log.

9. Decide if your injury can be repaired or if it is going to consume money and time.
    a. Injuries such as hairline fractures, minor cuts that need stitches, Eye flushing, and other easily repaired injures call your claims

manager after researching the award for your type of injury and as for twenty thousand more dollars. Be sure that the award specifies that your injury is treated until it is completely healed. Once you are speaking with the claim manager he realizes that you know what you are talking about. Get the best deal possible and return to work as soon as your injury has healed.

    b. If you have suffered a severe work-related injury your course of actions will be much more complicated.

    c. You must decide to retain an attorney. The attorneys that offer the best results get the worse results. Choose an attorney without close relations, contacts, or such with Labor & Industries, they are honest and have to earn their money the hard way.

    d. Be sure that you research your attorney carefully before retaining the Firm.

10. Keep good records and your log updated.

11. Create your own plan and stick to it.

12. Learn the laws in this book.

13. Carefully avoid the pitfalls mentioned in these books.

14. Prepare your family for the future. Discuss with them this book and that it will be a rough road.

15. Save your money.

16. Research each new Doctor you are referred to be examined and if the credentials are shady demand a new evaluator.

17. Avoid foreign Doctors as evaluators.

18. The best time to arrive at a decent award is before negotiations. It is best for you or your attorney to settle the compensation quickly. The only hang-up there is that your attorney will lose a lot of monies, more then a lot.

19. Always comply with procedures but use your influence to get the clinics and tests that you desire and not where L&I want to send you.

20. Do not try and do something that you cannot do, this goes for all matters. Know what is possible, what you can expect, and then what you get.

21. Accomplish good relations with all parties involved in your workers compensation case. This task is a difficult duty because at times the persons that you are sent to see can have their own attitude problems and mood changes.

22. Secret files at this point are beginning to accumulate. These files will bring on your first L&I profile.

23. Always say as little as possible and get to the point quickly.

24. Keep your personal life private. Do not tell of domestic problems or money shortages. This is useful information to L&I and your attorney is bound to pass it on.

25. The more evaluations you attend the more your case weakens. Begin complaining that these evaluations and stress tests are complicating your work related injury.

26. Do not consent to physical therapy if you know it will only worsen your injury.

27. Get copies of all your medical records as they are filed. Medical records easily can get lost. All your actions are being monitored

and recorded into your secret files.

28. Build a network of support.

29. Knowledge replaces ethics within the private circles of attorneys involved with your compensation case.

30. Secret files have notations and remarks by persons privy to your private information.

31. Keep out of the public eye.

32. Do not engage in sports.

33. Hire a private investigator if you can afford to hire one.

34. Expect more delays.

35. Trust no one.

36. Manage your prescriptions.

37. Truth is in the eyes of the believer.

38. Never compromise your ethical beliefs or principles. If you allow this to occur then you can lose your identity to be shaped by your living experiences.

39. The Doctor that can most hurt your cause is a D.O.

40. Be good to yourself.

41. Stay objective and be sure to maintain your mental health.

42. Remember that you are in control and you call the shots. Never

allow your attorney to these rights from you no matter what he tells you, stay the captain of your ship.

43. Be in charge of your life and never be discouraged.

44. Have power over your emotions.

45. Be in command of your appeals by staying informed and asking to be present at the hearings. Courts frown upon this because private deals and exchanges are made affecting peoples lives not present at the hearings.

46. Avoid seeing or seeking psychiatric treatment if possible because this will weaken your case and bring your honesty into question.

47. Remember that you must be strong-willed to win your workers compensation case.

48. What you do not know will hurt you.

49. Attorneys know one another well on first name basis. State and private attorneys share cases and stories at places like exclusive clubs, golf courses, tennis courts, and of course at trials.

50. Stay in contact with your family.

51. If you have no family join a support group.

52. Get in touch with agencies and organizations that will help you. If you are a Veteran then you can find organizations to help you if you search hard enough you can get monies from Grants.

53. Get through the head games and stay with the facts.

54. Get a message to Congress that you have been injured and your circumstances of the injury. This truly can change the way your workers compensation case is handled by your claim manager. All you have to do is get noticed by one Senator or State Representative to get quick results. I can give you a list of politicians that will certainly investigate your case but I can not list these names.

55. Connect with your local politicians and send a detailed letter of your injury. These letters are screened and then read. They are recorded same as point 54.

56. Arrive at sound conclusions about your state of affairs. Use logic and do not fool yourself into believing that it soon will be over.

57. Closing stages means do not bother your attorney. Your attorney will quit if you try to tell him what to do or go after. Then you are up a creek without a paddle with a hole in your canoe.

58. Wrapping up, is for attorneys and not for injured workers. Attorneys milk your case for every penny and when they drag it on for too long pass up opportunities to settle your compensation case. Each time you receive a workers compensation check your attorney receives a percentage. The more money you get on your check the more your

attorney gets. Attorneys will pack three to a thousand caseloads so that these monies add up to a regular substantial amount of profits. If they settle your case it is one less payment to your attorney.

59. Contesting your appeal decision in court will cause more delays thanks to your attorney and your employer.

60. Self-Composure, Self-possession, Self-control, Calmness, Level-headedness, Poise, commit to memory these words and keep them close to your heart and on your mind.

61. Collections of files, documents, and reports about you and your work injury now number in the volumes. Remember that your secret files are open to examination by any official with the proper clearance, from any Government Department.

62. Fight back if you are falsely accused of lying, fraud, or threatened by over payments. They can truly place fear in you through threats of you having to pay back the compensation monies. This tactic is for the broken, the persons whom lost their will to fight injustice.

63. Cannot agree on settlement so your case gets continued and the process begins again. Issues are raised by your claim manager and your injury has not been recorded as stable.

64. Remember that Court Officials can legally lie to you and misrepresent you with incompetence. They can be lazy or stupid and it is legal for them to make mistakes. They have protected themselves by surrounding themselves with laws protecting them. An attorney must

anger other attorneys to be prosecuted and even then Justice is not always doled out.

Secret files decide your case by persons without names. We live in a world filled with conspiracies but you better not say the word conspiracy at your attorney's office.

Book three will continue into the lives of these attorneys and court decisions that should be bloopers or laughed out of the justice system. Each book will give new statistics and expose more hidden truths. We will explore secret files that you cannot imagine exist and bring you to a point of writing your congressperson to complain.

Files are misplaced, lost, stolen, shredded, and exploited.

Book three will continue with topics such as child labor laws, ways you can file charges against your attorneys for poor ethical behavior. What the local governments contribute to advancing employer domination of the job market and more.

"Special Thanks goes to Troy Kohls, Audley Hargraves," and my nephew Bruce Keller whom contributed his time and his profession, and moral support.

I would also like to give mention and special thanks to my proofreader who read and reviewed most of the books I have published when they were only short stories in 1999-2002. Holly Hunter lives in the wonderful state of Washington with her husband Leroy and their pets. .

Troy Kohls witnessed the creation of this book and through the years followed brfe news research. on labor and industries. Troy is a witness to the truth of this book.

Labor Industries affects every human being in our country. Side-effects of long-term miss use of power and bending our laws will be our downfall.

Never forget that if you have ex-wives or girlfriends etc with your personal information they will use this information to cause you hardships. Your attorney knows it is unethical but he will not hesitate to talk to your ex. The attorney will record it all and pass it on to labor & industries claim manager.

Remember that a well told lie will travel the globe before it is disproven. Attorneys and claim managers take advantage of these persons and damage your compensation case.

Proof of this is that it happened with my custody attorney and three years later with my L & I attorneys. Your attorney is almost as bad to your case as your claim manager. Do not give marital information or list girlfriends for your attorney or claim manager. The best way to win your workers compensation case is to represent your own case. Book Five will go into detail with ten easy steps to accomplish this feat along with several examples of others that have won their cases in this manner.

Your attorney schedules many hearings and drags negotiations on for years or decades. This manner of business weakens your case but raises profits for the law firm you have retained. You want to control the direction of your compensation case; the attorney will never tell you seriously what direction he is taking. Sometimes you learn of a hearing the day before it convenes or learn that you checks have stopped when you look in the mail box. Your attorney keeps you off balance to protect the Firm.

We hope that once our series of books are completed you will be able to litigate your own compensation without an attorney. I will not become an attorney because I studied law to defend myself against attorneys and not become an attorney. You must sell your soul top be an attorney in a country that writes its own policies county to county, state to state.

We will compose book after book for other services that you can do yourself to eliminate attorneys from litigation in Social Security, AFDC, Welfare, and survival books for our brave military personal that return to this country only to be forgotten by those that sent them to war. Our objective is to eliminate attorneys from controlling and ruling the United States of America.

Military personal are released from the military in fairly good health unless they were wounded in combat or had an accident on the job.

As an ex Delta I know what these men and women have to go through and endure. I have the confidential clearance and common sense to know what the long-term effects will be for Service related injuries. As a Delta I observed more then I participated in the loading and unloading of artillery shells, tank ammunition, cannon fire, I can not go into specifics but I will tell what I can without breaking my code of silence.

First allow me to explain that injuries that you receive in the military do not have side-effects for years and the treatment at best is marginal. Studies are ongoing to develop treatments and vaccines that will be effective on these ailments. Now they are called syndromes but us persons who commanded or were specialists in these fields know that every syndrome is a side-effect of a injury while serving in the military.

It amazes me that dangerous and toxic work is passed off as ordinary duty. I had this duty once because I had to replace a lost soldier and yes sir; the side-effects started five years after I done this duty.

Public information has everything I am speaking about but you have to connect the dots. Ask any combat soldier and he will inform you that everything everywhere they go is radioactive or toxic. Residue is drawn in by skin pores and digested into your body.

We and they have biological and chemical agents that are designed to activate ten years after infection. There are others that awake twenty or thirty years after infection.

"After reading this do you believe as I do that once these persons are released from military duty that they fall under the jurisdiction of labor & industries, I am sure you do."

Congress and the House have proven that they are ignoring these facts or are sleeping on the job. Liberal lobbyists hand out gifts and cash so that these laws will continue to be ignored.

We are a nation of laws that our politicians decide which laws to enforce and which laws to ignore. We are at war and our government better provide for its citizens, take care of their soldiers. While Americans lose their rights more rights are given to those illegal aliens that flood our borders. Before long foreigners will have more rights in America than Americans. This being the case we still have time to find solutions to these problems so our leaders better stop wasting time. We are a nation of laws and all our laws need to be enforced, and not compromised.

Which laws do we begin with? This is easy, all the laws are used selectively whether you are small business, Mega Corporation, or the average Joe or Jane. If you have the clout and the money you can get laws enforced, if you do not have those things then you are S.O.L.

Child labor should be our number one priority because you can bet that McDonalds, Burger King, and a large number of corporations hire the vulnerable, they hire children who do not know their rights.

Children make up a huge part of our work force but slowly, surely being replaced by alien workers who do not care about their rights, only their jobs.

Last week we did a survey of injured workers at Standford University and found that in the dinning facilities the average wait is nine years to reach a settlement. This does not reflect the employees of Standford University because only employees from private contractors were interviewed. You will find similar results from every University in our great nation.

Everybody knows somebody who is or was injured on the job, this is a growing phenomena yet official reports do not reflect this with there statistics.

My conclusions lead to one verdict, and that is that our politicians think us stupid because we allow them to bully the people of the United States of America.

Addendum

    I am completing this message with a note of caution. These attorneys ultimately have the power of life or death. In their own minds they are gods. Attorney ethics that they secretly adhere to protects them thus forming a wall that keeps us out and them safe. I consider attorneys a threat; my own attorneys had threatened me on several occasions in the past with my businesses. Let me assure you that if a layer threatens you it is a real threat that will be carried out if you do not comply.

    Ethics is a thing of the past replaced by rhetoric and corruption. I am numb to their threats because I have hardened and this cause is worth fighting for. I was in the wringer and it was turned on high, it has made me a man with few emotions, wrecked principles and compelled to make a difference for the people that matter; the working person.

Bonus Book
City Laws ignore Federal Regulations

City Laws is supposed to be for the people living in the city protecting their right to safety and justice. Does the City truly protect with following Federal Regulations. *"Hell no it does not."*

City Politicians work with Attorneys to assure the large bundles of monies and distributed equally between them ignoring Federal regulations to accomplish their goals.

I will be frank with you; some cities take advantage of the situation at hand with the war exhausting Federal Government time and resources. Washington D.C. does not have the time or Agents to watch and enforce Federal Laws pertaining to mandated city laws. Some politicians believe they are above the law because of their knowledge and input into mandating, passing, and writing laws that suit special interest groups who truly control the atmosphere of every city in the United States of America.

"This book will kick ass and tell names!" It is about time that people that is or infiltrate the inside of the circle of corruption reveal the truth to the American public. At a phenomenal rate brfe will ensure that we do the best we can to reveal truth while exposing corruption. These crooks have gotten fat and lazy, believing that we are too stupid or afraid to stand up to them.

I founded the L.O.D. I cannot reveal the definitions of the initials because it is classified. I was inspired by a nephew of the President. I will not reveal which President nor does the name of his nephew who I am sure support this book.

The L.O.D. is a covert Intelligence network of soldiers and civilians alike globally watching and intervening in crisis situations. We represent the power of the best of the best experienced in hundreds of allocations and intense training in the best law schools and combat designations. We represent the weak and the hopeless to one day prove that America has not forgotten Americans. We are the elite that have seen what happens once corruption consumes Government. Some of us know what it feels like to be expendable or abandoned. *"I really do not know which is worse?"*

The point is that we knew in 1980 what was waiting for America if America continued on the path it was in. That is why we organized and grew in numbers quickly. Our children have united and represent the cream of the crop of children.

All colors and races we fit in perfectly and have the support of some military units.

I know that something's are written indistinctly but there is so much I can say before I step over the line.

In the year 2004 I announced our movement to the Miami Herald. Since that time recruitment has been intense.

Let me give you an example of Government corruption; there always will be secret societies within secret societies, this system will save our great nation. This book was written to strengthen our Nation and allow the peoples to see that they are but dollar signs at the present time and being thrown into the great sand lottery. No one is exempt so I guess this system could be called equal opportunity extermination.

Salinas, California bus 29 MST

Authorities and the system need to be regulated. Perhaps if they were regulated then misuse of power would be difficult to maneuver.

It was a pleasant day and I was waiting for the bus. I was on my way to Kinko's to complete a major project. The bus driver was on his last route. All that he could think of was getting into his car and getting home. I entered the bus and noticed that the driver was in a foul mood.

I was carrying a file case and sitting sideways facing the side on a bench seat. The driver was traveling 40mph and coming up to a light. At the last second the driver slammed the breaks and the bust abruptly stopped. The riders in the bus hurtled forward, jolted from their seats. I was launched from my seat, jolted and believe that a flying object hit my head as by brain slammed against my inner skull. I was dazed and when we gotten to the Terminal I filled out a form as the driver scowled at me and cussed at the accident report he needed to fill out. In a moment he was gone in his car and on his way home.

The People that control the Atmospheres
BOARD OF DIRECTORS
MONTEREY-SALINAS TRANSIT

Monterey-Salinas
Karen Sharp City of Carmel-By-The-Sea
Kristin Clark City of Del Rey Oaks
James Ford City of Marina
Libby Downey City of Monterey
Vicki Stilwell City of Pacific Grove
Thomas Mancini City of Seaside
Fernando Armenta County of Monterey
Lisa Senkir City of Gonzales (Ex-Officio)
Absent: Sergio Sanchez City of Salinas
Staff: Carl Sedoryk General Manager/CEO
Lyn Owens Director of Human Resources
Hunter Harvath Director of Administration
Michael Hernandez Chief Operating Officer
Robert Weber Dir. Transportation Services
Sonia Bannister Office Administrator
Mary Archer Planner
Tom Hicks CTSA Manager
Mark Eccles Director of IT
Carl Wolf Facilities/Capital Projects Manager
Others: Dave Laredo DeLay & Laredo
Charles Armbruster Communication Systems Specialist
Mike Cargile Communication Systems Specialist
Gary Wilmot City of Marina
Andy Cook TAMC
Jim Fink Salinas resident
Apology is made for any misspelling of a name.
Chair Armenta welcomed Ms. Karen Sharp, new representative for the City of Carmel.

brfe investigators questioned several MST bus drivers. Some were glad to pass on information freely, others complained about the passengers and the city. These are the facts were learned from these drivers. Some drivers are the top of the line and proud of their jobs but these were few.

1. Not all but some bus drivers get heavy-footed on their last route of the day.

Comment; "This causes many unreported injuries and injuries whisked under the rug."

2. In San Francisco, CA. Police enforces the laws and often ticket bus drivers.

3. In Salinas California the Police ignore the laws blatantly broken by MST bus drivers.

4. The city is out of money and tight with its funding.

5. There are five to seven cameras on most MST buses.

Federal Regulations require these cameras with strict enforcement of the recordings and maintenance of the cameras.

6. The bus driver is on video via camera and mirror at all times on the bus.

7. Some passengers are singled out and harassed by certain bus drivers. Several times the bus driver received Police assistance and the passenger was jailed.

8. Some bus drivers are polite while others are rude.

9. An Investigator filmed a bus driver drinking liquor from a thermos bottle.

10. Bus Drivers in a broad-spectrum drive recklessly.

Politics that allow this to transpire roots chaos in the Health Care System of the city and physicians are compelled to refuse some patients that were involved in a city related accident. Insurance companies back away from paying the medical bills so it comes out of your pockets. Politicians give themselves raises as undeclared monies are dispersed. Medical clinics are pressured to go with the flow or else. Medical facilities must be certain that they receive compensation for their services. I agree with these medical professionals because it is the corrupt politicians that force these conditions pressuring physicians to learn how to live with mandated policies. Indeed, Washington Leaders in Congress and the House of Representatives are studied under a microscope, is it not time that all level of politics are audited and evaluated on their performance? I believe that the life of our nation depends on us, the people, to take action.

We must make them all accountable if this nation is to survive the many crises it is facing. A time when something very important for the future happens or is decided is the time that we must hold them all accountable for the many persons or families it has handicapped because of their self-righteous and uncompassionate attitude toward the same people they were elected or appointed to serve.

Misinformation and Lies

The main body of Government no matter how big or small cannot properly monitor subcommittees and private secret committees created from these sub committees, now you tell me. *"Is this too much idle wild Government?"*

Times are hard for our country during our present State of Affairs and we should all carve up this burden together. It is a fact that the poor, middle-class, and the upper-middle class suffer as the elite class get benefits out of this fiasco. There are many issues on the minds of politicians and voters these days, terrorism and military operations overseas, the economy and jobs, health care. Environmental issues do not seem to level very high on the Concern-O-Meter, but to a large extent, that is a self-righteous prophesies due to the underreporting of ecological problems by the mainstream corporate media. Lies are difficult to discern from the truth. If ten experts swore that green is red then it can not be disputed.

We all are distracted by the billions of dollars we spend to feed this war on terrorism and as long as the city does not complain that city is ignored by Washington. March 22, 2008

Not that they need encouragement; politicians were given the green light to lie about their opponents by the Washington state Supreme Court last week This decision allows city politicians to exploit their ability to misappropriate city funds.

"The notion that the government, rather than the people, may be the final arbiter of truth in political debates is fundamentally at odds with the First Amendment."

Our Supreme Court deciding that what we think is right as a majority is wrong; is definitely not American.

Let's let our troops know how proud we are of them and that it is time our politicians took lessons from them in running this great nation of ours.

Lying politicians threaten our freedom of speech. Most people would agree that, for the sake of better government and everyone involved, politicians should not surely lie not to each other, and especially not to the public.

"The majority's decision is an invitation to lie with impunity."

This gives us; **"We the People"** the shaft on every bill passed. With terrorists operating from within our own borders and the national debt it is impossible to police our own nation. I know this for a fact; immunity given to high risk terrorists for their cooperation. Some have been given high positions and Grants for school along with an easy life. Immune from persons like me who know where some of them work and live. What do we get . . . more taxes? It is not fair but any politician will tell you that life is not fair.

Blatant Lies and False Accusations

MONTEREY - An American journalism icon told a sold-out audience of 500 Tuesday night that both journalists and politicians have drifted from their shared role of serving citizens.

Perhaps if the people were supported by the press then blatant invented laws designed for special interests groups would be curbed. Normal citizens would not be judged as liars and made suspects during accidents of buses, sidewalks, potholes, and other accidents due to city negligence.

I was a passenger on a bus accident that happened February 11, 2008. I suffered a severe head injury. It was not called in to the Police and I am doubtful that the bus driver filled out the accident report.

This afternoon I was walking my dog on Van Buren with a 25mph speed limit as a bus passed me traveling at a rate of 40mph or more. Children play on this street and skate-boarders often are seen riding Van

Buren here in Salinas California.

I can report these events because the residents that live on that street and in the neighborhood all have their own stories to tell about reckless MST bus drivers, and the reckless driving throughout the city.

I called Ben Newman; he the hot shot at MST and complained that he was not sending the filing forms for the accident. He said he sent them laughing as he did so. I explained that it was going on two weeks and he said there seems nothing wrong with me from his observation on the phone.

I decided to test him because I will be suing for millions of dollars. I said to Mr. Newman . . . "I bet the city would be better off if I were dead." Newman said this sarcastically, "I wouldn't say it that way," I heard him smirk. This man knew I had a head injury and how to push the buttons to bring on stress,. I told him that I would keep calling until he sent me the forms. Mr. Neman reported this as a threat.

I sent my CFO to get the forms and they played head games with him, amused and acting coy they gave Mike the forms.

I will scan the forms into this book now for you to see.

PROOF OF SERVICE

I, the undersigned, state that I am a citizen of the United States and employed in the County of Monterey, State of California; that I am over the age of eighteen years and not a party to the within action; that my business address is One Ryan Ranch Road, Monterey, CA 93940; that on February 21, 2008, I served:

<u>Blank government claim form and explanation letter</u> (English) on the person(s) listed below, addressed as follows:

        Mr. Kal Keller
        18671 Eisenhower Street
        Salinas, CA. 93906

Executed at Monterey, California, this 21st day of February 2008. I declare under penalty of perjury that the foregoing is true and correct.

_____
Kathy Medina
Human Resources Assistant

_____   _____
accepting documents for Kal Keller   Print name

259

MONTEREY-SALINAS TRANSIT

JOINT POWERS AGENCY MEMBERS:
City of Carmel-by-the-Sea • City of Del Rey Oaks • City of Marina • City of Monterey • City of Pacific Grove
City of Salinas • City of Seaside • County of Monterey

February 14, 2008

Mr. Kal Keller
18671 Eisenhower Street
Salinas, CA. 93906

Dear Mr. Keller,

    Enclosed is a form which, should you choose to file a claim, must be returned to our office filled out in its entirety before it can be submitted to the Monterey-Salinas Transit for consideration. Providing you with this information and form should not be construed as an admission of liability by Monterey-Salinas Transit. To be considered complete, your claim must include all elements required by government code §910.

    Please be advised that the Monterey-Salinas Transit investigates each claim fully. If it is determined that neither the employee nor Monterey-Salinas Transit caused or contributed to the incident which resulted in your alleged personal injury and/or property damage, your claim will be rejected.

In order to file a claim for money or damages against the Monterey-Salinas Transit you must comply with Government Code § 911.2, which provides:

    "A claim relating to a cause of action for death or for injury to person or to personal property or growing crops shall be presented as provided in Article 2 (commencing with Section 915) of this chapter not later than six months after the accrual of the cause of action. A claim relating to any other cause of action shall be presented as provided in Article 2 (commencing with Section 915) of this chapter not later than one year after the accrual of the cause of action."

    While the Monterey-Salinas Transit has investigated or will investigate the accident/incident and may possibly enter into settlement negotiations with you, Monterey-Salinas Transit does not waive your obligation to comply with Government Code § 911.2.

    If you have any questions or concerns regarding this, please feel free to contact me at 831-899-2555.

Sincerely,

Ben Newman
Risk & Security Manager

One Ryan Ranch Road • Monterey, California 93940-5795 USA • Fax 831.899.3954 • Phone 831.899.2558 or 424 769
www.mst.org • e-mail: mst@mst.org

CLAIM AGAINST MONTEREY-SALINAS TRANSIT
(Government Code §910)
Claim # _____

TO: Monterey-Salinas Transit

ATTN: Secretary to the Board of Directors
One Ryan Ranch Road
Monterey, CA 93940

1. **Claimant's Name:** _____

   Claimant's Address/Post Office Box: _____
   _____

   Claimant's Phone Number: _____

2. **Address to which notices are to be sent:** _____
   _____

3. **Occurrence:** _____

   Date: _____ Time: _____ Place: _____

   Circumstances of occurrence or transaction giving rise to claim: _____
   _____
   _____

4. General description of indebtedness, obligation, injury, damage, or loss incurred so far as is known: _____

   If additional space is required, check this box and attach supplemental material to this form.

   Name or names of public employees or employees causing injury, damage, or loss, if known:
   _____

5. Amount claimed now .... $ _____

   Estimated amount of future loss, if known .... $ _____

   TOTAL .... $ _____

Basis of above computations: _____
_____
_____

_____   _____
CLAIMANT'S SIGNATURE (or Company   DATE
Representative or Parent of Minor Claimant)

Note: Claim must be presented to the Secretary to the Board of Directors, Monterey-Salinas Transit.

I have six months to file this claim.

After the accident violent rage consumed my mind and body. It was agonizing but common sense told me it the jarred brain settling down. I could feel a tingling electrical current like a bowl atop my head. At times, a hot fireball burned in my brain.

Temporary amnesia came and went, I am still healing and feel that these headaches are a burden forced to carry. Friends with many global CEO's, I find it easy to learn the new trends and the battles and wars engaged between billion dollar corporations. People become numbers and a satellite tracks your car, your phone is moderately monitored and every day new laws are passed through the house. It is becoming a farce; have they passed a law yet that they can film you from your own computer screen. *"We need to think about these things and reconsider the course of action that is destroying our great nation."*

Perhaps it is time for a change. Politicians believe that since you can never please everyone then they better please themselves.

Sometimes it seems that California has as many vehicle-related laws as it does cars – besides the hundreds of infractions listed in the California Vehicle Code, there are a host of more serious offenses such as DUI / DWI, hit-and-run, and evading arrest. These are serious crimes with severe repercussions and require expert legal help.

Bus accidents are self insured meaning not insured in Monterey County. This means that you fight the city for compensation for your injuries the bills will be paid by you. You will have to pay because all insurance companies have policies not to insure city accidents. Insurers know that the city will avoid paying them or pass a new law denying payment for services. If you are middle class this can break you, if you are poor you do not have a chance for compensation.

In Dec 05 I was parked when car was hit by city bus. She claimed I was parallel parking & I was not, I was parked. The front of my bumper was pulled off my car & @ the time of the accident the driver said she was fine & nobody was hurt. Well she changed stories & claimed injury when I saw she perfectly ran & walked w/no problems. My insurance company says is still waiting on finalization of the workers compensation claim & because no law suite has been filed by the bus driver or compensation insurance...they can't subpoena any information. What are my rights? My witness would only give me an address & won't respond to letters sent. Any advice of what my rights would be I would appreciate it. My state is California

A prime example of accidents that people refuse to contest because the power of the bus companies. Corrupt bus drivers with influence to sue innocent persons, by chance in the wrong place at the wrong time, taking advantage of their knowledge of MST and secret unwritten policies.

brfe operates a Think Tank with members from all regions of this great nation. Many ex-members will be surprised to learn that the D.O.D.

are alive and well.

We know of older and better structured then we is but everybody knows who is anybody know whom these persons are. L.O.D. has broken into factions and has spread globally.

Photo of Author

Well now I feel like we know each other much better, don't you?

My dog Killer is now 12 years old and has gone everywhere I have gone for his whole life. He still acts like a puppy and runs like a five-year old.

Attorneys are politicians too. I studied law by private tutor at Hastings College of the law. My good friend now practices law in New York city where he was born. I have tried to get an honest attorney to take my case but I know more then they know about the law. After they try to scam me and try to put me through the wringer I put out their misguided efforts and the letter of the law. I meet them they swing their arms wide and say we will sue for millions. I correct them and explain the accident was filmed and I was handing them a silver platter. This Attorney backed out of my case because I wanted to settle the case fast. With the help of my friend I will litigate this case myself.

Riders of buses and trains that are involved in accidents that are not caused by the bus driver or train are not covered by the mass transit system if the accident was caused by an uninsured motorist, or if the motorist that causes the accident does not have enough insurance to cover the loss to all passengers.

Imagine it; you are on a bus that flips over because an uninsured or underinsured motorist runs a red light. You basically have no real way to be compensated for your losses because the bus was not at fault, and the driver who was at fault was either uninsured, or underinsured, and there is not enough money to cover everyone's losses

As it stands right now, passengers of mass transit are at the mercy of the road, and have no legal means to protect themselves if an accident is caused by someone other than the transit system. I feel that it is discriminatory to the riders of mass transit, not to provide them with appropriate legal protection and insurance in the case of accidents which are not the fault of the transit system

I hope that the California State Legislators hear my call for mandatory seatbelts, and mandatory insurance for mass transit riders.

"My case is different, the bus driver was at fault, and everything that happened shows it on the cameras."

BOARD OF DIRECTORS

January 8, 2007

Chairman Armenta called the meeting to order at 10:00 a.m. in the Monterey-

Present: Michael Cunningham City of Carmel-By-The-Sea
Kristin Clark City of Del Rey Oaks
Gary Wilmot City of Marina
Carl Anderson City of Monterey Alan Cohen City of Pacific Grove

Robert Russell City of Salinas
Thomas Mancini City of Seaside
Fernando Armenta County of Monterey
Absent: Maria Orozco City of Gonzales (Ex-Officio)
Staff: Carl Sedoryk General Manager/CEO
Lyn Owens Director of Human Resources
Hunter Harvath Director of Administration
Michael Hernandez Chief Operating Officer
Robert Weber Transit Services Manager
Sonia Bannister Office Administrator
Mary Archer Planner
William Morris Contract Transportation Manager
Janet Madler Fleet Manager
Dave Sobotka Controller
Roger Vandevert Maintenance Supervisor
Tonja Posey Human Resource Supervisor
Others: Dave Laredo DeLay & Laredo
Marc Friddle Coach Operator
Ken Walker Coach Operator
Mark Griffin AMBAG
Rich Deal City of Monterey
Belem Cruz Salinas resident
Jean Friddle Seaside resident
Jim Fink Salinas resident
Ron Golem BAE
Graham Carey Lane Transit District
Apology is made for any misspelling of a name

Corruption, dishonest exploitation of power for personal gain. Bribery; the offering of money or other incentives to persuade somebody to do something especially something dishonest or illegal can come in many forms and some are illegal. Fraud: the crime of obtaining money or some other benefit by deliberate deception.

All of these words apply to the Monterey system of Government.

Yes, I believe that the buck passes around the world and then falls on deaf ears. Indeed it does.

City's corrupt cops may lose pensions
By Bharat Ayyar

Bad boys, bad boys, whatcha gonna do? Whatcha gonna do when they wear uniforms, flash badges and work for the city? In the last year, four city police officers have been implicated on corruption charges, from embezzlement to accepting bribes to forgery. So for months, city officials have worked to restore the image of the New Haven Police Department by cracking down on corruption in its ranks.

"Give me a break! They should go to jail for a long time, perhaps meet with some of the inmates who were set up as patsy's."

Patsy here and a patsy there makes the bucks go around. Ben Newman is a fall-guy and gets paid for it well, an easily victimized, cheated, or manipulated person but a loyal yes man. The freedom of Speech Act gives me the right to my opinion.

Salinas is the county seat and largest municipality of Monterey County in the U.S. state of California. The most current estimate from the California Department of Finance, places the 2006 population at 148,350, showing a slight decrease since 2000 which is largely credited to the city's high cost of living. As of 2005, the city has been identified as the least affordable municipality in the U.S. The largely suburban city is located at the mouth of the Salinas Valley roughly eight miles from the Pacific Ocean and enjoys a kind climate. Salinas is known for being an agricultural center as well as being the hometown of famed writer and Nobel Prize laureate John Steinbeck

Indeed . . . I can write a book on Monterey County and its relics. There can be some pretty nasty storms out here and it can get cold. This year we have an early spring. The murder rate is high, 19 people were murdered in Salinas in 2007, at a par with Los Angeles. Twelve-hundred car thefts, perhaps a pleasant introduction forgets to mention that in Monterey County you must fend for yourself. It is a dangerous place to live with a melting pot of Aliens from the world over. Many are from Nepal who utters their hatred for Americans. There are the Paki, the Korean, and all the people with families in hostile nations. Can they be defenseless by the communist parties in Nepal to spy on Americans selling the information to the highest bidders?

Common sense overwhelms bad luck, what were our Leaders thinking when they embarked on mission impossible, beats the bees-wax outta me.

This costly war is costing civilians their livelihoods and some their lives, we need laws to enforce the Constitution so that our law-makers never get carried away.

Intelligence is faulty, perhaps the wrong character of recruits makes them impossible to see the whole picture, I don't know. I know that there are not enough of them to go around and that deficiency has weakened our security as a nation.

I speak through experience not through theories.

Ben Newman told me there was one camera on the bus and it was in the back of the bus. He said that it showed no injury. Federal Regulations state there must be five to seven cameras operating on the bus, with the mirrors everything is filmed. Ben New said to me as an Official a blatant lie. I counted the cameras and verified my doubt.

I told him I was a Press Agent and yes, off the mainline but I can get my articles into major papers. I ran two newspapers for two years and know what is expected of me. I do as my great forefathers had done and follow the Constitution. If the Press give up their rights to report what they see and know then the American people lose whatever is remaining of their cultural structure.

It is all politics, there is little justice and I know this too through experience by using my influence or others having it used on me. Sometimes I get caught off guard and nearly lose my life but destiny must like me. ***"Damn the torpedoes, and full speed a head."***

I hear CEO's and V.I.P.'s in the corporate world scream in outrage about the state of affairs this country is enduring. In public they hold their peace. Where is this strong attitude and outrage going to take us? Possibly, to a point where Americans create city-states, it seems we are regressing in history and our borders weakening because of this fiasco called Political order.

The innocent always suffer and it has always been this way. Perhaps it is time to change the order of Government utilizing less politics creating more positive action.

After keeping its number of homicides in the single digits for the past two years, the city of Salinas saw its murder rate surge in 2007.

This is because of the atmosphere created by insurgents running cheap motels and illegal actions that border on National Security invents recklessness, poor police response and greed complicating this crisis more. Many of these compromised individuals work in the hospitals, restaurants that are frequented by the powerful, rich, and famous. They act dumb and work for little wages but most have college educations, most loyal to their home countries.

The world hates Americans and if you do not know this by now you are a recluse person, indeed.

City politics in a nutshell means surviving the game.

How can the victim of a bus accident survive their game?

1. It all depends on your injury and your financial position in life.

2. Brain injury is the injury that they defend the hardest. City Officials will blatantly lie assuming that the average person is stupid the henchman is backed by all their staff and chain of Government. I listen to these persons as they lie in my face with impunity.

3. There are so many loop-holes in the laws and liars in the system that the average person, unless the injury is minor will not be compensated.

4. Medical bills will add up into the tens of thousands or more and you better have the monies to pay for it or do not bother filing a claim.

5. All the Attorneys I interviewed see you as an easy piece of meat to be thrown into the wringer.

6. If you do not have transportation then if you ride the bus and the

city claims the during the bus ride you threatened the bus driver. Numbers will overwhelm you as together they paint a false picture of you.

7. Try to keep your spirits up and keep in mind that your injury might cause you to be irrational.

8. Be polite to all and do not argue with them as they lie to you.

9. Pray to your God if you have one.

10. Buy a pet.

Due to the ever increasing congestion on our roadways and highways commuters are using rapid transit and public transportation more and more each year. In accordance with the growing number of people using buses as their main source of transportation, the number of injuries and deaths resulting from bus accidents is also rising.

I am sure that by now you have the idea. Americans are second best to the greed consuming our Political leaders. We are expendable in their eyes as if we are bugs that buzz around and bother them.

Bus accidents and school bus accidents often result in serious personal injuries or death. Bus accidents can be caused by such contributing factors as driver negligence, inadequate security, dangerous roadways, weather conditions, negligence, defective products and improper maintenance, among others like bus driver's long hours and alcoholism among some bus drivers. Older bus drivers take medications that affect their performance and some are heavy-footed.

A. California Constitution, Article XIV.
B. California Labor Code Section 3700.
C. Consent to Self-Insure, California Labor Code Part 5, Rules & Regulations.
D. Administration of Self-Insurance Plans, 8 California Code of Regulations SS 15000-15463.
E. Letter regarding changes in the rate additive assessment from Associate Vice President Pastrone to Administrative Vice Chancellors, July 27, 1988.
F. University Policy on Environmental Health and Safety, October 22, 1986.

A. **Director Risk Management, Office of the President, or Designee:**

1. Manages and administers the Workers' Compensation Self-Insurance Program.
2. Assures that self-insurance rules and regulations established by the State Department of Industrial Relations are followed.
3. Reviews program performance of the Workers' Compensation Claims Administrator.
4. Supports the information, coordination, and communication needs of Workers' Compensation Managers and participating University departments.
5. Works with the Workers' Compensation Claims Administrator to uphold and carry out claim management activities, including the making and reviewing of decisions relating to the furnishing of benefits and the maintenance of records.

B. Chancellor or Designee (Workers' Compensation Manager).
1. Establishes campus assessment rate for loss prevention activities and advises the Payroll Department.
2. Coordinates cost center program management activities, including advisory oversight of local Workers' Compensation Claim Administrator.
3. Defines, implements, and assists in the operation of effective loss prevention and control programs that meet local needs and State law.
4. Ensures that all eligible employees receive required notices and workers' compensation benefits to which they are entitled, in accordance with the California Labor Code and University policy.
5. Ensures that employees who have suffered injury or illness in the course and scope of employment are treated fairly and equitably, and returned to work as soon as they are medically able, consistent with vocational rehabilitation requirements and cost center capabilities.
6. Advises departments and campus/hospital/Laboratory administration of the status of claims, loss experience trends, and campus/hospital/Laboratory program costs.
7. Promotes cooperation and coordination with and between departments and administrative management, and oversees direct and indirect costs arising from employee work-related injury and illness.

    8. Provides training and education in conjunction with participating University departments.
C. Department
    1. Maintain a place of employment which is safe and healthful.
    2. Provides and enforces the use of safety devices, personal protective equipment, and safeguards.
    3. Adopts and uses methods and processes reasonably adequate to assure work performed and place of employment are safe.
    4. Takes every reasonable precaution to protect the life and safety of employees.
    5. Provides to Workers' Compensation Manager with timely information as needed and assistance to meet legal and University requirements for claims management.
    6. Maintains communications with work-injured employees and cooperates with efforts to return employees to productive employment.
D. Supervisor
    1. Encourage the proper attitude toward job safety performance, in himself or herself, and in his/her subordinates.
    2. Trains employees in job safety and health practices.
    3. Reports work-related injuries and illnesses in accordance with University procedures and State law.
    4. Investigates every accident and report of injury promptly and thoroughly to determine cause and prevent recurrence.
    5. Require all employees to comply with the Occupational Safety and Health Standards and all rules, regulations, and orders applicable to his/her own actions and conduct.
E. Employee
    1. Complies with all Occupational Safety and Health Standards and rules, regulations, and orders which are applicable to his/her own actions and conduct.
    2. Takes every reasonable precaution to protect the health and life of other employees.
    3. Does not remove, displace damage, destroy, or carry off any safety device, notice, or warning furnished for use in any place of employment or interfere in any way with the use thereof by any other

person.

4. Reports work-related injuries and illnesses promptly to his/her supervisor and cooperates with University efforts to provide timely, fair, and equitable benefits pursuant to State law and University procedures.

BUS-73, Workers' Compensation Self-Insurance Program
UNIVERSITY OF CALIFORNIA

The State Transit Assistance (STA) program is one of the state's primary sources of financial support for public transportation. The program will provide about $96 million in the current year to over 100 transit operators statewide, largely to support public transportation operating costs. For 2003-04, the budget proposes $100.4 million for STA, an increase of 4.6 percent over the current-year level.

The Monterey-Salinas Transit (MST) Board of Directors elected Fernando Armenta as Chair and Thomas Mancini as Vice-Chair at their February 11, 2008 meeting. Fernando Armenta represents District 1 on the Monterey County Board of Supervisors. He has been on the MST Board since 1996, and has previously served as Chair and Vice-Chair. Thomas Mancini is a City Council Member for the City of Seaside. He has been on the MST Board since 1999, and has previously served as Vice-Chair.

The Board of Directors is composed of one representative from the County of Monterey plus one representative from eight cities MST serves, including; Carmel-By-The Sea, Del Rey Oaks, Gonzales (ex-officio), Marina, Monterey, Pacific Grove Salinas and Seaside.

Monterey-Salinas Transit was formed in 1981 when Monterey Peninsula Transit absorbed the Salinas Transit System. The City of Salinas became a member of the Monterey Peninsula Transit joint powers agency, and the Board of Directors renamed the system Monterey-Salinas Transit

Monterey-Salinas Transit serves a 280 square-mile area of Monterey County and Southern Santa Cruz County. MST's 37 routes serve an estimated 352,000 population based upon the area within 3/4 mile of established routes within the county

MST currently operates out of two major facilities. Built in 1978, the Thomas D. Albert Monterey facility has outgrown its original design capacity by nearly 40%. In Salinas, the Clarence J. Wright facility was constructed in 1986 with parking for 23 buses. Today, there are a total of 35 buses stored, inspected and serviced at this location, exceeding design capacity by over 50%. Clearly, MST has outgrown both its operating divisions in Monterey and Salinas, as the risk of in-yard collisions increases due to the congestion. In addition, fleet expansion to meet growing community needs requires upgraded maintenance, operations and administrative facilities to provide adequate support, including space for 60-foot articulated buses. At full build-out, the facility will support a fleet of 205 buses, 50 para transit vehicles and 60 support vehicles and 550 employees. Also included are a body shop, paint facilities, central warehousing, dispatching office, driver training facilities, customer service center, and employee/visitor parking. MST owns a 13.15-acre property on the former Fort Ord that will serve as the site of the Frank J. Lichtanski Monterey Bay Operations Center. Estimated cost to design and construct the facility is approximately $25 million. MST will award a contract for final design, engineering and environmental analysis in early 2008, with completion of construction anticipated by 2011. The Frank J. Lichtanski Operations Center is named after MST's long-time General Manager/CEO who served in that capacity for nearly a quarter century. He was a part of the MST family for over 30 years and a leader in the public transportation arena. He passed away suddenly on June 9, 2005.

"Have you seen any opportunities thus far for greed to manipulate decisions, people are only people. None of us are perfect; perhaps this kind of money invites political opportunists."

I understand that by knowing this laws a person can see plainly that they are not enforced. Favoritism and what you know about who decides future chain of events at MST.

MST self-insurance policies are supposed to be public but yet, they are nowhere to be found. This is a sure sign that Salinas has a bum deal and monies exchanged hands behind private doors. The word is out that MST has no money, it is broke. MST needs to be investigated and I will make sure that they will be investigated by State and Federal Departments.

"Sure, I have a nasty headache and the Doctors predicted that it will take tears to heal. Makes me want to dig deep into MST and learn for myself what happens to the monies, and who gets all the city contracts."

MST will put the careers on the line for Doctors, Attorneys, Physical Therapists and the list goes on. Those who ignore the corruption are safe and get paid promptly. Others that provide findings for the injured victim of a bus accident never get paid our chance losing their license to practice their vocation.

Bus drivers are protected and mistakes covered up. They are above the law.

During 2007, an increase in crime was noted in parts of the MST service area. At the same time, homeland security remains a high-profile concern among transit agencies across the nation. In this atmosphere of rising crime and potential vulnerability, MST has taken significant steps to insure the safety and security of its passengers, vehicles and facilities. **MST buses are being outfitted with up to eight cameras each,** while the Salinas Transit Center and the new Marina Transit Exchange both have surveillance equipment that are linked via T-1 line to MST's Monterey communication center and other administrative offices. This enables staff to monitor conditions and activities in "real-time" at MST facilities. MST is successfully working with local law enforcement agencies to investigate, apprehend and ultimately convict individuals accused of violent crimes. This video equipment is also seen as an effective deterrent to illegal gang activities. Currently, MST is seeking additional resources to complete its comprehensive safety and security program, which includes additional cameras as well as the hardening of MST operations and maintenance facilities with controlled access security gates

"Ben Newman swore that there is only one camera in the bus, now you too can see the blatant lie he told me."

Benjamin Newman Risk & Security Manager

Ben Newman is the hatchet man with a deep staff trained to create confusion and throw blame on the bus accident victim.

The MST Board recognized Benjamin Newman, Risk & Security Manager, for 20 years of service.

The same man who laughed at my severe brain injury, the man that has an army to enforce his accusations or lies on any bus passenger.

We need a change for the better, get rid of Benjamin Newman and replace him with a younger, fresher, and ethical individual who will do what is right for the people.

Amanda Rouse, 15, was aboard a school bus driven for the Monterey Peninsula Unified School District about 8 a.m., when it went out of control after making a turn onto Sonoma Avenue at Contra Costa Street in Seaside

Covello said the bus - which was half filled with students - then struck two parked vehicles before coming to a halt.

Officers have determined that Graves was not intoxicated at the time of the crash; however, Covello said she was not wearing a seatbelt at the time and may receive a citation for that violation.

It is not uncommon for bus accidents to result in incredible personal injuries, medical expenses, or death. There are a multitude of elements that can cause a bus accident and they are often not the fault of the personal injury victim. These elements can range from negligent driving, an unsecure bus environment, damaged streets and roads, improper bus maintenance, broken bus components, dangerous weather and driving conditions, etc.

This brain injury from the bus accident that occurred on February 11, 2008 could kill me. I can not handle the Wringer with this head injury; it would stress me to death. Ben Newman knows this so he pushes buttons and people jump for him. I decided to make this part of my life a part of this law book.

I hope that this book will change things, yes, some people do speak English in Monterey County, and some of us will demand that justice be enforced at all levels.

Here is some interesting history of Monterey California.

The history of Monterey, California (population 29,674), begins in 1770 with the founding of a Spanish mission and presidio, making Monterey one of the earliest European settlements in California. In 1822, after Mexico seceded from Spain, Monterey prospered as California's sole port of entry for foreign trade.

When California became part of the United States in 1848, the city remained an important center for politics and trade, and was the site of the California State constitutional convention

Decades that followed and into the early 20th century, Monterey's economy was heavily reliant on the fishing industry, as immortalized by John Steinbeck's novel *Cannery Row*. But today, historic Fisherman's Wharf and nearby canneries has been adaptively reused for shops and restaurants that fuel Monterey's tourism industry.

Today Monterey County

It is a pleasure to present the 2006 annual Monterey County Crop Report which is prepared pursuant to the provisions of Section 2279 of the California Food & Agriculture Code. This report reflects a production value of nearly $3.5 billion for Monterey County, an increase of more than 4% over 2005. The increase is attributable to higher values for nursery products, head lettuce, strawberries, leaf lettuce, broccoli, artichokes and a variety of other vegetable crops and reflects the diversity and resilience of our agriculture industry. However, decreases were noted in spinach, wine grapes and salad products. While the overall production value has again increased, it is important to note that the figures provided are gross values and do not represent or reflect net profit or losses experienced by individual growers, or by the industry as a whole.

Now you see things under a new light, who runs this County Government? With the information you now have you can take a good guess if you connect all the dots it truly makes sense.

There is a crisis here and everybody has closed their eyes to it. A corrupting County can destroy a whole country.

Monterey County is the first California County to be registered as part of the new National Organic Program (NOP) establishing standards for certification of products from the ascending organic foods industry

Although only a fraction of its $2.8 billion output in all farm products during 2001, and Monterey County's organic production by 81 growers on more than 12,000 acres was valued at $108 million, up 18 million, or 20 percent, from 2000. Imagine what these figures proclaim today, in 2008.

According to the county's agricultural commissioner, Eric Lauritzen, at Salinas, certification goes into effect Oct. 21, concurrently with the national program. *"It means growers who receive a certificate are growing the commodity they say they're growing and selling, since they are exempt from certain labeling requirements."*

"Monterey County is a beautiful place to live and work and it is built around agriculture. Agriculture is geared to the geography and the climate. At the same time, this area has always been a popular tourism destination. As we see a smaller segment of our population directly involved in agriculture, the link between the two becomes even more important. But, looking ahead, I would have to say we will have both 25 years from now."

IMMIGRATION

Unhappy with a stalemate over immigration reform, Salinas Valley ag companies are more and more relying on Mexican soil. Stepped-up border enforcement and competition from other industries such as construction have created worker shortages for the Ag industry, which relies heavily on undocumented labor. This makes Mexico's fertile ground all the more tempting. "You are taking the product to the labor instead of trying to take the labor to the product," says Ken Silveira, president and chief operating officer at Tanimura & Antle.

This above statement is misinformation to the public; thousands of buses arrive from Mexico into Salinas valley wearing masks or hoods. Salinas is a boiling pot that has boiled over.

If you need a place to hide or operate an Organization illegally, Salinas, Monterey County is the place to be.

Of the California SAS workers who spent some time during the year not working and residing in the United States, 38% applied for unemployment insurance benefits. Of those who did not apply, 40% say it was because they did not qualify and another 5% because they did not know about unemployment insurance. Many workers who did not apply (22%) said their period of need was too short to bother, and others that they were on vacation (12%) or had readily found (or knew they could find) new employment (5%). The remaining non-applicants (16%) had vague reasons. A greater proportion, (46%) of workers, who spent time abroad while unemployed, filed unemployment insurance claims.

Draw your own conclusions, as I did.

Households of California SAS workers who are U.S. citizens and legal permanent residents are most likely to use needs-based social services (23% and 19%, respectively). In contrast, 9% of legal temporary resident households, 9% of other authorized worker households, and 4% of unauthorized SAS worker households obtained these services.

We have film proving our point if we are so called to do so.

I have showed you in this book that the only way to fight and win is through knowing what you are up against. Once you know than you can apply your own solutions to your case.

Again I would like to give some credit for the writing of this book to my loving nephew Bruce Csaba Keller. At 16 years old he is attending college. This proves my point that all children can be victimized and places such as the Burger King in Walworth Wisconsin should get stringent regular inspections so that our children can work in a safe environment when away from home. Bruce has not filed for a claim because he does not know how. Now he has a copy of this book and I expect that soon Burger King will be held accountable for any toxic injuries he may have suffered as a result of working for Burger King.

The child labor provisions of the Fair Labor Standards Act (FLSA) are designed to protect the educational opportunities of youths and to prohibit their employment in jobs and under conditions detrimental to their health and well-being.

Employers are subject to a civil money penalty of up to $11,000 ($10,000 for violations occurring prior to January 7, 2002) per worker for each violation of the child labor provisions. When a civil money penalty is assessed, employers have the right to file an exception to the determination within 15 days of receipt of the notice of such penalty.

When an exception is filed, it is referred to an Administrative Law Judge for a hearing and determination as to whether the penalty is appropriate. Either party may appeal the decision of the Administrative Law Judge to the Secretary of Labor. If an exception is not timely filed, the penalty becomes final.

The Act also provides for a criminal fine of up to $10,000 upon conviction for a willful violation. For a second conviction for a willful violation, the Act provides for a fine of not more than $10,000 and imprisonment for up to six months, or both. The Secretary may also bring suit to obtain injunctions to restrain persons from violating the Act.

U.S. Department of Labor
Frances Perkins Building
200 Constitution Avenue, NW
Washington, DC 20210

The FLSA prohibits employers from engaging in oppressive child labor, as defined by the Act. The FLSA also gives an employee the right to file a complaint with the Wage and Hour Division and testify or in other ways cooperate with an investigation or legal proceeding without being fired or discriminated against in any other manner.

Section 103.64-82 of the Wisconsin Statutes requires that the department promulgate administrative rules (**Chapter DWD 270** of the Wisconsin Administrative Rules) to establish hours of work, time of day and prohibited employment for minors 11 through 17 years of age and take enforcement action

Employers of minors are subject to certain restrictions when scheduling those minors to work. The time of day when they may be employed, including how early and how late, and the number of hours which they may work per day and per week are all regulated. These restrictions depend on the age of the minor and whether or not school is in session during the period they are employed. Only high school graduates and other minors who are exempt from school attendance may be employed the same hours as an adult. Although a given minor's required school hours may differ from another minor's required school hours, no minor may be allowed to work during hours they are required to be in school.

Form LS-119 - Labor Standards Complaint, use this form and send it with an explanation Statement addressed to the address above C/O Jim Doyle, Governor. Call Kendra DePrey At 608-267-9626

Wisconsin Department of Workforce Development (Worker's Compensation Division)

201 E Washington Ave, Madison, WI 53702-0001, United States
Phone: (608) 266-1340

Department of Workforce Development Division of Workforce Solutions Bureau of Workforce Programs P.O. Box 7972 Madison, WI 53707-7972 Telephone: (608) 266-5370 Fax: (608) 261-6968 e-mail: dwddws@dwd.state.wi.us

Department of Workforce Development management team
Lucía Nuñez, Deputy Secretary; Larry L. Studesville, Administrative Services Administrator; Frances Huntley-Cooper, Workers Compensation Division Administrator; and Micabil Díaz-Martínez, Equal Rights Division Administrator.

Main Office, Claim Files
Room C100
201 E. Washington Avenue
P.O. Box 7901
Madison, WI 53707-7901
(608) 266-1340
(608) 267-0394 (Fax)

Milwaukee Office
State Office Building
819 N. Sixth St, Room 330
Milwaukee, WI 53203
(414) 227-4381
(414) 227-4012 (Fax)

Appleton Office Associated Bank Building

**1500 N. Casaloma Drive, Suite 310
Appleton, WI 54913-8220
(920) 832-5450 (920) 832-5355 (Fax)**

To file a claim, an injured worker must complete an Uninsured Employers Fund Claim Application and provide the required documentation. In addition, a claimant is expected to provide assistance to the department or its agent, including copies of relevant payroll checks, check stubs, bank records, wage statements, tax returns or other similar documentation in determining whether their employer is liable for the injury. A claimant is also required to document any medical treatment, vocational rehabilitation services and other bills or expenses related to a claim.

Yes, the claim will be thoroughly investigated. In verifying information submitted in support of a claim for compensation, the department or its agent may share information related to a claim with other government agencies, including those responsible for tax collection, unemployment insurance, medical assistance, vocational rehabilitation, family support or general relief.

Within 14 days after receiving a completed UEF claim application, the department or its agent will mail the first indemnity payment to the injured employee, deny the claim or explain to the employee who filed the claim the reason that the claim is still under review. The department or its agent will report to the employee regarding the status of the claim at least once every 30 days from the date of the first notification that the claim is under review until the first indemnity payment is made or the claim is denied.

Call or write the Wisconsin Worker's Compensation Division, Bureau of Insurance Programs. Our mailing address is P.O. Box 7901, Madison, Wisconsin 53707-7901. Our telephone number is (608) 266-1340 or you can reach us by fax at (608) 266-6827.

INJURIES COVERED BY THE LAW

The worker's compensation law of Wisconsin defines an injury as any mental or physical harm due to workplace accidents or diseases, including accidental damage to artificial limbs, dental appliances and teeth. Injuries covered include:

1. **Physical harm** or injury such as bruises, burns, cuts, fractures, crushing injuries, hernias, sprains, strains, stiffness, amputation, loss or paralysis of part of the body, sudden loss of hearing, sudden loss of vision and disfigurement.

2. **Mental harm** including nervous disorders, hysteria, and traumatic neurosis. The effects of brain hemorrhage caused by an industrial accident may also result in such harm. If the injury is mental harm or emotional stress without a physical trauma, the injured employee must show that it resulted from a situation of greater dimensions than the day-to-day mental stresses and tensions which all employees' experience.

3. **Accidental injury** such as physical or traumatic mental harm occurring suddenly and unexpectedly as a result of some employment-related activity.

4. **Occupational disease** is chronic physical or mental harm caused by exposure over a period of time to some employment-related substance, condition or activity. Occupational disease includes loss of hearing and deterioration of bodily functions. Examples of common types of occupational disease are dermatitis (skin trouble), infection, silicosis, tuberculosis, pneumonia, lead poisoning, multiple **chemical sensitivity** and respiratory disease. In addition, occupational disease includes deterioration of bodily function caused by working conditions over a period of time. For instance, hernias and back trouble caused by repetitive motion or repeated strain over a period of time are considered occupational diseases under the law.

When a person is injured or suffers a disease that is work related the immediate goal is to take care of the condition through proper first aid treatment or medical attention. Remember, the injury and the need for medical attention must be reported to the employer to establish a worker's compensation claim. Even minor injuries should be reported because they may develop into something more serious.

As a general rule, an injury should be reported. A very late report may cause an employer to suspect that the accident occurred at home or, perhaps, not at all. Notice can be given verbally or in writing. It should include 1) the time, 2) the date, 3) type of injury or illness, 4) part of the body involved, 5) the circum-stances surrounding the injury or the first appearance of disease and 6) the need for medical attention. If the notice is verbal, the employee may want to keep a written record of the information and the person notified in case a question comes up later.

An injured employee should give notice to the employer within 30 days of any injury. In the case of an occupational disease, the employee should give notice within 30 days of the time the employee knows about the disability and its relation to the employment. However, if notice is not given within 30 days, it is still possible to give notice any time within two years of the date the injury occurred, the onset of the disease, or the date the worker first realized that such injury or disease was caused by his or her work.

If the employer receives notice within two years and the employer was not misled by the fact that earlier notice was not given, benefits may be payable. The two-year limit does not apply if the employer knew or should have known of the injury.

When an employee has stopped receiving weekly compensation benefits for temporary or permanent disability after an accidental injury, the claim may be reopened at any time within 12 years from the date compensation was last paid. This 12-year period does not apply, however, where a compromise agreement has been made and approved by the department or where a final award has been issued after a hearing.

In cases of occupational disease and some serious traumatic injuries there is no statute of limitations. The employee may make a claim against the employer or its insurance company within 12 years from the date of injury or the date on which compensation was last paid. If this 12-year period has expired, the employee may make a claim against the Work Injury Supplemental Benefit Fund, which is funded completely by specific case assessments on employers and insurance companies.

Complications can arise in a worker's compensation claim, and the amount of benefits is then determined by the specific facts of the case. It is important that the injured employee keep a record from the beginning. If the case goes to hearing, it is important that the employee's testimony is consistent with the earlier accounts of the accident such as his or her report to the doctor.

1. The date of injury or first indication of an occupational disease. The date is very important because benefit levels are based on the date of injury.

2. The accident's cause, such as being struck by an object, overexerting, strain, sprain, etc.

3. The nature of the injury or disease, such as cut, sprain, hernia, etc.

4. The part of the body affected, such as finger, low back or respiratory system.

5. The kind of action that was taking place, such as lifting, carrying, etc.

6. The source of injury, such as machinery, object, hot or flammable substance, etc.

7. The weight of the object causing the injury.

8. Physical symptoms, such as sharp pain, stiffness, loss of motion, rash, etc.

9. How long the symptoms lasted; if and when they recurred.

10. Names of any witnesses who saw the accident or who the injured employee spoke to immediately following the injury.

11. The doctors seen and the date of each visit.

12. All money spent on doctors, examinations, treatment, medicines and transportation. Receipts and bills are important documentation.

13. All days or parts of days lost from work because of the disability.

14. A written record of any statement made to the employer or the insurance company representative.

15. Copies of any agreement or final receipt signed for a worker's compensation claim.

An employee who is injured at work or suffers from an occupational disease is entitled to have all bills paid for all medical, surgical and hospital treatment relating to the injury including: doctor bills, hospital bills, medicines, medical and surgical supplies, crutches and artificial limbs, training in the use of artificial limbs, and lost time and traveling expenses for treatment or examination.

All reasonable and necessary medical expenses must be paid by the employer whether or not weekly benefits are also due for temporary or permanent disability. If an injury requires medical treatment and there has been no lost time, no lost wages and no disability, the employee is still entitled to have medical treatment costs paid. Necessary treatment expenses must be paid unless the claim has been settled through a compromise agreement.

When a worker reports an injury, the employer shall offer the worker the right to select a doctor of the worker's choice for treatment. The employee may select any physician, psychologist, chiropractor, dentist or podiatrist who is licensed to practice in Wisconsin. If the injury creates an emergency situation, the employer may make whatever arrangements are necessary for immediate treatment. Once the emergency passes, the worker has the right to select a doctor for future treatment.

Expenses will not be paid for treatment by a physical therapist, masseur or masseuse, or pain clinic unless the treatment is ordered by a doctor or unless the employer or insurance company specifically agrees in advance to pay for such treatment.

On written request, an employee should submit promptly to a reasonable examination by any doctor (physician, chiropractor, psychologist, dentist or podiatrist) named by the employer or insurance company. The written request must notify the employee of the date, time and place of examination and give the examining doctor's name and area of specialization. The request must also advise the employee of the procedure for changing the date, time and place of the examination. It must also advise of the employee's right to have a doctor of his or her own choice present at the examination, and of the employee's right to request and receive a copy of the doctor's report. The employee may also have a translator present if help is needed speaking or understanding English.

No compensation is payable for the death or disability of an employee if the death was caused by, or the disability aggravated by, an unreasonable refusal or neglect to submit to or follow reasonable medical or surgical treatment. However, an employee may refuse surgery which might endanger life or limb.

With the consent of the insurer, the employee may treat with a medical practitioner not licensed in Wisconsin. The insurer's consent is not necessary if the out-of-state treatment is based on a referral from a practitioner licensed in Wisconsin.

An injured employee is entitled to two-thirds of the actual average weekly wage up to the maximum average weekly wage set by the law at the time of injury. The maximum rate for permanent disability is set by law at a lower monthly figure, and the rate depends on the date of injury.

An employee may work with toxic or hazardous materials or conditions that cause some physical changes which are not yet disabling but might become disabling with further exposure. That employee may be entitled to benefits if he or she leaves that job through discharge, transfer or simply quitting. To be entitled to benefits, the employee must show that it was inadvisable to continue in that job and that by leaving the job the employee had a wage loss. The benefits are paid as the wage loss occurs. The maximum for these benefits is set by law.

If employees suffer from any serious work-related injury or disease that makes it difficult or impossible to do the work previously performed, they may be eligible for vocational rehabilitation services. These services may come from the Division of Vocational Rehabilitation or from private sector vocational rehabilitation specialists referred to them by their insurance carrier or the Worker's Compensation Division. The return to work services may include career planning, job placement or retraining of up to 80 weeks. Additional benefits could include the cost of transportation and maintenance if retraining occurs outside the employee's home community. Any employee who has a permanent disability and cannot return to his or her job should contact the local Division of Vocational Rehabilitation. The employee may also contact the Worker's Compensation/Rehabilitation Unit for further information.

A major purpose of the worker's compensation law is to ensure prompt and proper payment of claims. Administrative rules hasten the process and protect the parties involved. Under Wisconsin law, the employer or insurance company takes the initiative by paying benefits in non-disputed cases. The division insures that correct payments are made by requiring complete reports from employers, insurance companies and doctors, and by careful examination of the evidence

In some cases, if there is doubt that the claim is due to or aggravated by the employment, or if there is a dispute about the extent of disability, or if there is uncertainty on both sides about how the case would turn out as a result of a hearing, a compromise agreement may be made. Under this type of agreement, the employee is not allowed to ask to reopen the claim after one year from the date of the agreement. Unless an actual dispute arises, the parties should not attempt to make a compromise agreement, but should stipulate to the facts without using the word "compromise." For all practical purposes the case cannot be reopened once an order on compromise is issued.

A disputed claim occurs when an employee, surviving spouse or dependents believe they are entitled to worker's compensation benefits, and the employer or insurance company denies liability.

An employer's or insurance company's unwillingness to pay benefits may arise from an honest difference of opinion among witnesses or a conflict of medical testimony between doctors. If there is no settlement, a hearing is held before an Administrative Law Judge (ALJ)

The ALJ is to resolve the dispute on the basis of the relevant facts in the case. The ALJ's decision is based on the testimony of all parties, as well as doctor's reports, other documents, or other pertinent testimony submitted in the case. In most instances, the insurance company or employer is represented by an attorney and has expert witnesses. Typically, there is only one hearing. All further appeals are based on the record created in this hearing.

When an employee or employer wants to request a hearing, three copies of a form entitled "Application for Hearing" (WKC-7) must be filed with the division. The form can also be obtained from the division

The division sends one copy of the WKC-7 to the employer or insurance company for an answer. If an employee is not represented at the time of a scheduled hearing, the ALJ will ask the questions to record all testimony and evidence that is available at the time of hearing. The division and the ALJ cannot prepare the claim in advance, cannot see that the proper evidence is available at the time of hearing, or act as legal counsel to represent any of the parties.

After an Application for Hearing is filed, the division may schedule a pre-hearing conference. The purpose is to permit the parties to discuss the claim informally with an ALJ. The ALJ will try to have the parties agree on exhibits which may be introduced at a hearing and to reduce the number of issues that are in dispute. As the issues are reduced, it is often possible for the parties to come to an agreement that will eliminate the need for a hearing.

Welcome to the wringer and the pain and suffering associated with it. Either party may be represented by an attorney; most are represented. If an attorney is hired, he or she should be experienced in worker's compensation litigation. An attorney is entitled to legal fees up to 20% of the amount of benefits in dispute or, if there is no net gain over the amount the employer offered, the attorney is entitled to up to $100 as determined by the ALJ.

One of the most common types of cases to go to hearing involves a conflict of medical testimony. There may already have been a number of examinations and reports at the time of hearing. (The employer has the right to ask that the employee be examined and re-examined a reasonable number of times.) Both employee and employer have the right to obtain medical reports submitted on their behalf, or to have health care practitioners appear as witnesses at the hearing. Doctor reports may be submitted on the "Practitioner's Report on Accident or Industrial Disease In Lieu Of Testimony" (WKC-16-B)

If a party wishes to appeal the ALJ's Order, a "Petition For Commission Review" (WKC-28) must be filed within 21 days of the mailing date of the ALJ's Order. On this form the appealing party states points of disagreement. The three-member Labor and Industry Review Commission (LIRC) will review the hearing record. LIRC can affirm, set aside or modify the ALJ Order. All parties will receive a copy of the LIRC decision.

After LIRC has decided the case, any further appeal is to Circuit Court. Such appeal must be made within 30 days. A lawyer should be consulted to handle the case, since only questions of law are taken up by Circuit Court. If the appealing party loses the court case, he or she may be liable to pay court costs. If the appealing party wins, the court can assign costs as it sees fit among both parties.

Usually, only exceptional cases are appealed to the Court of Appeals and eventually to the Supreme Court. A lawyer should be consulted since only questions of law are taken by the court of appeals and the Wisconsin Supreme Court.

Food for thought

Burger King ejected 25 low-income residents who were waiting for the Red Cross to arrive after their Minneapolis apartment caught fire and burned to the ground. An assistant manager explained that the fire had slowed foot traffic to "virtually nothing," and that the crowd had to either wait somewhere else or deal with the police.

They were dealt yet another blow when the Assistant Manager received a call from the Manager of Burger King, telling staff to close the restaurant due to the traffic slowed to virtually nothing. Street traffic had been blocked off for a 1-block radius. When the Assistant Manager informed the Manager that the Red Cross was processing the residents that had been evacuated, according to my source, the manager told her to ask everyone to leave and if they didn't comply, to call the police. The Red Cross worker ended up talking to the manager, and a rescue bus was called to the scene.

Why not dress up the assistant manager as the king and send him over to the displaced folk to apologize with a few free whoppers? They're waiting at the Days Inn over on University Avenue.

The U.S. Department of Labor's Wage and Hour Division concluded its three-month child labor strike force by assessing $130,200 in penalties to companies in Pennsylvania and West Virginia. Investigations were conducted May 1 - July 31, 2000 at more than 100 randomly-selected businesses to determine employer compliance with federal child labor laws.

The initiative uncovered child labor violations at 24. Companies-- country clubs, restaurants, recreational resorts, grocery stores and other retail establishments. The following violations were found; 135 minors illegally employed, 112 minors working illegal hours, 31 minors working in prohibited occupations, 25 minors were involved in occupations deemed too hazardous by the U.S. Labor Secretary.

"Our strike force revealed that 23.5% of the companies investigated were not complying with the child labor provisions of the Fair Labor Standards Act," says Richard Clougherty, district director of the Pittsburgh Wage and Hour office, "Our goal is to ensure that all workers, regardless of age, are legally employed, paid fairly and working in safe and healthy environments."

Additionally, Wage and Hour investigators determined that 521 employees were owed back wages due to minimum wage and overtime violations in the following amounts.

Each year, 210,000 minors between the ages of 14 and 17 are injured on the job; 70,000 of them are injured seriously enough to require hospital emergency treatment.

The Fair Labor Standards Act (FLSA) protects young workers from employment that is detrimental to their health or well-being or interferes with their educational opportunities.

Burger King was one of the corporations fined.

The Supreme Court of the state of Washington has allowed a girl to sue a local Burger King restaurant for damages she suffered in the womb as a result of an on-the-job accident suffered by her mother.

According to the Associated Press, the case involves Patricia Meyer, now 6 years old and living in Yelm, Wash. Her mother, Verona, was working in a Burger King restaurant in Lacey in April 1995 when she lost her footing and struck her lower abdomen on a table known as the "Whopper Board."

When Jans landed his fast-food job three months ago, the 16-year-old figured getting scalded with hot oil from the French fry cooker was the biggest risk he would face.

Then come the gang members   .

They would filter in off the streets of downtown Seattle at night, strut up to the counter and demand money and free food..

It happened so often that the young workers knew the drill: Say nothing to provoke them; discreetly call for the manager.

"They're loud, but I'm not afraid," says Jans, who asked that his full name not be published. "We were taught to call the managers, and if things get ugly we'd call the police. They're always patrolling around here."

And if a gang member who doesn't get his way suddenly pulls a gun?

Jans suddenly looks worried. He'd never thought of that.

Welcome to the real world of teen summer jobs. Most aren't as safe as they seem.

Eight out of 10 teenagers in America hold jobs during high school, most commonly in the summer. Right now, in Washington State, more than 100,000 teens are working.

Most parents think twice before letting their children go to a Friday night party. But few have similar reservations about allowing their sons and daughters to get a job at a McDonald's or Burger King.

In the past 10 years, there were 27,000 reports of teenage workers suffering on-the-job injuries statewide, according to the state Department of Labor and Industries. Seven teens died.

There were more than 3,000 serious injuries -- requiring hospitalization or time off work to recover -- involving 16- and 17-year-olds in 2001 and 2002, Labor and Industries records show. Although the overall injury rate has been declining, it is still significantly above the national average, according to the AFL-CIO.

The state's list of those injuries, spanning more than 400 pages, ranges from bruises to amputations.

Sampling of the victims' accounts

1. "Cut fingers, then passed out, hit head on chair (and) table."
2. "I was crushing boxes, it crushed my right hand."
3. "Burned by deep fryer."
4. "I was reaching for tacos in a bin and at the same time a (co-worker) dumped a basket of hot grease and fries on my hand."
5. "On the side of a Dumpster cleaning off roof, slipped and cut left leg on concrete edge."
6. Teens get injured on the job two to three times more than adults, statistics show. Most experts attribute that to a simple lack of safety awareness.
7. Restaurant work is No. 1 on the state risk chart in terms of total

injuries 1,200 over two years. Teens working construction jobs reported 160 injuries.

"There is a good and a bad side to telling them everything that's going on," he says. "The good side is they become aware, but the bad one is that they might become too afraid to push the button."

"It's difficult for an adult to speak to his boss -- it's twice as difficult for a child," said Darren Linker, the University of Washington's School to Work program manager.

$525,000.00 Settlement

Settlement with Burger King in Capitola, CA for a young boy who was injured in the parking lot. A trucker got inpatient with traffic on 41st Avenue and tried to cut through the Burger King parking lot to get to his destination. In his rush the trucker failed to see a young boy crossing the parking lot. The young boy suffered major injuries which were complicated by the fact that he was a hemophiliac.

Across Florida and around the country, members of the Coalition of Immokalee Workers (**CIW**) and the Student/Farm worker Alliance (**SFA**) are hitting the streets for two months to mobilize workers and consumers to call on Burger King fast-food chain to improve farm workers' wages and working conditions.

This email was released by unknown persons and we are stating our opinions on the merit of these stories. Email warning claims that a child died after being injected with a heroin-filled hypodermic needle left in a McDonald's ball pit and that another child died in a Burger King Ball pit after being bitten by venomous snakes. It also claims that HIV infected needles are being deliberately left under gas-pump handles.

McDonalds, Chuck E Cheese, Discovery Zone... All places with ball pits in the children's play area. One of my sons lost his watch, and was very upset. We dug and dug in those balls, trying to find his watch. Instead, we found vomit, food, feces, and other stuff I do not want to discuss. I went to the manager and raised hell. Come to find out, the ball pit is only cleaned out once a month. I have doubts that it is even done that often. My kids will never play in another ball pit. Some of you might not be parents, but you may have nieces, nephews, grandchildren, or friends with children. This will pertain to you too. As I read the following, my

heart sank. I urge each and every one of you to pass this on to as many people as you can. I cannot stress how important this is! I do not know if these stories are true but know that I examined a ball pit and found it clean, I examined another pit and will not state what I found.

On October 2nd, 1999 I took my only son to McDonald's for his 3rd birthday. After he finished lunch, I allowed him to play in the ball pit. When he started whining later on, I asked him what was wrong, he pointed to the back of his pull-up and simply said "Mommy, it hurts." I couldn't find anything wrong with him at that time. I bathed him when we got home, and it was at that point when I found a welt on his left buttock. Upon investigating, it seemed as if there was something like a splinter under the welt. I made an appointment to see the doctor the next day, but soon he started vomiting and shaking, then his eyes rolled back into his head. From there, we went to the emergency room. He died later that night. It turned out that the welt on his buttock was the tip of a hypodermic needle that had broken off inside. The autopsy revealed that Kevin had died from a heroine overdose. The next week, the police removed the balls from the ball pit. There was rotten food, several hypodermic needles: some full, some used; knives, half-eaten candy, diapers, feces, and the stench of urine.

Don't think it's just McDonald's either. A little boy had been playing in a ball pit at a Burger King and started complaining of his legs hurting. He later died too. He was found to have snake bites all over his legs & buttocks. When they cleaned the ball pit they found that there was a copperhead's nest in the ball pit. He had suffered numerous bites from a very poisonous snake. Repost this if it scares the crap out of you!! Repost this if you care about kids!! Please forward this to all loving mothers, fathers and anyone who loves and cares for children!! What has this world come to?? If a child is not safe in a child's play area then where is the child safe?

In Florida and other places on the East Coast a group of people are putting HIV/AIDS infected and filled needles underneath gas pump handles, so when someone reaches to pick it up and put gas in their car, they get stabbed with it. 16 people have been a victim of this crime so far and 10 tested HIV positive. Instead of posting that stupid crap about how your love life will suck for years to come of you don't re-post, post this. It's important to inform people, even if you don't drive, a family member might, and what if they were next? Burger King denies all these allegations and has utilized its vast billion dollar assault force to prosecute persons repeating these allegations. I do not know if these events happened but common sense tell us that it can and it might happen in the future. If these allegations against fast food restaurants are untrue we apologize but what if they are true and billions of dollars covered it up in shredded files, secret files and large pay-offs, the powerful King is truly the King of the hill.

We do not agree with this email because I know politics and everybody has a price. Silence can be bought, and these emails can be lies. I do not know one way or the other but know that Americans are afraid of Burger King and Burger King thinks they are all mighty, powerful and invincible. I believe them to a certain point but sooner or later the truth will show through the cracks and we will see who is telling the truth.

Kids abusing liquor and drugs while on the job make anything possible. I wonder if Burger King has given large sums of monies for the fight against terrorism. I hope they have but if they had done so it would be recorded in a secret file.

My opinion is based on suppositions.

This email forward combines three widely circulated messages into one. Firstly, it claims that a child died of a heroin overdose after being pricked by a heroin filled hypodermic needle in a McDonald's ball pit. Secondly, it claims that another child died in a Burger King Ball pit after being bitten by venomous snakes. Thirdly, it claims that HIV infected needles are being deliberately left under gas pumps handles. All three of these claims are entirely untrue. So claims million dollar attorneys employed by Burger King.

Former Burger King Worker Accepts $4 million Settlement for Burn Injuries

The plaintiff was injured at a Burger King Restaurant in West

Seneca, NY. The accident occurred when the plaintiff was working on the hamburger line and another employee was using a portable machine to filter grease from the restaurant's three fryers. An aerosol can apparently fell into the uncovered portable filter unit during storage and, approximately 15 minutes into the filtering procedure, exploded suddenly, spraying Ms. Krollman with oil that had been heated to 350 degrees.

The Beltz firm argued that the portable filter, manufactured by defendant Food Automation Service-Techniques, Inc., lacked an in-line system, an interlocking lid, and warning labels, and that Burger King and Resser Management Services, Inc. were negligent in the selection, storage, and placement of equipment, and in the operation of the restaurant, including failure to properly train and instruct employees.

The settlement was reached shortly before jury selection was set to begin. The global settlement was brought about after extensive negotiations spearheaded by Martin J. Violante, chief attorney for the Eighth Judicial District's Alternative Dispute Resolution program.

A 58-year-old teacher at Newark High School is facing sexual harassment charges.

Delaware state police said Frank Smith, of Wilmington, sexually harassed a 17-year-old student at Burger King on the 2900 block of Philadelphia Pike in Claymont Saturday night.

Police said Smith went to the drive-through window and asked the manager if the 17-year-old girl could take his order, but the manager said that she would take his order. After placing his order and getting his food, police said Smith parked outside the fast-food restaurant.

The 17-year-old came outside to deliver food to another customer and police said she recognized Smith as a teacher at her high school and said hello. Police said during their conversation, Smith made several inappropriate comments and the girl returned to the restaurant visibly upset and crying.

Police concluded their investigation Thursday and formally charged Smith with sexual harassment and released him on an unsecured bond.

"I strongly advise you to keep your children safe by keeping them away from fast food restaurants. I can write a book of incidents that

occurred at Burger King and fast food restaurants that would cover this planet with paper."

Fifteen-year-old Kim Charbonneau has a summer job at the Burger King on Montreal Road. She flips burgers and cooks fries. She takes orders at the register and works the drive-through.

Every fifteen minutes, she checks the dining room and the bathrooms, wiping tables, cleaning toilets and taking out garbage.

Kim makes $7.50 an hour, and spends a lot of those hours worrying about getting hurt.

Buried in the clear plastic garbage bags she hauls are beer bottles, crack pipes and syringes. Last week, a co-worker was pricked with a needle.

Kim knows she is at risk, but she needs the job. She needs to get work experience for college.

The discarded drug paraphernalia she finds in the wet paper towels are the neighborhood's not-so-secret secret. Like several neighborhoods' in Ottawa, Vanier has a drug problem.

Attorneys for Jennifer Winder filed the claim Dec. 29 in Judge David Gibson's Dallas County Court at Law no. 1. According to the lawsuit, Ms. Winder bought several kids meals for her son at a Dallas area Burger King restaurant solely for the Pokemon toys that were included in the meals. Burger King recently acknowledged that the toys contain a hazardous defect.

Burger King issued a recall of the popular toys on Monday, Dec. 27, following the suffocation death of a 13-month-old girl in Sonoma, Calif., on Dec. 11. The young girl died after a piece from a Pokemon toy covered her mouth and nose, causing her to suffocate. All the toys sold by Burger King include round plastic balls that come apart in two halves. A press release issued by the restaurant chain acknowledges that either half of the ball can become stuck on a child's face, causing possible suffocation among children under three years old.

The tradeoff for workers compensation is that the injured worker trades a personal injury lawsuit against an employer for a quick, no-fault remedy for a workplace accident. In other words, workers compensation bars a worker from suing in tort. In some cases, this has led to uncomfortable results. For example, a worker who is rendered sterile on the job can still work and thus has no right to workers compensation but cannot sue in tort for what is a real injury.

One difficult question has been whether a fetus that is injured by its mother's exposure at work is also barred from a tort remedy. The Washington Supreme Court ruled that workers compensation does not bar the child's tort claim against the mother's employer for injuries suffered in utero in Meyer v. Burger King Corp., Case No. 70015-0, (Wash. July 12, 2001.

Attorneys cannot know them all or keep up with changes, in our compensation laws So many laws in the books that attorneys will never admit to a mistake; it will always be your fault.

I was a mercenary and saw horrible atrocities happening in third world countries. They are poor countries with sufficient natural resources that if they were properly governed there would be no revolutions. When I returned from my six months contract I studied law at Hastings College of the law under an alias name I used to become a mercenary.

I studied law for one reason; I was tired of being burned, betrayed, or sold out by respected high-priced attorneys. I never had any intensions on taking the bar examine only to know how to combat injustice in my world. There has to be a war to return our nation back to the people who built it, we must use their own laws to beat them and show the insiders that this time we mean business. Are there any persons that can represent us without being sucked into corruption? With the greed allowing bribes, and powerful organizations expressing threats, and pressure. Indeed, Pressure can be used in thousands of ways by these powerful people against you or anybody to make you comply. I do not know that we can find anybody that will not compromise the American people and their rights. I hope we do but the people do not elect politicians, "established old time organizations decide who will be President and the policies that will be followed. I call this American terrorist group the New Order. They have been around since America has become a nation and as secret as they are they also are as deadly if you bring them into the light. I know who these persons are that operate the policies for their end objectives but dare not mention their names. The most lucrative and secure job or vocation today is being an arms dealer. Can the law correct our crisis, no, because law does not apply to these power hungry worlds dominated by ivy-league Masters?

The people in the United States must insist that our laws be followed or in a few more years there will not be a United States of America.

I will continue telling secrets which in law school were forbidden to be told. You are better off not having an attorney and learning on your own how to fight and win your compensation case whether it is a city, state, or Federal issue on trial. My plans are to write law books that get to the point and show you the corruption and the way to win your case in the mist of corruption.

We will become a third world country if we do not stand up for our principles and traditions. Book four will begin naming the persons who are deciding global issues and control our country. I will connect them with secret organizations that they all are members of. I hope that by now you see that the war overseas comes in a close second to the war we must wage to regain our dignity and self respect as a nation.

It is more than being victimized by Labor Industries or city lawsuits; these are only signs of what is to come in our future looming before us.

Our guaranteed rights! Rights given to us in our constitution are being ignored, our right to privacy has been trampled on and civilian corporations have followed suit with our elected and appointed politicians. Did you know that some appointed Officials carry more power then elected politicians? We are showing you that this wringer is not happening only to us but encompasses the political system as a whole. We have politicians wanting to focus on the more important issues but the system shuts them up. The system is World Order that does not exist controlling and what they cannot control then manipulating their will on all the people. We have the right to our own opinion but not the right to enforce it. The majority of people should decide but we know that we have been over-ruled as a nation thousands of times through vetoes and regime-styled maneuvers made by private interest groups and influential organizations.

To find a cure for injustices to the people corruption among attorneys, politicians . . . we must enforce the laws on everybody and not just the selectively chosen. What does a billionaire care about your health insurance? Billionaires want cheap labor, low tariffs, and expect you to pay your own Doctor bills. Wealthy politicians are influenced easily by super wealthy private interest groups. American people are suffering. Wages should be raised with the gas prices, easy enough to me. This would take the pressure off our leaders and regain the respect of the American people.

We have interviewed thousands of Americans and 80% do not trust the Government. Many fear the Government and disagree with most of the policies that they themselves must follow. Government has teamed with mega corporations to make ends meet. In the long run the American people will carry the burden and suffer the hardships. Is it a wonder that the people are beyond even caring?

EXAMPLE

However, self-government and sovereignty are at risk when control over these matters is turned over to a newly created North American body headed by the representative of another country. It's an additional problem when the entire Plan is a spin-off of the Security and Prosperity Partnership, an arrangement **created in secret** solely by White House press releases, without Congressional approval or oversight.

The 2007 Plan acknowledges that it is based not only on the Influenza Partnership, but also on the guidelines, standards and rules of the World Health Organization (WHO), the World Organization for Animal Health (OIE), the World Trade Organization (WTO), and the North American Free Trade Agreement (NAFTA)

Legislatures wonder why the people distrust Government. They need to connect the dots, what they do in our world if Americans knew about it they would protest the way business is carried out. Americans are intelligent and deserve to know why Government acts secretly deciding billion-trillion dollar deals that change our rights, and changes the world. One change would be that under Plan 2007 we will have no rights at all and will be segregated and infringed upon our religions destroying our culture while collapsing our systems of governments in our Cities, Counties, and States. I supposed this elite group will get there way one way or another right? Not if **We The People** of the United States of America know about it. That is why these operations are planned and carried out in secret if possible.

Our Government says that we should be glad for what we have because most countries are oppressed and or living in poverty. These same nations that America gives millions, billions, trillions of dollars for Aide and employment. . . . Hey, what about the unemployed Americans or the starving right here in the United States. We are visible but you ignore domestic issues covering them up with botched reform and excuses. If it is not broken then leave it be but if it is broken then please fix it. Easy, not so difficult, all you need is self-respect, integrity, and some pride in your work and love for the people politicians serve. Not the monies people have to offer politicians. There is the saying "It is better that they do not know."

An even higher percentage of the population think the government doesn't care in Poland, Japan, Germany, Belgium, the Czech Republic, and Hungary. America, eighty-percent of the people do not trust the leaders in government, in general, our government.

Asked how widespread corruption in the public service is, 80 per cent of Poles, 63 per cent of Israelis, 42 per cent of Japanese, 30 per cent of Americans, and 16 per cent of Australians answered "A lot of people" or "Almost everyone".

Our polls showed 80% of Americans do not trust our government. If you do not believe me then do your own poll at work, places you eat, shop, and wherever and you will learn what we had. These people will not admit it publically they will tell you privately. I held one pole on Market and Pole Streets in San Francisco, California. To win your injury compensation case you must be fearless and never give away your strategies or tell about your home life. Fight fire with fire, keep secrets with people you know you can trust and always be prepared to organize with your friends and or family to expose the corruption that throws you into the wringer. Speaker of the House I know will investigate your case if you bring it to her attention. I know this to be fact. There are many of our

Leaders that will take on your cause so write letters, send emails, phone them if need be, but it usually takes only one letter sent to the right Senator or House Representative to solve your issues with Labor & Industries or the city, anything addressing national security issues and corruption in government. You must send proof of your case number and court dates; "this is the best way to win your case if you were injured on the job, negligence of the city, county or state."

ATT aggressive door to door sales managers

Watch out because they will not take no for an answer. One of my Officers were an ATT manager and nearly collapsed our company before absconding with our secret contact files, Business Plan, installing expensive ATT communications into our company before absconding. An ATT Fraud investigator is at the present investigating Stephen Hermida. An example of blatant corruption spreading to those who want to live the easy life, at the expense of your sweat and blood off your back they smile as they steal the shirt off your back. Lying and corruption is commonplace with people using the example of our corrupt government. If they can lie and cheat then why we can't, they adopt the ways used against them spreading discourse and corruption among themselves.

    AT&T is currently hiring full-time, Door to Door sales people in the San Francisco Bay Area to sell our residential communications and entertainment (TV) services. This is a direct 1 to 1 sales position for aggressive individuals who can exceed sales targets and are looking for career advancement with a Fortune 20 company. We are hiring sales hunters who are motivated, energetic and driven to succeed in a fast-paced environment. Successful applicants will sell AT&T services door to door to residential customers and will experience tremendous earning potential based on performance. Top sellers can make in excess of $100K annually. Previous Door to Door or TV services sales experience is highly desired, but not required. Qualified candidates must be available to work Monday-Friday until 8 p.m. and Saturdays. **"Must possess reliable transportation and valid driver's license and the job is yours."**

    Once this case is closed we will publish all documents relating to this case. ATT is not responsible for what their employees do, if they are breaking the law. Book 4 will include this exclusive story with scanned documents and exclusive litigation with interviews.

The December immigration raids at Swift & Co, and increased enforcement activity elsewhere, are a body blow against labor's attempt to organize low wage workers.

"Are you seeing it now?" This book is a trail that leads to the source.

Undocumented workers comprise a significant percentage of the workforce in many of the industries targeted for organizing by unions including cleaning contractors, hotels, meatpacking, food processing, light industry, and commercial laundries. The raids will make workers feel more insecure and may make them less willing to take the chances required to organize. The raids may also make employers more willing to use immigration status as a club to thwart organizing and more willing to cooperate with immigration authorities to protect themselves from prosecution or lawsuits. If a significant percentage of the workforce feels vulnerable, all workers will be hurt since chances of successful organizing campaigns will be greatly reduced.

"It is a game of life with little or no control over your own future."

In fact, the raids also provide a good opportunity for labor to reframe the immigration debate with fresh ideas and new action.

"There is a simple rule one must never forget; 'every action' creates a reaction."

Global newspapers pay close attention to what is happening in the United States, *"we must change our domestic arena to a war-like Nation as the nation we become during world war two, the war to end all wars"*

Separate one person or group from the rest, or divide a group into smaller units that are kept apart is the best way to keep Americans under Government control. I want to remind you that Government and Federal have dissimilar meanings. Federal relating to a political unit established on a federal basis, especially its central government. Government is a group of people who have the power to make and enforce laws for a country or area. Federal henchman once was a term used for Federal Government personal.

We must give applause to the Federal Government for trying to keep up with the great demand for their services. With a few simple changes in our present day laws and more security measures being taken without invading on the citizens of the United States. Their burdens could be lifted and everybody can relax.

"Americans do not approve of being pushed around. Our main body is our soul to act as one."

Can you believe that Civics is taught in few High Schools in America? It should become a mandatory status at every High School. Business and science classes increased and expanded in most High Schools while knowledge of our Government and political leaders was at an all time low. *"What they do not know they will not miss."*

Politicians will not have to worry about what they say because our next generation will not know anyways, I guess you can call them ignorant and it would be politically correct.

We will take you step by step through the Appeals process. Fight & Win Book 3 will show ways to avoid the Appeals process. I have friends with Attorneys and wonder why they are tricking their clients, it has become impossible to get a straight answer. My books will give you tips and give away strategies employed by Attorneys they use to beat money out of all parties involved during litigation. It will break down these parties into groups and lists.

Labor Economics makes or breaks a country.

The expression "sweatshop" conjures up images of cramped, dangerous, and filthy factories in New York's Lower East Side. Immigrant women and children worked long hours in these factories for no benefits and little pay. To make ends meet after 15-hour workdays, many workers brought more work home in the evenings.

"How far ahead have we come from those days?"

Sweatshops are also common in other cities with large immigrant communities. Greater Los Angeles is a major example.

OSHA requires employers to record information on every occupational illness and injury that involves one or more of the following: loss of consciousness, restriction of work or motion, transfer to another job, or medical treatment (other than first aid). Employers who are selected for the SOII sample but who are not usually required to keep these records are provided with a copy of instructions and recordkeeping forms for the survey.

The Department of Labor is the sole federal agency that monitors child labor and enforces child labor laws.

Once a youth turns 18 years of age, there are no special federal rules on how or when they can be employed. However for youth under 18, there are specific rules on the wages they may be paid, the occupations and industries in which they are allowed to work, and the hours they may work. All states also have child labor standards. When federal and state standards are different, the rules that provide the most protection to young workers apply. *"This you have to remember Bruce."*

Learn both and use both standards if possible.

I have agonizing headaches that keep me from sleeping for up to three days. I was insulted and threatened by the bus co. and my attorney lied to me so I dropped him. I will write my Congresspersons to get results, what are you going to do to get positive results in your compensation case?

I hope that it will not affect my life more then it all ready is doing. Lapses of memory, spotted amnesia, and these headaches, it is easy to offend a person if your brain miss-fires.

My goal is to expose the system and how it functions so that you can understand how to go about your injury compensation claim.

We hope that this book has given you understanding of the system so that you can fight and win. Do not fool yourself, once you are injured at the work place or injured through government negligence it becomes a war to get justice, and it can be a long and agonizing path you will walk. After we publish all the books in this series you will win your case with or without an attorney.

Kal Keller **III**

Summation

My argument leads to here and now. Are our politicians dishonest or does private interest groups manipulating our elected leaders? Here is an example of how the people behind the disorder in our country seem to get a free ticket to ride each time they lie, cheat, or miss-lead our politicians and we the people of the United States.

Mark Penn, the pollster who has advised Bill and Hillary Clinton since 1996, stepped down under pressure on Sunday as the chief political strategist for Mrs. Clinton's struggling presidential campaign after his private business arrangements again clashed with her campaign positions.

Mr. Penn, who was widely disliked by Mrs. Clinton's fiercest loyalists and had bitterly feuded with many of them, sealed his fate last week by meeting with officials from Colombia, which hired him to help secure passage of a bilateral trade treaty with the United States that Mrs. Clinton, a senator from New York, opposes.

Mr. Penn met with the Colombians in his role as chief executive of Burson-Marsteller, a global public relations firm. He has refused to sever his ties to the company, which also represented Countrywide Financial, the nation's largest mortgage lender, and through a subsidiary represented Blackwater Worldwide, the military contractor blamed for numerous civilian deaths in Iraq.

Mr. Penn's work on the trade treaty with Colombia threatened to undercut Mrs. Clinton's support among the blue-collar voters who are a crucial part of her base, as well as call into question the sincerity of her populist economic message.

A statement from Maggie Williams, the campaign manager, and comments from aides suggested that Mr. Penn voluntarily stepped aside, but other knowledgeable aides said that Mrs. Clinton was furious when she learned of the Colombia talks and insisted on Mr. Penn's demotion. Mr. Clinton concurred in that judgment, aides said.

In a terse statement Sunday evening, Ms. Williams, the campaign manager, said, "After the events of the last few days, Mark Penn has asked to give up his role as chief strategist of the Clinton campaign."

Special interest groups include some covert congresspersons and

Senators deeply involved in these organizations and their influence reaches the Oval office and our Presidents desk.

"If this were you or I committing these crimes and backstabbing our employers then we would be heavily fines and spend time in prison."

This man earned profit and made shady contacts, I am sure he received huge payoffs. *"I guess our Government employs liars and corrupt dignitaries so as to spread the buck out. If everybody is the blame and anybody can get set up in our once great nation then none of us are safe, secret agendas hidden in secret files."*

April 7, 2008 The nation's employers eliminated tens of thousands of jobs for the third month in a row, the government reported Friday, and top Democrats immediately called for new measures to help suffering American workers.

After the early-morning report from the Bureau of Labor Statistics that 80,000 jobs had disappeared in March, the speaker of the House, Nancy Pelosi, said she would propose a second economic stimulus package. Hers would supplement the $150 billion measure that includes the mailing of tax rebates to millions of Americans beginning next month.

I am an avid supporter of Nancy Pelosi; she listens and acts using logic sticking to her principles giving off an aura of security. Other politicians should use Nancy Pelosi as an example of what is expected out of our elected Officials.

(With Americans losing jobs and Labor Industries Department receiving a record number of claims the cuts will have to be made somewhere). We need to eliminate these self-interest individuals from our government to protect our elected politicians from persons such as Mark Penn. We must have strict enforcement with long prison sentences for those politicians who or aids that misinform the American people for self interest reasons, for those who miss-lead or misinform our elected Officials nothing less then a firing squad is sensibly adequate.

Our elected officials need our help, our protection from power-hungry special interests groups. This book is a warning that Americans have had enough, we poll them, interview them, and call them with a general response of a quiet rage that would not take much to erupt.

Government has us numbered, inventoried, and watched so they are comfortable now in the beginning our new millennia.

I have written books about genetic breakthroughs, therapies and anti-rejection medicines. This will improve humanity for some and end life for others.

Labor Industries sees much to gain from these new medicines. Book 5 will explore this avenue in our industrial and corporate Xeno Chapter along with the implications of what laws this will change and the new laws that will be drafted once Xeno-therapy has been openly declared a miracle in medicine.

Please note this example of milking the American people. Fortunately there are enough organizations and the masses in New York to prevent this type of discrimination.

We as Americans pay trillions of dollars in taxes, in would be politically correct to use these taxes for the American peoples throughout the world. This example is about a huge city; imagine the small cities and their governments.

Mayor Michael R. Bloomberg's ambitious dream to remake New York City streets with an elaborate plan for congestion pricing died on Monday, after Democrats refused to put the bill to a public vote on the floor of the State Assembly.

"Through the will of the peoples somebody was thinking, miracles do happen."

Perhaps speaking out and voicing our opinions is not enough anymore. We need to find non-violent ways to show our outrages and make them follow their own laws focus on winning the war not prolonging the war. Persons in power now do not want monies diverted from arms dealers and the pentagon. The Pentagon is the largest arms dealer in the world. Check it out online . . .

In Thoreau's 1849 "Resistance to Civil Government," he advocated tax refusal as a way to stand up against slavery and what he saw as an unjust war with Mexico. Thoreau had a "noble doubt," then acted on it. As he wrote in the essay, "Under a government which imprisons any unjustly, the true place for a just man is also a prison."

People once in time stood up against corruption, now the American people are afraid of their own government.

Seoul, Korea (Nov. 22, 2006)--An American delegation of peace, labor and social justice activists led by Cindy Sheehan is in Seoul to join the nationwide mobilization against the U.S.-Korea Free Trade Agreement currently being negotiated. The delegation is joining the Korean Confederation of Trade Unions (KCTU) who has called for a General Strike from all sectors of South Korean society to demand that the Roh government seriously address the needs of workers and peasants.

Hind-sight is always 20-20. Soon this country will become divided between the rich and the poor.

The delegation of 18 includes trade unionists, students, journalists, and peace activists from the Working Families Party; American Federation of State, County and Municipal Employees (AFSCME) Union; International Longshore and Warehouse Union; Via Campesina; Gold Star Families for Peace; Code Pink; and Veterans for Peace.

"Once the peoples of America truly see the truth and the correct direction this country is on, this scenario can be America."

Immigration; Salinas and many other cities in the United States, *"The surrounding community has tolerated this abuse for decades, watching more and more tax-payer funneled give-always thrown at these out-right Illegal Aliens until we're ready to puke!"* But economic times were good and there appeared to be enough work for everyone ... until now. Beyond the illegality of these border-jumpers, the jobs they continue to take are increasingly important to our community. As this recession deepens, like before – there is no job an "American" won't do.

"Are we blind, lazy, or ignorant to these issues that eventually will destroy this great nation? I wonder if it is not already too late for us."

Illegal Fugitives is more like it. Immigration is when you do what is required to become an Immigrant. Some wealthy Liberals seem to forget that not everyone can take advantage of these poor people and work them to the bone for their own greed. Do not try to make me feel bad because you want you're Slave Labor.

It seems that we have pampered and spoiled our policy-makers to the point they cry like babies when confronted with the truth. Perhaps we need to tether them so that they never stray from their posts.

Apr 2, 2008 ... Senator's Husband Admits Hiring Prostitute. According to a police report the husband of U.S. Sen. Debbie Stabenow told police he paid a prostitute $150 for sex at a hotel. *"Was this a set-up?"*

Sen. Larry Craig (R-Idaho) was arrested in June at a Minnesota airport by a plainclothes police officer investigating lewd conduct complaints in a men's public restroom, according to an arrest report obtained by Roll Call Monday afternoon.

Craig's arrest occurred just after noon on June 11 at Minneapolis-St. Paul International Airport. On Aug. 8, he pleaded guilty to misdemeanor disorderly conduct in the Hennepin County District Court. He paid more than $500 in fines and fees, and a 10-day jail sentence was stayed. He also was given one year of probation with the court that began on Aug. 8.

Tim Droogsma, a former press secretary to a U.S. senator and a Minnesota governor, was arrested Tuesday in a mid-afternoon prostitution sting on St. Paul's East Side.

He allegedly arranged a deal for sex from an undercover officer through Craig's List, police spokesman Tom Walsh said Wednesday.

Authorities cited Droogsma, 50, of Red Wing, on a misdemeanor charge of engaging in prostitution and jailed him for about 12 hours before releasing him on his own recognizance early Wednesday. Droogsma denies the allegation.

NEW YORK (CNN) -- Republican Sen. Charles Grassley of Iowa is hoping to stamp out the sex trade by taxing pimps and prostitutes, then jailing them when they don't pay.

Days after Senator David Vitter apologized for using an escort service in Washington, D.C., a woman who once worked as a prostitute in Louisiana said he was a regular client of hers several years ago while he was a state legislator.

"Where were the Secret Service Agents?"

CITY ATTORNEY MURDERED; Ex-Senator Moody's Son Shot by Gamblers -- Appeal for Troops . . . All day the town has been in the hands of a mob, and in the last twenty-four hours three men have been killed.

These fortunate few - seven senators and one congressman - are political allies of President Alvaro Uribe, and all are charged with collusion with illegal rightwing militias. Some also face charges of conspiring to commit electoral fraud, murder, kidnapping and even organizing massacres.

Indeed, Columbian politicians are bosom buddies to some of our great leaders, go figure. Others in this same sprawling prison do not fare so well as these Senators.

In the cramped and dirty cells of La Picota prison in Bogotá, some of Colombia's most hardened criminals languish, existing on the barest amenities. The prison is notorious - the scene of bloody feuds and riots, contract killings.

This example on, "if you know the right people" rings true with Senators everywhere.

It is difficult to manage Labor Industries as long as our elected leaders take advantage of the power we give them. Soon we will have a professional army and that is when the Government will truly gain control over America. I know I was there and recognize how I felt and becoming general issue made me numb. Following orders and moving out while moving in, ready to strike without thinking staying on your toes a person does not have time to think about a future.

SULLIVAN, Ind. -- The City Council president faces a preliminary drunken driving charge after police said he marooned a city patrol car in the front yard of a home in a nearby town.

Police said Lamb registered a blood-alcohol content of 0.12 percent, above Indiana's 0.08 percent limit to legally drive.

Lamb was released from the Sullivan County Jail on $3,000 bond on Tuesday, said Brant Ford, a Sullivan County dispatcher.

Lamb was re-elected to the Sullivan City Council in November and recently reappointed as president. "I guess it is cool to drink and drive if you are a politician. Unless you are stopped by my brother, he will ticket anybody breaking the law.

A few months ago, Delaware State Rep. John C. Atkins was pulled over in Ocean City Maryland under suspicion of drunken driving. Immediately after getting pulled over, he flashed his Delaware Legislature

ID, after which the officer assured him that he wouldn't be arrested. Problem is, Atkins took a roadside breath test which came back at .14, well over the legal limit.

Atkins wasn't arrested. His car wasn't impounded. He wasn't even fined. Instead, he was allowed to call a friend, who came to pick him up and take him home. Atkins was arrested hours later after a domestic dispute with his wife. He pled guilty to one count of "offensive touching."

I wonder how many other people who blow .14 in a roadside breath test, go home and "offensively touch" their wives, then publicly lie about it get such staunch public support from MADD?

"Must be nice, check out this fact, I do not drink but approve of responsible drinking."

Tennessee Senator Jerry Cooper pleaded no contest to DUI charges after he crashed his car last February. Cooper was found guilty of DUI, but speeding violations were dismissed. Cooper rolled his vehicle last February and was found by state troopers hanging upside down from his seatbelt. Cooper was sentenced to 24 hours of community service and a $350 fine.

Entertainment Tonight has reported that Al Gore III, son of former Vice President Al Gore, has been formally charged with speeding, two counts of felony drug possession and three misdemeanors after he was stopped by Orange County, California police in early July. News reports have stated that police searched Gore's car and allegedly found marijuana plus the prescriptions drugs xanax, Adderal, Soma, and 140 tablets of Vicodon.

I guess politicians do not have time to teach their children about drugs? This kid must be holding a hell of a burden on his shoulders to be this mixed up.

I believe that the psychopathic reactions of Al the III are the direct result of living with the unknowable, a living hell. Labor and Industries should take the blame and responsibility of what Mr. Gore suffered because of political pressure from his father' job responsibilities.

A spokesperson for Martin O'Malley, the Governor of Maryland, has confirmed reports that Maryland Budget Secretary T. Eloise Foster was arrested and charged with DUI in Howard County. Foster, 60, was reportedly stopped by state police for "failing to drive in a single lane" and was charged with DUI and driving while impaired. Blood alcohol content results, if taken, were not disclosed. Foster is reportedly a key advisor to the Governor. "Secretary Foster immediately disclosed the incident," an O'Malley's spokesperson said. "She has been treated like any other state employee and has the Governor's full confidence as the legal process continues."

Marion Barry, former Mayor of the District of Columbia, has been acquitted of DUI by a DC Superior Court judge, who said Barry's apparent difficulty with walking and speaking was caused by age and not alcohol. Barry, 71, testified in court that he takes several medications and has trouble walking because he has high blood pressure, diabetes, and edema, which is swelling of the legs. A blood alcohol content test showed that Barry's blood alcohol level when arrested was only .02, which is below the legal limit of .08 in District of Columbia. Barry had served six months in prison on drug charges in 1990. ***"Once a person is singled out they better watch their steps."***

A Criminal Court judge has ruled that Tamara Mitchell Ford, ex-wife of Tennessee State Senator John Ford, will not have probation revoked because of a February DUI, because Ford has complied with the judge's orders to get counseling, take alcohol treatment classes, and wear an ankle bracelet, among other conditions. Mitchell Ford was arrested in February for DUI and pleaded Guilty last month. Ford's DUI reportedly violated her probation from a 2001 assault case against her ex-husband's girlfriend.

Politics immeasurably affect the persons involved with politicians whether they are family members, friends, or ***"We the people of America."***

Ben Harbin, a Republican State Representative in Georgia, has been charged with DUI after his vehicle hit a utility pole in downtown Atlanta, Georgia. Harbin, 43, was arrested and charged with a DUI after failing a field sobriety test, according to Atlanta-area newspapers. His blood alcohol content was not reported. In the past, Harbin has voted in favor of DUI crackdowns, especially for repeat offenders.

"I bet Harbin will ease up on the DUI issue after this lay-over."

Arizona State Representative Trish Groe has agreed to a plea deal in which she will be charged with misdemeanor DUI and will avoid having to resign from office. Groe was arrested for felony drunken driving and driving on a suspended license in late March outside of Phoenix, Arizona. She has agreed to plead guilty to a lesser charge, spend one day in jail, and pay more than $1,500 in fines. The charge of driving on a suspended license will be dropped, as will the felony DUI charge. Groe was charged with a DUI in 1999. A felony DUI charge would have forced her to resign from her office. Groe's license was suspended for not paying a parking ticket, not for her prior DUI charge.

Politicians love their liquor, and they love to drive expensive cars bought with our taxes.

The Mayor of Carson City, Nevada is facing a recall petition from his constituents after he was charged and pleaded guilty to a DUI. Mayor Marv Teixeira, 72, pleaded Guilty after being stopped for speeding and failing a sobriety test in early March. This was his first offense. Carson City resident Rheba Montrose has filed a petition against the Mayor, to recall votes cast three years ago. She would have to collect 5,529 signatures in 90 days to oust the Mayor from office. Although the Mayor claimed the DUI incident was "the biggest embarrassment" of his life, Montrose believes further action should be taken. She told the Nevada Appeal newspaper, "He didn't apologize to us. I think he should resign because he committed a crime and was convicted."

Tennessee's former State senator Kathryn Bowers was indicted by a state Grand Jury reckless driving stemming from a car accident last August. Bowers had originally been charged with a DUI, but those charges were dismissed when toxicology results failed to show a significant amount of drugs or alcohol in Bowers' system. In August of 2006, Bowers hit a UPS truck. Reckless driving is a Class B misdemeanor in the state of Tennessee. An arraignment date has not yet been set.

Jade Riley, 31, the Chief of Staff for Dave Bieter, the Mayor of Boise, ID, was arrested for DUI. Riley is also the former director of the Idaho Democratic Party. He was released shortly after his arrest and was placed on two weeks of unpaid leave.

Republican activist Robert Vellanoweth, appointed by California

Governor Arnold Schwarzenegger, has been arrested for felony DUI and gross vehicular manslaughter after allegedly causing a head-on crash that killed three adults and a toddler. Vellanoweth, 63, of Sacramento, CA, crossed into oncoming traffic and hit a vehicle carrying five people, four of whom were killed instantly. Vellanoweth's blood alcohol level has not been released. Governor Schwarzenegger's office has said that Vellanoweth will be immediately removed from his political post at the state Board of Optometry. Vellanoweth also served as an activist with the Republican National Hispanic Assembly and was Vice Chair of that group for Schwarzenegger in Northern California. According to the Governor's office, he also had served on the Youthful Offender Parole Board and in the California departments of Economic Opportunity and in Parks and Recreation.

A South Carolina judge has ruled that Fulton Fletcher Taylor, 23, son of former Georgia Lieutenant Governor Mark Taylor, will serve one year in jail plus five years probation and a $15k fine after Taylor pleaded guilty to felony drunken driving for a 2005 incident that killed his friend. Taylor's vehicle was traveling at a high speed when it hit a concrete barrier on an Interstate highway in August 2005. The vehicle flipped over, killing Joseph Victor Gennert, 22, of Charleston, SC. The two men reportedly spent nearly $200 on alcohol before the crash. Taylor's blood alcohol was .25, which is more than three times the legal limit of .08. Members of both Taylor's and Gennert's families urged the judge to be lenient, however South Carolina law requires a minimum jail sentence when a DUI death occurs. Taylor was sentenced to three years in jail but the sentence will be suspended upon completion of one year of jail time, according to the Associated Press.

The Tampa Tribune has reported that Steve Cole, 53, the spokesman for the U.S. Attorney's office in Tampa, FL, was charged with a misdemeanor DUI after he crashed into another car that was stopped at a traffic light. Police reports show that his blood alcohol content was .11, which is above the Florida legal limit of .08. Cole reportedly said, "I plan to deal with this responsibly through the court system." He was released on $500 bond shortly after his arrest.

Drinking while working is in, everybody does it, almost. Ask anybody in government off the record and they will tell you the same thing.

An Alpharetta, GA city councilwoman was rushed to the hospital after being found unconscious in her home just one day after being charged with DUI. Debbie Gibson, who serves on the Alpharetta, GA city council, was taken to North Fulton Hospital after she reportedly overdosed on prescription medication. According to police, her daughter called 911 to report the incident. Gibson was cited with DUI after a car crash in which nobody was hurt. Alpharetta Mayor Arthur Letchas was reported to have given Gibson a ride home after she was released from jail. Gibson is up for re-election this year.

Lawmakers should follow the laws or these examples encourage our youth to follow their examples. This list goes on and on forever. We need to audit our lawmakers and we need to do this soon. Audit their ability to litigate, negotiate, and judge others before we can trust anyone of these elected Officials in our government today. .

Newly elected Nebraska State Senator Danielle Nantkes, 29, was arrested after she crashed into a snowplow, and may face charges of driving while intoxicated. Nantkes has two prior DUIs, according to a Channel 6 News report in Lincoln, Nebraska. Nantkes issued a statement that admitted "alcohol was a factor" in the crash and apologized for the incident. The vehicle she was driving reportedly sustained more than $1,000 in damage, however the city snowplow that she crashed into was not damaged. Lincoln Police Captain Genelle Moore said Nantkes may be charged with a DWI when she appears in court

Ashley Garamendi, 20, the daughter of California's Lieutenant Governor John Garamendi, has avoided a DUI charge because a toxicology report showed she was not driving above the California legal limit of .08 when she rolled her SUV in December while on her way home from a party. According to a Garamendi spokesperson, the Yolo County District Attorney will charge Garamendi with driving under the influence of alcohol as a minor. The legal drinking age in California is 21.

A Northumberland County, PA assistant district attorney was arrested for DUI January 5 by Point Township Police and has reportedly checked into an in-patient rehabilitation program. According to the county's district attorney, Tony Rosini, John P. Muncer, 47, was charged with DUI after a minor collision. Rosini said the case will be handled by the Attorney General's Office. Muncer is taking a voluntary, paid leave of absence while reportedly participating in a 30-day alcohol rehabilitation program. Must be nice getting paid for drinking and driving . . .

A Miami-Dade state attorney's office prosecutor has been charged with a DUI and released on $20,000 bond after he hit two people on New Year's Eve who were riding a motor scooter. George Cholakis refused to take a roadside sobriety test but was booked into the county jail on two counts of DUI with serious injury. The state's attorney's office has reportedly asked the Governor, Charlie Crist, to appoint another office to investigate the charges.

Fla. Assistant U.S. Attorney Arrested In Child Sex Sting

John David R. Atchison, 53, an assistant U.S. attorney from the northern district of Florida, was arraigned in U.S. District Court in Detroit Monday afternoon.

According to police an undercover officer posed as a mother offering her child to Atchison for sex.

The detective, acting as the child's mother, allegedly arranged a sexual encounter between Atchison and her 5-year-old daughter, police said. In deposition, detectives said Atchison suggested the mother tell her daughter that "you found her a sweet boyfriend who will bring her presents."

Protect and serve, yep, that's what they do . . .
Former U.S. Attorney Sam Currin walked into the courthouse Tuesday where he prosecuted criminals in the 1980s, this time facing charges of his own.

Federal prosecutors said Currin, a familiar face in the state's political and legal circles, was involved in a scheme to help people set up offshore bank accounts, offshore credit cards and foreign trusts, all to help them evade federal income tax.

They also accused Currin, 57, of Raleigh, of lying to and withholding evidence from a federal grand jury in Charlotte that is investigating a complex securities fraud scheme.

Currin faces seven felony charges, including tax conspiracy, witness tampering and perjury.

"These are true events that you would think to watch on cable but this is real life."

Currin, a protégé of former U.S. Sen. Jesse Helms, is well-known in conservative Republican politics in North Carolina. His connections were on display in his law office, which has featured photographs of Currin with such luminaries as Helms, former President Reagan and former British Prime Minister Margaret Thatcher.

Wow! This guy was in on the action. He must have been taught by the best.

"You're kidding me?" said state Republican Party chairman Ferrell Blount. *"You mean, Sam Currin, who was party chairman? I'm speechless, and I'm not speechless much."*

Currin and Graves were each released on a $100,000 unsecured bond.

An attorney the FBI wrongly arrested after the 2004 Madrid terrorist bombings because of a misidentified fingerprint has settled part of his lawsuit against the U.S. government for $2 million.

Now let us stray into L&I realm of nightmares: Merino, 51, a former Westport mayor, state trooper and state Department of Labor and Industries investigator, is on trial in Thurston County Superior Court for one count each of attempted first-degree theft and conspiracy to commit attempted first-degree theft. *"I wonder if he had any part in the miss-handling of my Washington State Compensation case, who knows?"*

Labor Industries spends the majority of their budget investigating claimants for fraudulent activity while decisions about laws and your compensation case are decided by persons above the law. Unless, they get really stupid these persons are never exposed.

The charges stem from Merino's alleged participation in a scheme to report a $60,000 1949 Chevy Woodie stolen when the car, according to an insurance investigator, did not exist.

If Merino is involved in illegal activities now then what about the way he handled high public positions in Olympia, Washington. Merino's character exposed makes you ponder the question: how many powerful persons called Merino a friend.

Disbarred
Charles O. Bonet (WSBA No. 19717, admitted 1990), formerly of Tacoma, was disbarred effective April 1, 2003, by order of the Supreme Court, following a hearing. For additional information, please see In re Bonet, 144 Wn.2d 502, 29 P.2d 1242 (2001). This discipline is based on his offering a prohibited inducement to a witness.

Disbarred
Jason J. McCarty (WSBA No. 15985, admitted 1986), of Olympia, was disbarred effective May 13, 2003, by order of the Supreme Court, following a hearing. This discipline is based on his conduct from 1995 through 2002 involving dishonesty and criminal acts.

Disbarred
Kenneth R. Mitchell (WSBA No. 17401, admitted 1987), of Tacoma, was disbarred effective July 8, 2002, by order of the Supreme Court, following a hearing. This discipline is based on his conduct in 1999 and 2000 involving lack of diligence, failure to refund unearned fees, misrepresentation, and failure to cooperate with the disciplinary process.

Reprimanded
Janet A. Irons (WSBA No. 12687, admitted 1982), of Bellevue, received a reprimand on September 13, 2002, based on a stipulation approved by the Disciplinary Board. This discipline was based on her conduct during 1998 through 2000, involving lack of diligence, advancing financial assistance to a client, negligent misrepresentation, and failure to cooperate with the disciplinary investigation.

"These persons were caught because they became lazy. Attorneys need to follow actions and they never are caught. I studied law but would never become an attorney, but it is good to know the laws of California and Federal laws to live in the millennia. You need to know when to duck; you need to know the truth and the last person to tell you are a lawyer."

OLYMPIA, Wash. - The state Department of Labor and Industries paid more than $600,000 in pension benefits to dead or otherwise ineligible claimants in the last fiscal year and lost more than $180,000 in equipment, including laptops, digital records and camcorders, according to a state audit released Friday.

"This is just an educated guess but it certainly seems that most of this fraud is committed by employees within the Department."

The Department does not have adequate internal controls in place to ensure gasoline purchased is for authorized purposes. ***"Free gas anyone?"***

One vehicle supposedly received a tank fill-up of 40.7 gallons when the tank capacity is only 33 gallons.

(Good thinking, take some extra gas with you so that you may burn secret files and some more for your personal car. With gas prices these days stealing seven gallons a day can earn you some extra cash).

By KEITH BRADSHER

For two generations, Americans have imported goods produced ever more cheaply from a succession of low-wage countries. But that free ride may be coming to an end.

It is also a threat to Western consumers because Asian exporters, even in very poor countries, are passing their rising costs on to customers.

Winning your lawsuit is impossible unless you know the right persons in the right places. Otherwise you will lose your compensation case and watch your case is closed. Reading this book will give you an attitude that you can win if you make everybody, Doctors, lawyers, caregivers, everybody involved in your case honest. This book will not be easily dismissed and it will allow you to understand how to fight and win your award. Globally the world is on a downhill slide and we are heading the charge for apocalypse with our insensitive and self-righteous policies being forced by our elected and appointed leaders on the will of the people.

Lawyers can turn on you for a million reasons, most having to do with trading you off or betraying you, your case could be bad for the law firm or for greed.

To me, and to those who want freedom and liberty, the roll of our government is to simply be there when we need them! The roll of these employees of ours, the roll of those we hire and have decided to put in charge, the people we are in charge of... their job is to be our safety net.

They are here to enforce OUR laws and OUR ideas. They are not here to tell us what to do and when to do it! We all live in a constant fear of a Big Brother Government, where those in the government can look up anything and everything we do, that they track our every move. Yet among their own ranks our leaders create laws that provide immunity. Example:

While the prosecution thumps former L&I inspector Frank Antico with charges he got nookie for looking the other way, one witness wonders why City Hall's eyes were closed too.

That's why the *United States v. Frank Antico*, currently being heard in Philadelphia's Federal Courthouse and predicted to last until the end of May, is already shaping into a historical event—one of the most revealing and embarrassing views we've had into the greasy inner gears of Philadelphia politics. The more the prosecution builds its case against Antico, the more it builds a case against City Hall's nudge-and-wink Boys Club: How could Antico possibly have gotten away with such stunts for so long without anyone—the Mayor, the L&I Commissioners, the City Council overseers, the District Attorney—doing anything about it?

Proof is in the pudding.

The top U.S. commander in Iraq told Congress on Tuesday he plans to stop U.S. troop withdrawals in July due to fragile security gains and heard appeals for quicker action to find a way to end the war.

"When our elected officials refuse to act and lives are lost the army decides for them."

Consumer morale fell in March to its lowest levels in four years, according to a survey from the Nationwide Building Society on Wednesday. Today's date; April 8, 2008.

It is no wonder that politicians operating local Departments are not overseen by mainline U.S. Government. Our Government cannot trust their trusted aides and chaos has invaded and rotting our sense of justice. They are as busy watching their backs as they are doing their jobs.

The gap between rich and poor in many states has broadened at a quickening pace since the last U.S. recession, which could make it difficult for low-income families to weather the current economic downturn, according to a report issued Wednesday.

Since the late 1990's average incomes have declined 2.5 percent for families on the bottom fifth of the country's economic ladder, while incomes have increased 9.1 percent for families on the top fifth, said the report from the liberal-leaning Center on Budget and Policy Priorities and Economic Policy Institute

The result is that the average incomes of the top five percent of families are 12 times the average incomes of the bottom 20 percent.

"The report's bottom line is that since the late 1980's income gaps widened in 37 states and have not narrowed in any states," said Jared Bernstein, one of the report's authors. "In fact, we've found that the trend toward growing inequality has accelerated during this decade."

Things are not going to get better for the majority in America; in fact it will get worse. This makes me see clearly the future becoming a place without workers compensation. You will be fortunate to have a job and if you are wealthy now, you will be wealthier in the future.

You can hire investigators to investigate the investigators investigating you. You can do the same with your claims manager or agent and others involved in your compensation case. Learn who the key players are in your case and research these persons, searching for anything that can make them bias toward your case.

Profile these people and learn how they operate while searching for weaknesses in their offensive. We have to keep our elected officials honest by weeding out the crooks. *"Meanwhile, the middle class has remained virtually stagnant, with average incomes growing by just 1.3 percent in nearly eight years, the report said."*

A study indicates Washington state has the tenth largest concentration of illegal immigrants nationwide -- and also the highest average household income. The Center for Immigration Studies estimates the number of illegal immigrants at nearly 38 million (37.9 million) nationwide, including 277-thousand in Washington. The think tank in Washington, D.C., favors strong immigration control. According to the group's report, legal as well as illegal immigrants in both the state and the nation use welfare programs at higher rates than native-born citizens. The study also contents that they are twice as likely as natives to be uninsured and to live in or near poverty, and nearly four times as likely to lack a high-school diploma.

The Mason County Sheriff's Office was presented with a $1,500 check from Wal-Mart Tuesday. Wal-Mart donated the money to aid the Sheriff's Sex Offender Registration Program, Search and Rescue Program, and the Mason County Search and Rescue Dive Team which is a non profit organization that performs emergency search and rescue dive operations. The dive team intends to use its portion of the money to conduct needed repairs on its dive van which is used to transport divers and equipment to diving emergencies. The Sheriff's sex offender registration program will use its portion to purchase a digital camera to replace the obsolete camera currently used by the sex offender registration detective. The search and rescue program will be purchasing maps for its search and rescue coordinators with its portion. All of the items were not provided for in the current budget and will significantly aid the Sheriff's Office abilities to perform its sex offender registration and search and rescue functions. In a written statement, Sheriff Casey Salisbury said "We cannot adequately express our appreciation to Wal-Mart for its continuing support to the Mason County Sheriff's Office. Wal-Mart's community partnership with the Sheriff's Office contributes significantly to public safety in Mason County."

This kind of monies is special interest agendas. This is a way of paying protection money against law suits and other favors, protection from the public that they serve when they screw up with a customer. I was in a store and my cell phone was stolen at the check out stand. Walgreens manager refused to allow me the use of the store phone to call 911. Bad publicity is not good for these stores.

"I believe that nothing is free; everything has its price even charity."

A Western Washington pharmacy owner has been sentenced to five years and three months in prison after being convicted of billing Medicaid for drugs and services that he never provided. Alexander D. Milman, of Kirkland, ran A-Z (A-to-Z) pharmacies in Bellevue, Kent and Tacoma, and he secretly held a stake in another pharmacy in Kirkland.

Prosecutors say he fraudulently billed Medicaid nearly $1.7 million, an amount that U.S. District Judge James L. Robart ordered him to pay in restitution during the sentencing yesterday. Three other people, including Milman's wife, have already pleaded guilty to involvement in the scheme.

"Corruption is an easy way to get the map that leads to Easy Street."

A Canadian man died yesterday in Vancouver, British Columbia _ four days after police used a Taser stun-gun on him because he reportedly was acting erratically in a store. He's the third person to die in recent weeks in Canada after being shocked by the hand-held weapon. Police say 36-year-old Robert Knipstrom died in a hospital after two officers used pepper spray, a Taser and their batons to subdue the British Columbia resident. Police earlier said Knipstrom was agitated, aggressive and combative with officers who responded. The cause of death has yet to be determined. Inspector Brendan Fitzpatrick says a Taser was used against Knipstrom, but it's not immediately clear what role, if any, it played in his death. The case comes as Canadian police face criticism over the death of Robert Dziekanski, a Polish immigrant who died at Vancouver airport last month after officers used a Taser and manhandled him. A Nova Scotia man also died earlier this week, 30 hours after being shocked with the Taser at a jail where he was being held for investigation of assault.

"Special interest groups receive special attention."

Puyallup High School principal Mike Joyner has been reprimanded for his hugs and kisses. Last week's reprimand by the Puyallup School District comes after a district investigation last month that found the 58-year-old Joyner inappropriately kissed three female employees and a student, and ``lightly swatted'' one teacher on the head. A Nov. 16 letter says the district plans to survey the employee climate at Puyallup High School. The letter was written by assistant superintendent Larry Serna of the Puyallup schools' human resources. Serna told Joyner future physical contact with a woman that might be perceived as inappropriate or unwelcome in the future could result in discipline up to and including his firing. Sera's letter noted it was Joyner's second reprimand for similar conduct within a year. In November 2006, the district reprimanded Joyner after a teacher at another Puyallup school said he inappropriately squeezed her shoulders and arms as she tried to move away from him at an athletic coach seminar. *"Status and control over others makes some crooks overconfident and reckless. They actually believe themselves to be above the law. This man should have been jailed and L&I should be paying compensation to the victims."*

Zero Tolerance Policy on Government corruption.

A claim seeking $1 million in damages has been filed against the Fife School District by a 17-year-old Fife High School female student and her mother. They accuse the district of failing to protect the girl from retaliation on campus after she accused a teacher of sending sexually suggestive text messages to her. Their tort claim is a preliminary step to filing a lawsuit. The girl and her parents first reported Fife High business teacher Steven Weidenbach's text messaging to Fife police on Oct. 4. The 27-year-old Weidenbach was placed on administrative leave on Oct. 5. Weidenbach recently pleaded not guilty to seven gross misdemeanor counts. Fife Superintendent Steve McCammon says the district is enforcing its zero tolerance policy against harassment.

"It needs to be the same in local and Federal policies and laws. So that we can trust knowing that our backs as Americans is covered." I say this; 'we the people' need to adopt a zero policy toward government corruption. I have shown you that they are getting more control over the American people daily, and that even the army is protesting the lack of action of Congress. "Where do we stand with labor and industries?" We need to stand together making sure that they follow the laws, which protect us, "watching and if we have to shut down then so be it."

Politics have put us at ends with each other with the poorly drafted immigration laws and the lack of jobs. "Labor and Industry is frightening peoples into not reporting job related injuries and closing out high award cases. I promise you that as we toil in our labors our elected leaders get rich and fat." affluent and prosperous digging in for the future while we are left with our butts in the wind.

"Zero policy would save our great nation and win the war against terrorism." The fastest way to collect a billion dollars in cash and assets is to be the President of the United States, or so it seems. If we do

not take action soon then we will lose our great nation to shrewd thugs and our laws will mean nothing. It will be controlled anarchy.

"Our Space Programs are a great accomplishment but were it not a global endeavor then it too would be corrupted."

A NASA astronaut has been charged with attempted kidnapping after driving 900 miles to confront a woman she believed was a rival for the affections of a space shuttle pilot, according to police documents.

"See what I mean, NASA has its problems but corruption is rare because of their zero corruption policies."

We do get serious if the world is watching and playing a role in a Project. We have to realize that as long as government keeps Americans in a confused state then its easy money in their budgets or pockets or both.

City Secret Files, indeed. I know of some and am in some just through being a CEO. These files locked in private safes with information on millions of peoples of the world. I opted to get out of this organization because of my principles and ethical values.

Error gave terror suspect secret files

The US Government has mistakenly given secret documents to the only man charged so far in connection with the 11 September attacks, Zacarias Moussaoui.

According to newly-released court records, the classified documents - FBI interview reports - were given to Mr. Moussaoui along with materials to which he was entitled for his legal defense.

Once the discovery was made, federal officers searched Mr. Moussaoui's cell in Alexandria, Virginia, to retrieve the material in late August and early September.

"Makes me want to know just how many phone calls Zacarias Moussaoui made before this alleged error was corrected?"

It is that easy to pass your private information along to the opposite side; to the people you are suing. Accidents and errors are legal within the law in Washington State and Wisconsin.

A Denver-area man filed a lawsuit today against a member of the Secret Service for causing him to be arrested after he approached Vice President Dick Cheney in Beaver Creek this summer and criticized him for his policies concerning Iraq.

According to the lawsuit filed at U.S. District Court in Denver, Howards and his son walked to about two-to-three feet from where Cheney was standing, and said to the vice president, "I think your policies in Iraq are reprehensible," or words to that effect, then walked on.

Ten minutes later, according to Howards' lawsuit, he and his son were walking back through the same area, when they were approached by Secret Service agent Virgil D. "Gus" Reichle Jr., who asked Howards if he had "assaulted" the vice president. Howards denied doing so, but was nonetheless placed in handcuffs and taken to the Eagle County Jail.

I wish that Abraham Lincoln and Ronald Reagan were in the crowd to see the way our government man-handles its citizens. Hinting that we can have our own opinions as long as we keep them to ourselves; Taking away our right of free speech.

A diverse group of authors and legal experts have announced their support for a lawsuit that demands the release of secret CIA records related to the assassination of President John F. Kennedy.

The authors and experts differ on who was responsible for the president's murder, but all agree that the CIA must now come clean about Joannides, a career spy who died in 1990.

Secret files are for persons who want control. It is for those who decide our fates, our well-being, and our family's futures.

In the first case of its kind in the U.S., federal authorities have arrested a Seattle man on charges of committing identity theft and fraudulent online transactions using personal information harvested from peer-to-peer (P2P) networks.

In a four-count indictment unsealed Thursday in the U.S. District Court for the Western District of Washington, federal officials said that Gregory Thomas Kopiloff used P2P software such as LimeWire and Soulseek to snoop for and steal identity, banking and credit information belonging to other users on file-sharing networks.

Secret files have your names in them; I hope you are worried because you should be. For every person caught at least a hundred get-away with this theft of secret files. Secret files are used for more then making a buck; there are a million ways to extort private information.

It can be used on bids, land deals, or to destroy you if they have a mind to.

I found the stolen video cameras, check this out . . . Charges were filed Tuesday against a former Gardena aerospace parts manufacturing worker who allegedly videotaped a female colleague as she used the company restroom. Well oh well; I guess there is much to do over nothing. "Perhaps he was only searching for stolen secret files?"

"8 teens charged with 'animalistic' beating of girl for a YouTube video." As our nation corrupts our children soon will follow suit learning through example.

Victoria Lindsay was attacked on March 30 by six teenage girls when she arrived at a friend's home, authorities said.

One of the girls struck the 16-year-old victim on the head several times and then slammed her head into a wall, knocking her unconscious, according to an arrest report.

Later, according to a clip of the video that was released by the Polk County sheriff's office, the teens can be seen blocking a door and hitting Victoria.

"They lured her into the home for express purpose of filming the attack and posting it on the Internet." Where do you suppose that these girls learned to act in this manner?

The sheriff's office said that after the attack, three of the teens forced the victim into a vehicle and drove her to another location, where she was told she would be given a worse beating if she contacted police.

There is something in corruption which, like a jaundiced eye, transfers the color of itself to the object that it looks upon, and sees everything stained and impure. **Thomas Paine, The American Crisis (1776-83)**

Housing prices in Silicon Valley remain rebelliously high. New BMWs and Saabs cruise Highway 101. But for the first time there are signs that the current economic downturn is taking its toll on the country's cradle of technology and innovation.

Job growth has slowed, start-up companies are hiring and spending more cautiously, and early-stage investors who nurture the start-ups with money and expertise are growing more frugal.

During the first three months of the year, only five companies backed by Venture Capital investors went public on Wall Street, the National Venture Capital Association said last week. That is down from 31 in the fourth quarter of last year, and is roughly the same level as at the all-time low of the dot-com bust.

With those options increasingly off the table, investors must spend money and time nurturing or on the whole salvaging -- existing companies rather than building new ones.

Persons in power are taking what they can now while the taking is good. Our rise to power has hit a brick wall that must be climbed over. Save and cover your own ass seems to be the slogan because soon new businesses will be a thing of the past.

WASHINGTON, April 9; The dispute between the White House and Democrats on the economy escalated sharply Wednesday over a surprise move by House Speaker Nancy Pelosi to scrap the House's rules and hold hostage a trade accord sought by the administration until President Bush agrees to more economic relief for Americans.

No doubt about the agenda now, special interest groups in Columbia and the United States will push this Columbian deal through no matter what, damn the torpedoes, full speed ahead. Washington is refusing to help Americans and address those issues, which Americans are demanding solutions, and a method of successfully dealing with problems or difficulties facing this nation as a whole.

Ms. Pelosi's action, which appeared to stun the White House, came just two days after Mr. Bush attempted to gain the upper hand by sending the bill to Congress with the understanding that current trade laws required a vote this year.

We do have elected officials that try to do the right moves for Americans but the majority of politicians are in government are there not to help the American people but for financial freedom, power, and status, basically greed has taken control of our political leaders. ***"You only live once right."***

Hastily assembling at the White House, Treasury Secretary Henry M. Paulson Jr. and a group of other cabinet members denounced Ms. Pelosi's action as threatening American relations with Colombia, encouraging anti-American forces in Latin America and jeopardizing the

American economy. *"Labor & Industries is on the bottom of the totem pole in reform and the least of Washington's problems so why care what happens to injured workers, if our elected officials do not give a damn then perhaps we should stop working for one day and see the impact on our elected and appointed officials."* This action would force the Pentagon to think of Americans first before sending our taxes abroad. The world hates Americans now, Columbia is run by syndicates and corrupt thugs *"why are we dealing with Columbia in the first place?"*

But the Democrats stood firm, saying that they had beseeched the White House not to send the Colombia deal, which is opposed by labor and environmental groups, to Congress and set in motion the 90-day timetable requiring an up-or-down vote.

Ms. Pelosi said she told the White House not to submit the deal because there were not enough votes to pass it. But the Bush administration has taken more than two dozen Democrats to Colombia in recent months and thinks that there are enough votes among them to make it possible to pass it if enough pressure is brought to bear. "Obviously the trips to Columbia were prosperous trips for these politicians and the threat of a Columbian necktie is a good endorsement to vote as you are told."

Do they really think that the American peoples are so stupid that we cannot connect the dots? 'By examining their actions,' it seems that they must believe Americans is simple clay in their hands.

While I served for my country I worked with N.A.T.O. and United Nations commanders and understand what cooperation can bring to America.

At the present time everybody is sweating, worried because politics in American has gone idle wild. We can only offend so many nations before one of them takes a swing at us. All of this is common sense, it once was anyways. Hillary Clinton felt the sting of non compliance and betrayal the same way that every American has, we are disappointed with our government officials and do not trust them to make the right decisions for America unless we begin a zero corruption policy now. Senators and Generals shook my hand and patted me on the back after passing a Bill through Congress with my successful completion of a Project. While I was in the Army hospital a General said that animals like me should be kept in cages until needed in the battlefield. Go figure?

As individuals we are doomed, as a united front we can create an atmosphere of cooperation and reach plateaus higher then we have ever reached before as a nation.

What Democrats do not want, many of them say, is a vote that would force lawmakers to choose between the labor and working-class opponents of the measure, who say that trade, has cost American jobs and led to wage stagnation, and the Wall Street and manufacturing interests that favor the deal.

While Democrats blame trade deals for the downturn, Republicans note that exports are now the fastest-growing sector of the economy and that whatever the losses from trade, the gains outweigh them. "What gains and where do these gains go, who do they benefit. Surely not Americans but the Columbians get more then they bargained for.

James 5-4 Behold the hire of the laborers who have reaped down your field, which is of you kept back by fraud, crieth: and the cries of them which have reaped are entered into the ears of the Lord of Sabbath.

There has always been labor and industries throughout the course of humanity. There are records of this in our history, evidence in the bible.

Proverbs 13-11 Wealth obtained by fraud dwindles, but the one who gathers by labor increases it.

Our corrupt politicians are not thrifty in their characters. Who misses a million here and a million there with Billions of dollars piling in stacks from every district in America? We do that is who, the people of America.

Proverbs 21-6 the getting of treasures by a lying tongue is a vanity tossed to and fro of them that seek death

"If you get caught. Confusion makes for an easy get-a-way for these deceivers of the truth."

Proverbs 22-16 He that oppresses the poor to increase his riches, and he that grivet to the rich, shall surely come to want. *"It is sad that these corrupt politicians are taking our nation down with them."*

Jeremiah 17-11 "As a partridge that hatches eggs which it has not laid, So is he who makes a fortune, but unjustly; In the midst of his days it will forsake him, And in the end he will be a fool.

Jeremiah 22-13 Woe unto him that buildeth his house by unrighteousness, and his chambers by wrong; that useth his neighbour's service without wages, and giveth him not for his work

Ezekiel 22-12 In thee have they taken gifts to shed blood; thou hast taken usury and increase, and thou hast greedily gained of thy neighbors by extortion, and hast forgotten me, saith the Lord GOD.

1 Timothy 6:10 For the love of money is the root of all evil: which while some coveted after, they have erred from the faith, and pierced themselves through with many sorrows.

With most of our politicians claiming to be church-going devoted Christians it is difficult to believe that they missed these verses in the bible. *"I am so sick of these people playing the roles but in reality believing they themselves to be gods."* In many ways they are gods and we made them what they are now so just as easily we can unmake them.

"I am a scientist, a researcher, a man who sees everything logically and does not dismiss evidence of any venue to prove my point."

A zero corruption policy is the best way to go; this would enable the people of American to have a voice in government.

President Bush said on Thursday that the senior commander in Iraq could *"have all the time he needs"* before reducing troops further.

With that said we know conditions here at home will worsen, and more Americans will be put at risk while more Americans die in Iraq.

Alarmed by the number of suicides among soldiers in Iraq, the Army has asked a team of doctors to determine whether the stress of combat and long deployments is contributing to the deaths.

"The number of suicides has caused the Army to be concerned," said Lt. Col. Elspeth Cameron Ritchie, a psychiatrist at the Army's Uniformed Services University of the Health Sciences in Bethesda, Md.

Most of the suicides have occurred since May 1, after major combat operations were declared ended. Experts say harsh and dangerous living conditions combined with a long deployment can worsen existing depression. And the accessibility of weapons in a war zone can quickly turn a passing thought into action. "It just takes a second to pull it out and put it to your head and pull the trigger.

From 2004 to 2005, 433 people who have served in the military committed suicide in Washington State. That's one of the findings of an investigation by CBS News on what the network calls an "epidemic" of military suicides. In 2005 alone, there were 6,256 suicides nationally among those who served in the armed forces - about 120 deaths per week. The two-part CBS report has shocked many members of Congress, because the figures compiled by CBS are higher than other studies have suggested

"Even for all of the tragic stories I have heard, these facts are astonishing," said Sen. Patty Murray, a Democrat and an advocate for veterans.

"Labor and Industries should expand and follow its own laws by offering treatment with compensation for these soldiers." These men and women hold jobs and provide for our safety. "You watch a friend lose his face standing a couple feet away from you this event can cause mental illness in anybody.

More startling, veterans between 20 and 24 years old — the group most likely to have been in Iraq or Afghanistan — killed themselves at twice the rate of civilians of the same age, CBS found.

So how many military members total have committed suicide? Who knows, Murray said.

"There's been no willingness to provide the information by the VA for five years," she said.

CBS producer Keith Summa noted that during the interview with the Dr. Ira Katz, the VA's deputy chief mental-health care services officer, Katz estimated from "a back of an envelope calculation" that there are about 5,000 suicides per year among those who had been in the armed forces; a higher figure than Murray had previously heard.

According to the CBS data, people who had served in the military account for about a quarter of the state's suicides, Dicks wishes it weren't so; and he wishes he'd hear about it from the VA, and not the media

This book is showing you that the way to win your injury compensation case is to know the laws. Never allow an attorney to completely control litigation, always watch closely that attorneys are truthful and give you choices. The laws in this book must be followed. If they are not you can file a complaint, asking for a new hearing, search for new appeals. If you fight hard and watch the system then you will win your injury compensation case.

We have the Departments and the man power plus plenty of good American cash. Zero corruption policy will put our nation back on our toes and eager to deal with multitudes of crisis caused by ham-fisted politicians in the last ten years.

Political corruption examples

We all know the story: As the U.S. industrial economy collapsed over the last half-century, a disproportionate number of cities in the Northeast and Midwest experienced significant population loss, including Philadelphia. This city has lost more than a quarter of its population over the last 50 years. In other cities, the population loss has been worse.

An ATOP Licenses and Inspections official, under investigation by both city and federal authorities, quickly resigned last month after L&I confronted him with irregularities on his financial-disclosure forms, according to sources familiar with the probes. Nicholas A. Sacerdote, 62, was pressured to quit his job as the $79,356-a-year executive assistant for L&I's contractual services, the sources said.

Inspector General Seth Williams' office uncovers petty corruption by city employees, as well as by residents.

SCHINDLER, A.C.J. — The Washington State Medical Quality Assurance Commission (the Commission) concluded Dr. Mary Ballard engaged in unprofessional conduct in violation of the Uniform Disciplinary Act, chapter 18.130 RCW, by (1) failing to document the medical treatment she provided one of her employees, Patient One, and (2) improperly using her status as a doctor to threaten and intimidate Patient One's treating physician in Florida. The Commission suspended Dr. Ballard's medical license for four years but stayed the suspension on condition that she comply with certain requirements. Dr. Ballard contends clear, cogent, and convincing evidence does not support the Commission findings and conclusions. Dr. Ballard also argues the sanction was excessive; the refusal to admit an exhibit was error, and the administrative Proceedings violated the appearance of fairness doctrine. Because clear and convincing evidence supports the Commission's decision, the sanctions are not manifestly unreasonable; the refusal to admit an untimely and irrelevant exhibit was not error, and Dr. Ballard waived any claim of appearance of fairness.

TUMWATER — King County prosecutors have charged the owner of Peak Performance Physical Therapy with first-degree theft, accusing James Gordon Aiton of falsely billing the Department of Labor and Industries (L&I) for over $375,000 worth of treatments his company never performed.

L&I began investigating the company in 2000 after an L&I nurse consultant noticed a billing discrepancy. An audit and investigation by L&I's Provider Fraud program determined that the company had billed L&I for thousands of therapy sessions that never occurred. The case is part of a broader effort to crack down on those who attempt to cheat the workers' compensation system.

TUMWATER — A 37-year-old former resident of Snohomish County, Timothy Smith, has pleaded guilty in Snohomish County Superior Court to first-degree theft after he was caught working for various employers while collecting workers' compensation for a workplace injury.

Alfred Galoustian, 34, was arrested on a felony warrant charging six counts of grand theft.

CDI investigators revealed that Galoustian allegedly worked as an insurance broker/agent in Tarzana, collected more than $7,500 in insurance premiums and failed to remit premium to insurance companies. The alleged actions exposed five consumers to the risk of loss.

Galoustian purportedly collected the full premium from one client, then financed the premium without the victim's permission. He placed his own post office box address on the application in order to prevent the victim from knowing the policy had been financed. Galoustian then reportedly failed to make the payments on the premium financing loan and the insurance policy was cancelled for non- payment.

"Who can an honest person trust now days?"

A Grays Harbor County, Wash. man has pled guilty to a felony charge of first- degree theft and for fraudulently receiving workers' compensation benefits.

Investigators allege that Elisa Guillermo, a billing clerk for Fremont Compensation Insurance Company, allegedly issued more than

$700,000 in claim checks to a non-existent vendor created by Guillermo.

"Once you file your claim you started a war against corruption. You can see that honesty is a thing of the past and that you need to know your rights, it is not good enough to have a lawyer know your rights for you."

"This following story sounds like an inside job to me."

The Washington State Department of Labor and Industries has ordered a 35-year-old Redmond man to repay $69,196.96 after an investigation revealed he had collected workers' compensation benefits illegally. Labor and Industries manages the state's workers' comp system, providing coverage for more than 163,000 employers and 1.9 million workers.

The Department of Labor & Industries (L&I) recently received favorable publicity for its safety program in the *Puget Sound Business Journal*. Rather than using a heavy-handed approach to enforcement of work-place safety laws, L&I is partnering with businesses to pinpoint problems and prevent accidents before they occur. For instance, L&I launched a cooperative program with the Washington Restaurants Association to reduce accidents among teenaged workers.

"Allowing Employers to police themselves is a big mistake. This gives L&I extra fat to spread around."

You have to fight for your rights if you want rights, and you cannot trust anybody in the system.

Labor & Industries "Fight and Win" Book 3 will be published in the winter of 2008.

Shrinking of hours and pay for millions of workers appears to be a bigger contributor to the economic decline than loss of jobs and the risk of layoffs.

Immigrant workers are standard policy, they work for little and never complain, and will replace the American workforce American middle-class will vanish as it is replace by wealthy immigrants and their cheap labor.

Work weeks of less then 40 hours to avoid paying benefits is destroying the United States of America along with labor & industries ethics. Immigrant workers are voluntary slaves ready to please for a place to live in America and a few dollars regressing to a time before the civil war.

American politicians should never forget the French Revolution.

The term **inalienable rights** (or **unalienable rights**) refer to a theoretical set of human rights that by their nature cannot be transferred from one person to another. They are considered more fundamental than *alienable* rights, such as rights in a specific piece of property

Inalienable rights may be defined as natural rights or human rights, but natural rights need not be inalienable. Life, liberty, and estate (or property), we as Americans should demand our rights instead of standing fast as other nations conquer our United States of America.

"Life, liberty, and the pursuit of happiness" is one of the most famous phrases in the United States Declaration of Independence. These three aspects are listed among the "inalienable rights" of man. Have we forgotten that these words created our great nation, example; *"So it's not surprising then that middle-class get bitter, they cling to guns or religion or antipathy to people who aren't like them or anti-immigrant sentiment or anti-trade sentiment as a way to explain their frustrations,"* Mr. Obama said.

"Obama said what all politicians or most also believe; so they are taking away our privacy, our firearms, and with it goes our poise, dignity, and trust in our elected officials!"

This book clearly defined the fall of the United States of America and if we do not stop it now all working Americans will lose their rights and pursuit of happiness will belong to the powerful and extremely wealthy Special Interest Groups, and the privileged few.

Email your comments about this book to keller2529@hotmail.com and we will post it in book three of this "Fight & Win" set of books.

We the People Demand a zero tolerance policy on political corruption, betraying our trust should receive the death penalty.

www.ingramcontent.com/pod-product-compliance
Lightning Source LLC
Chambersburg PA
CBHW030134170426
43199CB00008B/65